the Sharper Mind

Mental games for a keen mind and a foolproof memory

FRED B. CHERNOW

Prentice
Hall Press

*To my dear wife, Carol, who for more than 40 years
has made our days together worth remembering.*

Library of Congress Cataloging-in-Publication Data

Chernow, Fred B.
    [Memory plus]
    The sharper mind / Fred B. Chernow
        p. cm.
    Includes index.
    ISBN 0-13-24066-X (pbk.)
    1. Memories. 2. Memory. I. Title.
  BF385.C453 1997
  153.1'4—dc21   97-23322
                                          CIP

Printed in the United States of America

10 9 8 7 6 5 4 3 2 1

ISBN 0-7352-0287-7

This book is also available in hardcover under the title *Memory Power Plus!*
[ISBN 0-13-242074-0]

ATTENTION: CORPORATIONS AND SCHOOLS

Prentice Hall Press books are available at quantity discounts with bulk purchase for
educational, business, or sales promotional use. For information, please write to:
Prentice Hall Special Sales, 240 Frisch Court, Paramus, New Jersey 07652. Please supply: title of book, ISBN, quantity, how the book will be used, date needed.

 Paramus, NJ 07652

http://www.phdirect.com

Contents

Chapter One
Unlocking Your Memory Power—1

Chapter Two
Building Memory Associations—27

Chapter Three
Boosting Your Learning Potential—53

Chapter Four
Remembering What You Hear and Read—69

Chapter Five
Making Others Remember What You Say and Write—97

Chapter Six
Conquering Absentmindedness—121

Chapter Seven
Recalling Numbers with Speed and Accuracy—143

Chapter Eight

Using Five Surefire Techniques for Remembering Names—169

Chapter Nine

Age-Proofing Your Memory—189

Chapter Ten

Mental Math Shortcuts—215

Chapter Eleven
Mental Creativity Boosters—239

Chapter Twelve
Mental Aerobics Workouts—263

Acknowledgments

This book was conceived on the Long Island Campus of the Albert Einstein College of Medicine. Dr. Ronald Kanner, chairman of the Department of Neurology, and Dr. Steven Mattis of the Department of Psychiatry, were my co-panelists at a public forum on "Improving Memory Skills" at the Teaching Center. They encouraged me to put my strategies for strengthening memory into a book for the lay reader. My thanks go to them and to Dr. Seymour Cohen of the Department of Public Affairs of Long Island Jewish Medical Center for helping me reach a huge audience of memory-enhancement seekers.

Needed encouragement during the incubation process came from Sybil Grace at Prentice Hall who was my indefatigable coach and helped me make the manuscript user-friendly.

Jon Keith, an early leader in memory training for the business community, as well as Dr. John Mitchell, a consultant in memory and management assessment, made valuable suggestions.

Special thanks to Clara Blackman, coordinator of Lifelong Learning for University Seniors at New York University, and Dean John J. Brennan of Notre Dame College, St. John's University, for their faith in my ability to improve the memories of their students.

What This Book Will Do for You

"Did you say our meeting was on Tuesday or Thursday?"

"I was sure my car was parked on Level Three."

"Here comes the woman I met yesterday, and I haven't a clue as to her name."

Do these statements sound familiar? Are you wondering if this is the book for you? Take the quick quiz that follows.

1. Have you been turned down for a promotion or a raise you deserved because you weren't as "quick on the draw" as your competition?

2. Is it more difficult lately to quote prices, style numbers, interest rates, and premiums?

3. Are there more occasions now when someone addresses you by name and you can't recall his or hers?

4. Is it harder to complete all your daily errands and keep every one of your business appointments without error?

5. Are you more dependent on notes when making a speech or presentation?

6. Do you waste time searching for misplaced files, keys, letters, memos, and eyeglasses?

If you came up with one or more "yes" responses, chances are you are *not* using your potential memory power. This, in turn, blocks the full measure of success and financial fulfillment you want and deserve—at home and on the job.

FINALLY, A MEMORY SYSTEM THAT REALLY WORKS!

Here's a book with the latest breakthroughs in memory improvement. All you have to do is apply this three-step approach:

1. Look over each of the simple, proven memory strategies.
2. Next, select the approach that will be most natural for you.
3. Then, put to work those methods and techniques that are best for your learning style.

   That's it. You will gain the following benefits:

- Immediate help in meeting your toughest memory challenges: names, dates, phone numbers, price quotes, lecture notes, and so forth.
- The tools you need to get started—in every chapter. Scores of hands-on help are provided to help you translate these examples into your daily life. Everything is spelled out in simple English.

   Chapter 1 gives you an understanding of how your memory works. You learn to Register, Retain, and Retrieve.

   Chapter 2 helps you make memory associations. By using the easy-to-learn Link and Peg Systems you are able to memorize lists of items and to keep appointments.

   Chapter 3 gives you six techniques for better learning. You'll learn how to retain what you read for a longer period of time. As your personal trainer I take you through your individualized system for registering and retaining the facts and figures you need to get moving fast. You're not left on your own.

   Chapter 4 offers seven ways to remember conversations better and gives you methods for improving your concentration.

   Chapter 5 shows you how to make others remember what *you* say and write. Included are 12 ways to add chemistry to what you say.

   Chapter 6 offers eight simple solutions to the problem of absentmindedness. They are unforgettable! You'll now be able to use the information you already have mastered but seldom use, including vocabulary words, dates, and telephone numbers. Previously learned material will not be lost.

Chapter 7 shows you how to master remembering numbers with speed and accuracy. The simple exercises will give you confidence in recalling number associations at home and at work.

Chapter 8 provides surefire techniques for remembering names.

Chapter 9 gives you the latest discoveries in age-proofing your memory. It presents steps in clear, nonmedical language that you can take now to ensure a strong memory in later life.

WHAT THESE TECHNIQUES CAN DO FOR *YOU*

Unleashing your memory properly will get you what you want out of life. Here are a few benefits:

- Develop the poise and confidence that only a trained, razor-sharp memory can provide.
- Use your improved memory to help solve your most pressing problems and lead you to better decision making.
- Apply the memory tools acquired from these pages and free yourself from the frustration of not remembering.

Best of all—you will feel energized as you use these dozens of memory aids in your daily life. Friends will notice your increased vitality and enthusiasm. Each day will start with confidence and positive expectation.

AND, THERE'S MORE!

An enhanced memory is good—but not good enough.

To stay alert, be self-assertive, always make a good impression, and succeed in the workplace, you need a good memory, plus—

- An ability to handle mental computations with speed and accuracy.
- The mental creativity to find solutions to life's everyday problems.
- A collection of mental exercises you can do daily to reinforce your mental skills and keep them sharp.

Chapter 10 gives you 22 mental math shortcuts to strengthen your brain power when it comes to handling numbers. Learn to handle shopping chores with ease and accuracy; approximate investment returns; estimate the percent of your money being spent in different areas; and project profit-and-loss figures for your company.

Chapter 11 shows you how to apply mental creativity to problem solving. You'll get the most from your people skills, motor skills, language skills, and more. The ten training exercises included will help you distinguish yourself on the job.

Chapter 12 offers a mental aerobics workout. Included are seven daily warm-up exercises for mental agility and ten weekly workout exercises. Keep your memory buffed and in good shape with these seventeen practice exercises. They're simple to do and proven to work.

READY, AIM, SHOOT!

Take a moment to scan the table of contents. You'll find a logical, common-sense approach for getting ahead and achieving both personal and professional satisfaction from a memory that doesn't let you down.

When you have tried the techniques and selected those that suit your needs, your memory will be like the latest auto-focus camera—easy-to-use with sharp pictures. From now on, all you'll have to do is aim and shoot! Your brain will photograph what you want to remember. You'll be pleased with what develops.

Good luck and good memories.

Fred B. Chernow

Chapter One

Unlocking Your Memory Power

"I walked into the kitchen and suddenly wondered why I went there. What was I thinking of?"

"Now that I've reached middle-age, I can't expect my memory to serve me well. Forgetting just comes with the territory, I guess."

People can learn a variety of different things. We can learn to tie our shoes, ride a bike, swim, type, play the piano, program a VCR, phone numbers, names, master foreign languages, and so on. The list is endless. Yet, none of this learning is useful unless we can remember what we have learned. Without memory we would have to relearn each skill or fact daily as if we had never experienced it before. Your two-pound brain can store more than the average computer. But humans, unlike computers, also forget. We forget birthdays, phone numbers, names, and appointments, among other things.

This chapter presents those aspects of memory that will give you enough of an understanding of how your memory works to make the rest of this book meaningful.

Memory is a complex mental process with different facets. Understanding the three basic memory skills your brain performs is essential if you are to make the most of them.

Modern research has identified three kinds of memory. One declines with age, one remains fairly constant, and one, psychologists maintain, can actually improve throughout life.

Semantic memory refers to the general knowledge and factual material you store in your head. The information you use on the job as well as those bits of information you use to respond to TV quiz shows or crossword puzzles are good examples of semantic memory. This kind of memory actually improves as we go through life and acquire more general knowledge about the external world. Such improvement is afforded those who continue to keep their minds active.

1

Implicit memory does not decline with age; it stays fairly constant. It is a kind of motor or kinesthetic memory, including such skills as typing, playing the piano, swimming, and bike riding. If you were a good typist or pianist in high school, your fingers will feel comfortable on a keyboard now. A little practice will restore confidence. After a 20-year hiatus, you can still ride a bike if you had this skill as a child. The balance and coordination that took so long to master at age eight will come back with a little practice. Your body seems to "remember" how to ride, swim, type, and so forth.

The only kind of memory that seems to decline with age is *episodic* memory. This refers to personal, autobiographical incidents, such as what you ate for lunch yesterday, your neighbor's phone number, the place for tomorrow's meeting, and of course, "Why did I walk into the kitchen?"

Throughout this book you learn techniques for reducing the loss of episodic memory. Many of the strategies will help you compensate for the decline of episodic memory, and still others will help prevent such loss.

In this chapter you learn how to register, retain, and retrieve; how short-term memory works; how permanent memory takes over; how memory encodes data; how to distinguish between recall and recognition. You see how your brain uses your mind's eye to remember; how to use your memory to make a story chain; see how your memory works through its five senses; energize your memory by using color; and learn six ways to remove memory blocks.

Mastering the 3 Rs of Memory: Register, Retain, Retrieve

The first step in remembering anything is to register it. For example, a cheerful waitress approaches your table at the diner and introduces herself as Diane. You're engrossed in the menu. A few minutes later, when she brings the wrong order, you begin with, "I'm sorry, but I forgot your name."

Wrong. You didn't forget her name. You never registered her name. If you heard it, you didn't *register* the name. How can you remember something that you didn't access or attend to in the first place?

Registration is a form of input. If you skip input and don't put the name or fact into memory because you weren't paying attention, there will be nothing to remember. It is essential to input or register the thing you want to remember. Pay attention. Our inability to remember names, in most cases, is due to not attending in the first place.

Concentration is another handmaiden of registration. A mind free from distraction or worry, a relaxed mood, physically and mentally—all favorably affect your ability to concentrate on what you want to remember. If these conditions are not present, begin to blame them, not your memory, if you can't remember.

How You Can Store Information for Future Reference

If you do register the name, fact, or skill, you will now want to store it for future reference. Such efficient storage is called *retention.*

When placing items in your memory bank for retention, you can't just toss them in as if your brain were the Grand Canyon. Imagine trying to find your doctor's phone number if it were on a slip of paper tossed into the Grand Canyon! We need pegs or other devices to help us store all the information we register.

Well-organized people retain information better than disorganized people. If your doctor has evening hours on Thursdays, file that away in your mental file cabinet in the appropriate drawer and in the correct manila folder. Thursday is also your spouse's bowling night. "I can go to the doctor after he or she leaves for the bowling alley." Or, "He used to stay late on Tuesday, but Thursday is better for me." By doing this, you have now taken the first step to remembering the doctor's late office hours—you have made associations.

Retention, or the storage phase of memory, is strengthened by interest, observation, association, and repetition. The mere act of learning a term, price list, stock quote, or name so that is can be recalled once or twice is *not* sufficient for good retention. Data must be practiced, reviewed, or even relearned if they are to be remembered properly. Putting facts once learned into regular use also strengthens retention. The juggler who can toss three balls at once does not stop practicing the trick as soon as he acquires it. He continues, hoping to retain and improve his skill. So, too, with retention of information. Once registered, you must continue to review the information if you want to retain it.

Retrieval is the process of calling up an item from memory when we need it. When we remember something, we have retrieved it from the retention or storage phase of memory. This becomes easier if we classify or categorize the item at the time we place it in our memory bank. Then we have a variety of cues to help us access the information. A good way of calling up a memory is to recall all or part of the code that was used to file it away.

For example, you and your friend enjoyed seeing *The Phantom of the Opera* on Broadway. In your mind you classified it under Andrew Lloyd Webber, musical, or even your friend's name. Any one of these are retrieval cues. They refer to the information used to access a memory trace. These cues help you in the same way as key words help a librarian locate reference material.

Retrieval is the payoff. If you have registered and retained the information properly, you will not have a problem calling up the memory item when you need it. Occasionally, you may suffer from TOT, or tip-of-the-tongue syndrome. That is the experience of trying to recall a specific word or name but not quite being able to get it. Perhaps you can tell what letter the name starts with, what it rhymes with, or its length, but not the name itself. We explore this phenomenon in a later chapter.

HOW YOU CAN IMPROVE YOUR SHORT-TERM MEMORY

Short-term memory, as the name implies, consists of those pieces of information that your mind holds onto briefly. It is made up of the small amount of material you can hold in your head at any one time. It is sometimes called *active memory* because you must keep the short-term data active in your mind or you lose it.

For example, you look up your dentist's phone number in the directory. It's a seven-digit number, and like the average person, you can hold onto that data for about ten seconds unless you repeat it constantly, write it down, or transfer it to your long-term or permanent memory. You may look it up on the directory, shut the phone book, call, and get a busy signal. When you attempt to redial a minute or two later, you've already forgotten the number because you didn't write it down.

Short-term memory refers to how much a person can consciously pay attention to at once. It is your "attention span"; it also has a rapid forgetting rate. We combat this rapid forgetting rate by repetition, as in repeating a phone number, spelling a word, a person's name, a travel direction, and so forth.

Such repetition serves two functions: It keeps the information in short-term memory longer, and it can help you encode the information and transfer it into long-term memory.

In addition to a rapid forgetting rate, short-term memory has a very limited capacity, about seven items for most of us.

Determining the Length of Your Short-term Memory

You can determine your short-term memory capacity by reading these lists of digits aloud and then covering the page as you repeat them. Start with four digits and go up to nine. The average capacity of seven is true for all age groups and all levels of formal education. Neither has any significant effect on short-term memory. Here goes:

2893

74065

369748

8179543

53467986

765322498

After seven digits many people lose the first few digits to "make room" for the last few. This exercise can also illustrate the rapid forgetting rate of short-term memory. If you wait ten seconds instead of reading and then immediately repeating the digits, the delay will decrease your ability even more.

Exercise for Improving Your Short-term Memory

"What can I do to improve my short-term memory?" is a frequently asked question. The answer is learn to "chunk." This is the ability to group long numbers or long lists of data into smaller chunks.

For example, it would be difficult to remember 109244153, but if we break it up into three chunks, as we do Social Security numbers, we get a more manageable 109 24-4135. The same applies to phone numbers. You couldn't possibly remember Aunt Tillie's number as 3114536127 with any ease or accuracy. But when you break it up into three chunks you have 311-453-6127. These three chunks make it more accessible.

The same principle of chunking applies to verbal lists. Look at this list of nine separate words:

> desk, rose, marigold, elephant, cheetah, chair,
> zinnia, zebra, bookcase

Read them slowly and then cover the page to see how many you remember. Again, seven is average for most people.

Now, we're going to chunk these words into families of similar items. In everyday speech we call such verbal chunking by another term: *categories.*

Animals	*Flowers*	*Furniture*
elephant	rose	desk
cheetah	marigold	chair
zebra	zinnia	bookcase

You can remember the three categories (chunks) more easily than you can the nine random items. Each category is one thing, so you're remembering only three items. The items in each category will come to you easily because there are only three and you can associate them.

Your Benefits from Short-term Memory

In spite of its limited capacity and fleeting quality short-term memory has several uses:

1. Short-term memory reduces clutter. Imagine how jumbled your mind would be if you were aware of every name, number, date, and fact you ever encountered. It serves as a kind of temporary scratch pad. Once you have made the calculation, paid the bill, filled the order, and so on, the data leave your mind and you have a clean slate for more temporary or short-term information.

2. Short-term memory helps you keep a current picture of your surroundings. It gives you an instant photo of obstacles and pathways when you enter a new or unfamiliar place. Once you leave, it's gone and your brain is ready for its next assignment.

3. Short-term memory records your plans for the moment. By keeping your plans or goals in active memory, you are efficient in executing your daily objectives. Having accomplished them, you go on to other plans.

4. Short-term memory helps you follow a conversation. If a colleague mentions a customer's name and then goes on to call the customer "he" or "him" you know whom she is talking about. The customer's name is still in your active memory and you can follow the conversation. An hour later, in another conversation, the "he" refers to someone else and you can't follow because the earlier short-term or active memory is erased.

FIVE WAYS TO HOLD ON TO PERMANENT MEMORY

Many people confuse long-term memory with events that happened a long time ago. That may or may not be so. Long-term memory holds data that were learned 30 years ago as well as material learned 30 minutes ago. In recent years, the term *long-term memory* has been replaced with *permanent memory*. This is more accurate. Its basic difference from short-term memory is that it is permanent. It holds items as varied as the following:

- Your birthday
- What a now-deceased relative looked like
- Which keys on your ring fit which locks
- How to operate your microwave oven
- Your spouse's new phone number at work

Permanent memory refers to any data that are no longer in conscious thought or short-term active memory but are stored for future retrieval or recollection. Memory can be thought of as learning and storing information so that it can be retrieved in the future.

Short-term memory is like the in-basket on an office desk. Permanent memory is like the file cabinets lining the wall. The in-basket has a limited capacity. It can hold only so much and then the contents are dumped to make room for more. Some of it is discarded. Nothing goes into the file cabinet until it has been sorted in the in-basket. Our permanent memories are virtually limitless— although some of the file cabinets are hard to reach. More about this later.

"What Can I Do to Hold onto Important Items in My Permanent Memory?"

There are five ways you can keep from forgetting what you have stored:

1. *Use it or lose it.* Memories leave a trace in the brain that gradually fades with time. The basis of forgetting is disuse. You can combat this by repeating, rehearsing, using, or practicing what it is you want to remember.

2. *Maintain interest.* People with excellent memories have varied interests. There is a natural tendency to remember what we are interested in. We remember what we want to remember. Make the material more interesting or of greater value to you and your recollection of it will soar.

3. *Make it meaningful.* If it doesn't make sense it will be hard to learn. If it has meaning for you it will be easier to learn. When material has no real meaning for you, you learn it by "rote." Rote memory is tedious, like learning the multiplication tables in school.

4. *Think around it.* You know that word or name is stored in your permanent memory, but you're having trouble pulling it out. You can't recall the name of the female lead in a motion picture you enjoyed last year. The technique entails thinking of everything you can that might be associated in any way with the actress's name: her co-star, the film's title, whom you saw it with, the theater, the story line, the character's name, her face, other films with the actress, and so on. It's similar to the steps you would take to find your eyeglasses when they are misplaced. We sometimes call this *verbal elaboration.*

5. *Relax and take a deep breath.* Any kind of stressful situation can interfere with memory. The antidote is to relax. That's why minutes after a student turns in an exam paper the difficult answers occur to him. The stress ended and the memory returned. People speaking in public think of great points to make—after the speech is over and they are seated.

Taking a deep breath, relaxing the skeletal system, and closing your eyes can all help in retrieving the information you know is there.

How to Transfer a Number into Permanent Memory

We are accustomed to glancing at a word and getting its meaning in a flash. Numbers are harder to read than words. We can't access them in the same way. It is foolhardy to try to "get" a four or five-digit number with a glance. The word *number* is grasped in an instant. It has seven letters in it, but we know what it is the moment we see it.

The number "6927" has only four digits, but it seems longer and harder to grasp. In a way, it is longer. We have to take four words to enunciate that single number: "sixty-nine twenty-seven" or the even longer form: "six thousand, nine hundred, twenty-seven."

Instead of just reading the number like a word by glancing at it, take time to pay attention to each digit. Capture the number; "get" it by paying close attention to each digit. Speed is a saboteur of number memory; it interferes with accuracy.

Say the number aloud. By doing so you are involving your auditory sense as well as your visual sense. This will reinforce your memory of the number.

See the number in an exaggerated way. You may want to envision the number in six-foot-high numerals. You may choose to see the numerals in bright colors. You may elect to break up the four-digit number into two two-digit numbers in different colors: a red 69 followed by a green 27. This will keep you from mixing up the middle two digits.

Writing it down will help in two ways: You will have a permanent record and you will employ your motor memory as you form the numbers.

HOW YOUR MEMORY ENCODES INFORMATION

Our permanent memory is a huge storage space that is virtually limitless. The process of storing information in our permanent memory is called *encoding*. We all have a variety of encoding skills we choose from when we want to "learn" a name, number, or fact. Paying attention, making associations, applying reasoning, analyzing, or elaborating are just a few. We explore these and others throughout the book.

You strengthen your chances of remembering something in your short-term memory and transferring it to your permanent memory if you are truly *interested* in the fact; or if you pay *attention* when the information is presented; or you *elaborate* the details; or you *associate* the new data with something you already know.

Four Ways to Ensure Remembering Data

1. *Look for an interesting angle.* Being interested in whatever you want to remember is vital. You shouldn't expect that what you see or hear will magically sink into your memory by itself. Look for some interesting angle or fact in what you are reading or in the person you are conversing with. This level of interest will provide the glue to make the information "stick" in your mind. If you're reading something difficult, your mind may wander and you suddenly remember you must buy a quart of milk. Then, instead of concentrating on the reading material, you half think about remembering to buy the milk. One way to avoid such distractions is to keep a pencil and paper nearby when you read. As a distracting thought enters your head, write it down. The act of writing will serve to put it out of your mind, and you can return to your book without this gnawing distraction.

2. *Focus your attention.* Attention is influenced by interest. You pay attention to things you are interested in. We have so many free-floating bits of information aloft in our brain and competing for attention in short-term memory. The amount of material we can hold in our short-term memory is quite small. If we give just casual attention to a piece of information it will never make it into permanent memory. We have to decide which of these items we would like to transfer into our permanent memory and focus our attention on those.

3. *Add details to the item.* The word elaborate refers to giv͟ ͟
a subject fuller treatment and adding details. We talk about making
elaborate plans or we elaborate on a topic. Verbal elaboration is a
memory device for encoding information. For example, you are
introduced to Allison Brown. As you converse, you elaborate on her
name, mentally. Any one of these elaborations may pass through
your mind as you look at her and listen to what she is saying: her
last name is Brown but her hair is blonde; her eyes are brown; she
went to school in Rhode Island, perhaps Brown University. Her first
name is Allison, sounds like "Ali's son"; does she spell Allison with
two l's?; her initials are AB. When you use verbal elaboration you
are adding details to the name, word, number, or fact. The more you
elaborate, the better your fix on the data.

4. *Make associations with something you already know.* Making
associations between new and already learned data is frequently done
unconsciously. The more associations you can make the deeper the
processing, and the stronger the encoding. For example, you are
introduced to Barbara. Make associations with another Barbara you
know. How are they alike? How are they different? Associate your
new acquaintance with a celebrity such as Barbra Streisand. Does she
look like, or an any way resemble a Barbie doll? Think of someone
else you know with a similar hairstyle, smile, figure, or voice.
Associate her with someone else in her occupation or from her town.

In a like manner, you can use association to help fix the new
model of a piece of machinery. Make associations with the old
model: How is it the same? How is it different? What is the major
change? How will it impact your job?

These four techniques will help you hold on to the information
you need on the job, socially, or for your personal satisfaction.

HOW YOUR MEMORY RECOLLECTS DATA

Recollection, or retrieval, is the process of reaching into our vast
storehouse of encoded data to pull out the precise piece of information we're looking for. Most readers complain about their occasional
inability to retrieve something on demand. Actually, our ability to

pull out a fact from our vast storehouse of memories is the more common occurrence and is truly amazing.

The two methods we use to recollect information we have stored or encoded are:

Recall: A search through our permanent memory bank for information.

Recognition: A sensation that information presented to you is something you already know.

In school there were multiple-choice test questions where you were given four answers and had to choose the correct answer or sentence completion. This kind of retrieval is called *recognition.* You had to recognize or sense the correct answer.

Other test items were of the "fill-in" type. This was harder. You had to remember the fact and fill in the blank space with data from your head. You did not have four responses from which to choose one. This was a test of *recall.*

How to Pull Out the Information You're Looking for

We tend to remember faces more easily than names. That's because faces present themselves for recognition. Being able to come up with the name involves recall. Also, the face is concrete: a certain nose, mouth, shape, and so forth. These act as cues to recognition.

The name, on the other hand, is abstract: a John, a James, a Jane, a Ms. Jones. These are vague abstractions having no visual form or pictorial representation.

You never heard anyone say, "I remember your name, but I forgot your face." We see how much harder it is to recall a face than to recognize one in police situations. A crime witness tries to recall the face of the attacker. In response to specific questions a police sketch is drawn. This may or may not look like the perpetrator. When photos of suspects are given to the witness, however, or a line-up of suspects is arranged, the witness may easily recognize the alleged attacker. The poor recall of faces contrasts with the high recognition rate of faces.

The same is true of names and faces. Name memory is more difficult than face memory because name memory requires recall.

The face is already presented for recognition. You must recall the name from your long-term memory file of thousands of names.

The Benefits of Using Recall and Recognition

Is there a secret to enhancing recall and recognition? Many people, when told how they can improve both their recall and recognition of item numbers, book titles, machine parts, and so forth, dismiss it as too much work. You can better recollect your memories if you involve yourself in these activities:

1. *Meaningfulness:* Tell yourself "why" you should learn this fact.

2. *Association:* This is the single most important memory tool. Match up or link the new fact with something you already know.

3. *Visual imagery:* See the name of the product on the item itself. If it isn't there, put it there in your mind. Give people imaginary name cards. "See" the price quote superimposed on the name of the stock.

4. *Review:* Employ repetition or practice. You can't see an item or person once and expect to achieve instant recall the next time unless you review the data periodically.

Use these enhancers to improve your ability to recollect information you have stored.

EXERCISING YOUR POWERS OF RECOGNITION AND RECALL

1. Listed here are ten words selected at random. Read and study these words for three minutes. Then close the book and see how many you can *recall,* in any order.

tiger	prince	wheel	picture	suit
card	pencil	chair	lamp	fog

2. The following list contains 12 words selected at random. See how many of these words you *recognize* as being on the original list. Be sure to cover the previous words before you begin.

table	lamp	desk	pen	chart
suit	photo	tire	prince	light
chair	fog			

HOW YOUR BRAIN USES YOUR MIND'S EYE
TO REMEMBER

"A picture is worth a thousand words." This often-heard adage suggests a great memory booster. If you want to remember an errand, an unfamiliar name, a number, or an abstract item, you must first consciously create a picture and visualize it in your mind. Take the time to translate what you want to remember into a meaningful picture and hold it for a few seconds. You are then much more likely to remember it. The picture has to be vivid only for you. Feel free to create any kind of picture you like.

For example, you are sitting in the den watching TV when you get the urge to eat an apple. You get out of your favorite chair, shut the TV, walk into the kitchen, and then—you don't remember why you came into the kitchen! One way to remedy this is to retrace your steps and hope the thought will reenter your mind. But this does not always happen.

A better technique is to vividly visualize the apple when the thought of eating one first comes to mind. Close your eyes for a second if you are easily distracted. Visualize the apple in your mind's eye. Is it a green, red, golden? How big is it? Where in the kitchen will you look for it?

By creating a strong picture you will know precisely why you came into the kitchen and just what to do when you get there. Your mind has a strong, vivid picture that will guide you until your mission is accomplished.

How Visual Imagery Helps You in Everyday Situations

Here are four additional techniques for using visual imagery in your daily life:

1. *Completing errands.* Shopping lists are invaluable, but for just a few items you may not bother to write a list. Worse yet, you may leave your long list at home. You want to pick up milk, rolls, a newspaper, get gas for the car, and select a birthday card for your niece. When you use imagery you see yourself at the gas pump reading the birthday card and glancing at the first page of the newspaper. On the seat next to you is the grocery bag containing the

milk and rolls. You should also visualize the number "five" so that you'll know you're not finished until you have accomplished five tasks. If you should have just four errands done, you will know there is one more thing you must do before you return home. Your mind's eye will scan your memory until that fifth task comes up.

2. *Reinforcing names and faces.* When you meet someone for the first time, use an imaginary pen to write his or her name on his or her forehead. As you speak to your new acquaintance look at him and see his name superimposed. It will force you to make eye contact, always a plus in making an impression! Furthermore, by looking at the "name," you are checking spelling and/or pronunciation. By superimposing the name on the face you are also reinforcing the association.

3. *Navigating travel directions.* You want to drive from Customer A to Customer B. Visualize the route as you would see it from the air in a helicopter. This aerial view will vividly show you the main roads and streets where you make turns. A pattern will emerge of lefts and rights that will make the verbal travel directions more relevant. Also, picture the landmarks you will see from your car: a left at the church, a right at the bank, go two lights beyond the movie theater and turn left.

4. *Remembering punch lines.* We frequently enjoy a joke told by someone else but can't remember the punch line when we want to share the story with a friend. In this visualization, you pretend you are the director of a Hollywood movie. Cast the anecdote with your favorite movie or TV stars. Feed them their lines. Have them exaggerate their movements. We remember action scenes better than static ones. Visualize their scripts with the key words of the punch line in boldface type or highlighted in yellow. Reduce your punch line to four or five key words. Review these key words in your mind before you tell the joke.

FORGING MEMORY LINKS INTO A CHAIN

Through visualization, you can forge memory links into a chain of your own making. Because you make this chain yourself, it is stronger than a chain anyone else could provide.

In this technique, each item you want to remember becomes a link. You use your imagination to forge the various links into a chain by means of a story. These stories, of necessity, are silly because the separate items you want to remember do not usually lend themselves to a logical narrative. This is illustrated in the following exercises:

Linking Exercise Using a Sample Story

Assume you have a shopping list of these ten items. Here is the list and a sample fantasy or image story linking each item.

snow shovel	a dozen eggs	thirteen bagels
six wine glasses	talcum	lettuce
six oranges	a tube of toothpaste	a bunch of flowers
a bar of soap		

In creating your link story, remember to use all your senses, a vivid imagination, humor, and exaggeration. This is what ad executives use to help you remember their products on TV or in print media.

Here is one possible story to remember the ten items, in order:

"Imagine walking out your door holding up a *snow shovel* on which you are balancing *six wine glasses*. In each glass is a brilliantly colored *orange*. You can smell the citrus aroma. You step on a *bar of soap* and fall backward onto *a dozen eggs*. As you sink down, you hear the cracking of the eggs and see the yellow of the yolks.

You go back inside, shower and dust with *talcum*. You brush your teeth with *toothpaste*, trying to start your morning over. The fresh taste makes you feel better.

On the way to the store you pass a bagel bakery. The sight of fresh *bagels* piled high compels you to buy a bakers' dozen. The bag feels warm, and the smell is divine. Next door, you pick up a head of *lettuce*, looking and feeling for a firm, fresh one. Before going home, you renew your spirit by picking up a *bunch of flowers*. You stare at the many bright colors and enjoy their fragrance.

Now, close your eyes and review this image story. Use your fingers to count off the ten items. Notice how we used our various senses to reinforce the images. We will explore this in great detail in a few pages.

Exercise for Creating Your Own Link Story

Here we have a list of things you want to attend to today. Create a link story or image story for these ten items. Be sure to use your senses, a vivid imagination, humor, and exaggeration. Write your story on a piece of paper. Count to see if you have all ten items.

library book	bank deposit	dry cleaning
quart of milk	loaf of bread	cream cheese
laundry bleach	paper towel	fresh fruit
newspaper		

These stories have two important elements: imagery and linkage. You visually capture each listed item. Then, you string it to something else to forge a chain.

Visual imagery is a powerful tool in recalling verbal material because these mental pictures are processed in two different parts of the brain: a verbal location and a nonverbal location. We are more likely to remember words *and* pictures better than words alone. It's like the advantage of leaving two reminders to yourself instead of just one.

The linkage effect is still another memory aid. Instead of ten items in isolation, by making up a story, no matter how ludicrous or improbable, the ten items are forged into a chain. One link leads to the next, thus ensuring better recall.

ENHANCE YOUR MEMORY BY USING YOUR FIVE SENSES

"Verbatim memorization is not the only way to learn a part in a play," said Richard Burton when asked how he learned Shakespearean roles. He went on to explain how he used multi-modal learning; that is, a variety of approaches to the words he wanted to commit to memory. In addition to seeing and hearing the words he tried to touch, smell, and taste the part. He actually used all his senses in assuming the character's lines.

We're going to do the same thing in our daily lives—use our five senses to enhance our memory: sight, hearing, touch, smell, and taste.

Maximizing Your Sense of Sight

Obviously, you have to read your script, speech, sales pitch, and so forth, before you can learn it—and read it more than once. Then you have to "see" the key words on the wall of the auditorium, side of the product you are selling, or elsewhere. Seeing the key words or numbers in oversized, exaggerated format will make them easier to remember.

"Seeing is believing" is frequently quoted to prove that what we see is virtually infallible. People begin to trust too much this one form of perception. They overlook the fact that they don't always "see" everything that is there. We tend to see what interests us and ignore other things. For example, two people are invited to the home of one of their co-workers. One of the two visitors will "see" and remember the clothes worn by the hostess, the food served, the decor of the rooms. The other visitor may not see these items at all! He may vividly recall, instead, the car in the driveway, the landscaping, the type of windows and siding, and the den paneling.

Another perception error is when people get caught up in details and miss the larger picture. Here are three examples:

1. You want to learn a code number. You recall there were two zeros in the middle. What you overlooked was the number of digits. You came up with a six-digit number when there were actually seven digits. The whole should get your attention before the parts.

2. In following detailed traffic directions, it is helpful to sum up the sequence of turns. Is it "right, left, and left" or "right, left, and right"? This comes after you attend to the details of "the bank, the church, a school . . . "

3. Take note of the general price range of the stock, house, car, and the like. For example, you can't remember if the security traded at $19 \frac{1}{4}$ or $91 \frac{1}{4}$. You are sure about the $\frac{1}{4}$, the most insignificant part of the price. If you had remembered it was a low-priced security, you'd know it couldn't be $91 \frac{1}{4}$.

FIVE TECHNIQUES FOR USING YOUR SENSE OF SIGHT

1. *Take a snapshot.* Use your imaginary camera to photograph the item, person, or street sign you are trying to remember. If it's a number, photograph it enlarged so that each digit is six feet tall. If

it's a person, photograph her holding a nameplate with her name and firm listed.

2. *Use a name tag.* If this is an object, attach an imaginary price tag that also lists the model number, color, availability, and manufacturer. Visualize this "tag" whenever you think of the product.

3. *Paint with color.* Use a varied palette of colors to help recall people or things. Use green for model numbers, red for prices, as examples. Also, remember people by some distinguishing color: gray lady, golden girl, silver fox, carrot top.

4. *Locate a dominant feature.* If it is a piece of equipment, exaggerate some important control such as, for example, a button, lever, handle, dial. Visualize this as larger than lifesize.

5. *Look for a pattern.* A pattern is a relationship or rule that you apply to remember, as in the name MISSISSIPPI. After the initial letter M, you add I and double SS, then I and Double SS, and I and double PP, ending with the final I.

Recognizing the Importance of Hearing in Memory

Hearing is our second most useful sense when it comes to learning. Many excellent pianists respond to questions about their artistry with, "Oh, I learned to play by ear." They "hear" the melody in their mind as they play. This helps them remember the thousands of notes that make up a lengthy piece.

There are many situations where recognition of sound is of primary importance. In some cases, hearing may supplant sight entirely. This, of course, is true with blind people who depend on hearing to compensate for their loss of sight. Most sighted people are apt to miss some of the opportunities where hearing serves to augment learning through vision.

The shriek of a fire alarm immediately reminds the volunteer fireman that he is needed at the firehouse. Alarm clocks, door bells, kitchen timers, car alarms, ice-cream vendors all provide auditory cues to our memory. In memory development, you can use a person's voice as a cue to the name or the face. You can hear the voice of the directory assistance operator give you the telephone number. This will enhance your hearing it correctly and your ability to remember it.

So, too, the dieter can enhance her memory if she recalls the suggested food items in the voice of the lecturer or doctor. When in the supermarket, it's helpful to try to recall what it was your spouse asked you to buy in your spouse's voice. Such auditory elaboration makes it easier to remember.

Once you have cultivated the practice of trying to hear more as well as see more, you will broaden your path toward an improved memory. You will see that generally, hearing can be used to supplement sight, rather than to supplant it. This is similar to looking at an object and seeing extra things with it. In this case you add hearing as the main "extra," which at times can prove to be a vital factor.

THREE WAYS TO BENEFIT FROM USING YOUR HEARING TO REMEMBER BETTER

1. *Use rhyme.* Simple rhymes can give meaning to material that eludes memory. From your childhood, you may recall:

I before E except after C, or sounded like A, as neighbor and weigh.

Thirty days hath September, April, June, and November . . .

In 1492, Columbus sailed the ocean blue.

From your present-day encounters, you can remember people you met with keep-to-yourself visual reminders such as Plain Jane, Slim Jim, Fat Matt, or Ruth Tooth.

2. *Use similar sounding words or names to boost recall.* Mr. Saltz reminds you of "salts." Dr. Kissinger reminds you of a statesman who will "kiss the singer." The automobile, Acura, sounds like "accurate."

3. *Say it aloud.* Talk to yourself to enhance the encoding of the information. You will hear it as well as see it.

Using Your Sense of Touch to Enhance Memory

Just as the sense of hearing is an important addition to that of sight, so is the sense of touch a great aid to hearing, and in fact, to sight as well. Touch may even supplement or supplant both hearing and sight on occasion.

A darkened room or blackout where hearing is needed or when sight is impossible is such an analogy. Under those circumstances hearing, too, may be curtailed or even lacking if no sounds occur. Then touch takes over in full. We have heard the term "groping in the dark," and anyone who has gone through such an experience will recognize how important touch can be.

In the field of memory improvement, touch is interconnected with something we call *motor memory*. Our kinesthetic or motor skills are the last to leave us. Ask any senior who learned to swim and/or ride a bike as a youngster. We never "forget" how to do either even if it has been years since we last tried.

If you ask expert typists to call out the order of the letters on the keyboard he or she might not be able to do so. They know the alphabet in ABC order, but the keyboard letters simply jump to their fingertips in response to the linkage of memory with touch, with no conscious effort on the typist's part.

Many things with which we are familiar may be noted at a glance through sight; or sounds may be checked automatically, as when a radio operator reads a coded message. These are like typing, tying shoe laces, and many more complex uses of the sense of touch when it has reached the state of motor memory.

To improve memory utilizing the sense of touch, it is a good idea to try doing minor actions automatically or even in the dark, while putting your mind on other things. When you drive a car, you must be alert for things you see and hear; yet all the while, you are handling the controls by applying touch and linking it with your other senses.

TWO TECHNIQUES FOR HELPING YOUR MEMORY THROUGH TOUCH

1. *Get the feel of the word or name.* When you hear an unfamiliar word or name, imagine what the object would feel like. For example, to remember the film *Silkwood,* imagine the smooth feel of fine silk and combine it with a piece of rough-hewn wood. Apply "feel" to these names of people or objects: Sanders, Thorne, ironstone, Firestone, glass, Ruff, snow.

2. *Write the key number or word in your palm with your finger.* Kinesthetic approaches are a big boost to memory. Let's say you need to recall the number "eight." Write it in the palm of your hand using the index finger of your other hand as a pen. The motor memory of your "writing" will help you remember. Writing a longer number in the "air" with your finger will also serve as a memory aid.

Increasing Your Memory Through Your Sense of Smell

Utilizing smell with the other senses is an important memory adjunct, as it may provide just the needed difference in some essential matter. The smell of food tells when it is properly cooked. A burning smell warns of a short-circuit. Spoiled food gives off a distinctive smell, and so on. But the sense of smell can go much further. The scent of an exotic perfume can bring back a flood of treasured memories. A whole story might be written hinging upon the aroma of a fine cigar.

Two Techniques for Advancing Your Memory Using Your Sense of Smell

1. *Associate smell with certain people you meet.* Become aware of certain odors that seem to cling to some individuals, such as tobacco, onions, garlic, and the like. They may be pleasant aromas, as, for example, from perfume, or after shave lotion.

2. *Link smell with places.* After getting the notice of a meeting in a Chinese restaurant, link the smells of such a cuisine with the date of the meeting notice. If travel directions tell you to make a left turn at the fast-food hamburger place, make that image more vivid by smelling the burgers as you turn left mentally.

Using Your Sense of Taste to Improve Your Memory

There are many times when taste becomes important to memory, or depends on memory. A cook will pause to taste the food in the middle of preparation. His memory will ascertain that it tastes "right."

Many memories are induced by bitter or sweet tastes. Wine tasters make a profession of such distinctions. Tastes of various foods often bring back recollections of almost forgotten experiences or surroundings, all adding to the memory cross-index file.

Two Techniques for Getting Memory Results with Your Sense of Taste

1. *Match the new person you meet with the taste that his or her name may suggest,* for example, Mr. Rice, Dr. Burger, Frank, Ms. Lemmon, Olivia, Kevin Bacon, Sherri, Brandi, Mrs. Pepper.

2. *In preparing a grocery shopping list, pause to taste each of the items you plan to buy.* Taste the food briefly. This will enhance your chances of remembering each item on your list.

By using your senses, you will definitely enhance your memory. The advertising industry has known and practiced this for decades. We remember a product better when we perceive it from different sensory modes. TV commercials appeal to us via a "new car smell," "sensuous leather," or the "smooth taste" of a malt beverage.

Because each sense plays its part in observations that are transferred to your "memory file," it is important to use those individual senses to their full degree and purpose. It is important to cross-file. The findings from one sense amplify or validate the others. Overdependence on a single sense may limit your memory file, just as limiting the activity or observational range of a single sense is the reason why memory may "fail" a person later.

Using your different senses increases the power of your memory because objective and subjective sensations are working in an interlocking fashion. The more you use them along these lines, the stronger they will become. And your memory file of certain things will enable your imagination to fill in essential facts toward a completed whole when certain gaps occur.

USING COLOR TO ENERGIZE YOUR MEMORY

Why try to remember things in black and white when you can make your images more vivid and more memorable in living, vivid color?

When you are introduced to someone you never met before, listen to his or her name and visualize the spelling in colorful ink. If you haven't heard it clearly, ask to have the name repeated or spelled. Using your mind's eye, which is always 20/20, see the name spelled out. Be sure to select an appropriate color. Look at this list to get some ideas:

Mrs. Kelly—green	Rose—red
Mr. Silva—gray	Sonny—yellow
Mr. Blustein—blue	Pearl—pearl

When you use colorful imagery, you are also using association. The name or word is now associated with a color you are familiar with. You often use colorful language that does not necessarily involve a color yet is vivid, picturesque, and glowing. For example, your personal association can be sensual, exaggerated, action-filled, or humorous. These do not involve a tint or hue but are nonetheless colorful. You remember best when you use a whole arsenal of mnemonics, or memory aids.

Four Tips for Enhancing Your Memory Images

Here are some tips for making the images you use colorful and powerful:

1. *Exaggerate them.* Make the subject, number, or name bigger than life in size and in quantity. Use caricatures. Pick out salient features just the way a cartoonist does.

2. *Use humor.* Use funny associations to make the image absurd or nonsensical. You are more likely to remember some humorous connection. TV advertisers employ creative directors to do just that. You can do it—for example, Daniel (inside a lion's den), Dr. Hershey (melted chocolate dripping down his side), Frank (with mustard around his mouth).

3. *Add action.* Whenever you can, use motion. Moving objects stand out more than do stationary ones. For example, you meet people with these last names: Field (track and field athlete in competition), Stein (hoisted beer stein), North (compass needle jiggling and pointing north).

4. *Create a unique image.* Avoid using the same image for more than one thing. Create your own images so that it will mean more to you. The preceding examples are merely illustrations. Those you make up will work better for you.

While we have primarily used names, you can use these techniques to match products, street names, words, or numbers.

SIX WAYS TO REMOVE THE MEMORY BLOCKS
THAT HOLD YOU BACK

The psychologist Hermann Ebbinghause wrote about "curves of forgetting," which describes how, if we learn something today but don't use or review the information within 24 hours, we will forget a great deal of it. The following day, he found, we forget a little more, but not as much as we forgot the first day.

His good news was that once we review the material our memory will bounce back to its initial learning. We will forget it again, but the second time we will forget more slowly than the first time.

Just as memory gets stronger with use, it gets weaker with disuse. While this decay is a major factor in forgetting, there are others.

There are many situations in which we sabotage our own efforts at mastering business facts, figures, and names. By anticipating them, we can often prevent forgetfulness. Some of these blocks we put in our path ourselves. Others are beyond our control but not beyond our understanding. Here they are:

1. *Anxiety.* When we are anxious, our memory is diminished. If a family member or friend is undergoing surgery the next day, it's understandable if that's the day you misplace your glasses. When the anxiety is reduced, normal memory will return.

2. *Depression.* Depression is another emotion that weakens our memory. If you're mourning the loss of a close friend or colleague, you will inevitably see signs of increased forgetfulness. As the depression lifts, so too will the level of memory.

3. *Rushing.* A great source of misplaced or forgotten items is the hurried pace many of us maintain. Think of what you are doing *now* rather than ponder what you must do next. Time is saved when you take deliberate, thoughtful steps in your errands and routines.

4. *Tension.* Anger, rage, stress, and ardor all interrupt our usual unconscious encoding processes. They blur the mind temporarily. Taking a break, a refreshing drink, or participating in an exercise program will help restore memory.

5. *Interference.* Much forgetting is likely due to interference by other learning. This does not imply that you have a limited capacity in your memory bank where new data push the old data out. It is not so much the amount we learn as it is what we learn that determines forgetting by interference. Meeting people with similar names, ordering material with similar code numbers, or learning Italian after studying Spanish may lead to interference. You can, of course, build on the similarities to strengthen learning.

6. *Chemicals.* Caffeine, tobacco, alcohol, mind-altering drugs, even antihistamines have an effect on alertness and judgment. Stimulants such as caffeine and tobacco as well as depressants such as alcohol and over-the-counter drugs interfere with your ability to get the message recorded properly. For those hooked on these substances, brain cells are destroyed leaving permanent memory damage. A reduction or elimination of stimulants and depressants will enhance your memory considerably. Most alcohol-induced memory loss seems to disappear when the individual stops drinking. Of course, much depends on the degree of deterioration. Older people have more trouble rebounding because a lifetime of abuse can cause irreversible damage.

Coffee, and other caffeine sources, cause agitation, which interferes with memory function. In the best of circumstances, the mind is both alert and relaxed. When stimulants such as caffeine become addictive, they prevent us from becoming relaxed even though they promote alertness. Yet older people benefit from the elimination of drowsiness that a cup of tea or coffee may provide. People have their own tolerances and you must seek your own level.

Use these tips to keep your memory from being sandbagged.

MEMENTOS

1. Learn the 3 Rs of memory: register, retain, retrieve.
2. Do the exercises for strengthening short-term memory.
3. Work on transferring material into your permanent memory.
4. Encode information by using interest and elaboration.
5. Recollect memories using recall and recognition.
6. Include visual imagery in your daily activities.
7. Create link stories to forge memory chains.
8. Use your five senses as memory aids.
9. Add color to your arsenal of memory techniques.
10. Get rid of common memory blocks.

Chapter Two

Building Memory Associations

Memory is triggered by the thoughts we carry in our brains. These thoughts are intertwined in a web of associations. The process of relating what you want to learn to something you already know is called *association*.

Basic to memory improvement is the concept that all we wish to remember must be associated in some way with something we already know.

Very often we see or hear something that makes us say: "That reminds me!" The visual or auditory cue that reminded you may have had no obvious connection with the object it reminded you of. Yet there was an association there someplace. That's because many of our associations are made subconsciously.

For example, we briefly glimpse a face of a person on the street who vaguely resembles a long-deceased relative, and a flood of memories washes over us. Or, we hear the voice of a stranger that triggers a response to a voice of a childhood friend. A dozen early memories come back to us, all at once.

To improve our memory, we have to learn ways to make conscious associations. The focus of this chapter is how to make conscious associations between new information and information you have already stored.

HOW TO USE CONSCIOUS ASSOCIATIONS

When you went to school, if you wanted to learn the notes on the lines of the treble clef in music class you may have made a conscious association with the sentence: Every Good Boy Does Fine. This sentence, from each of the first letters, gives us: E G B D F.

Or, the word HOMES helped you remember the names of the Great Lakes: Huron, Ontario, Michigan, Erie, Superior.

These first-letter cues helped us remember the items themselves. Here are examples of other conscious associations:

1. *Simple rhymes:*
Thirty days hath September, April, June and November.
In fourteen hundred ninety-two, Columbus sailed the ocean blue.

2. *More complex rhymes:*
I before E, except after C, and when sounded like A, as in *neighbor* and *weigh.*

3. *Giving meaning to random numbers.* Personal information can help you remember otherwise meaningless numbers. For example, your friend's phone number is 234-1954. This is easy for *you* because 1954 may be a significant year in your life (for example, birth, marriage). You associate the year that you already know with the new phone number.

4. *Adding familiarity to the unfamiliar.* You learned to draw a reasonable outline map of Italy because you remembered it looked like the profile of a tall boot with the heel to the right. The "boot" is familiar. The shape of other European countries did not conjure a familiar shape with which we could forge an association.

Why Do I Sometimes Call My Children by the Wrong Name?

Paradoxically, association can occasionally cause us to confuse the names of children or grandchildren when we call an offspring by the wrong name. It also illustrates the power of association in memory.

This is easy to explain and easy to remedy. The names of children or grandchildren are easy to confuse because they are so strongly associated with one another in your memory. You have used them together so often in the same sentence, at the same time, and in the same place. When you are tired or distracted, you may open your mental memory box labeled "children" and grab the wrong name because they are so tightly interwoven.

You can avoid this in the future by pausing before you address one of your children. Focus your attention, for a second, on what you are doing—on the face of the child and then on the name. Instead of groping for a name from that "box" of related names, you

will reach for the correct name. That extra second you take to associate the face with the name will save you from embarrassment and
your child from frustration.

HOW TO PUT THE ASSOCIATION CIRCLE
TO WORK FOR YOU

On those occasions when you need help in retrieving something
that you know is stored in your memory but you can't quite pull it
out, you can use the association circle technique. It's called a circle
because you think around the subject. You think of everything you
can that might be associated in any way with the specific item you're
trying to recall. This is one of the few memory techniques you can
apply at the retrieval stage of memory. Most others are used at the
recording or encoding stage.

For example, you're trying to think of the name of a fellow student you knew in high school and haven't seen in years. You might
try thinking of the building itself, other students, facial characteristics of this student, and so forth. One of these items might have
become associated sufficiently to bring the name forth. If not, you
would go on to specific classes you took together, team or club
associations, the sound or length of the name, and so on.

The association circle has been used to help crime and accident
victims recall details such as height and weight of assailants and car
license plates. Often, a piece of incomplete information on a related
topic is enough to help them remember something more significant.

This technique of thinking around the subject is similar to what
you do when looking for a lost item at home. You start by looking
in the general area and circle around until it's found.

Reap the Benefits of Getting Personal

Personalizing events is one way of using association to remember. You can recall the date of the Apollo 13 takeoff because your
son was born on the same day. Perhaps your niece got married the
same year that you moved into your present home. People remember personal and public events better when they try relating them to
themselves and events in their own lives.

We even associate on an unconscious level. The phenomenon of *deja vu,* or of having the feeling of having been someplace before, is an example; also, the phrase "Hmm, that reminds me of. . . ." The reason for such feelings is that somehow in the past those two places or things became associated with each other. The surfacing of one thought drew the other with it.

Obviously, association plays a major role in memory. After this overview you may wonder how you can use association to help you remember lists of random items. We're going to test your ability to do that. After giving you some pointers on how you an make association pairs and clusters, we go on to show you how to maximize the use of association by means of visual and verbal elaboration, forging links, and hanging pegs.

LEARN THIS BETTER WAY TO MEMORIZE LISTS OF ITEMS

Most of the associations we make at work or in our personal lives are based on logic. We associate the patient with his illness, the client with her portfolio, the restaurant patron with what he ordered, the jury and its verdict.

A random list of isolated items such as the following presents us with associations that are not logical, if we read the items as written. Take a few minutes to read the 20 items on this supermarket shopping list. Take three more minutes to study the list, cover it, and jot down as many items as you can—in any order.

Supermarket Shopping List

eggs	cookies	paper towels	ground beef
milk	cat food	chicken	toilet tissue
cheese	sugar	butter	tuna fish
bread	coffee	ice cream	ketchup
flour	napkins	crackers	rolls

1. _____   6. _____   11. _____   16. _____

2. _____   7. _____   12. _____   17. _____

3. _____	8. _____	13. _____	18. _____
4. _____	9. _____	14. _____	19. _____
5. _____	10. _____	15. _____	20. _____

Putting Association Pairs to Work

You're going to have another opportunity to recall this list after we offer you some suggestions. You'll be amazed at your improvement.

Instead of attempting to memorize this list as written, try to make logical pairings wherever possible, that is, bread and butter, cheese and crackers. This way, instead of trying to learn 20 disparate items, you are reducing the task by half. Learning ten pairs is much more manageable.

You may want to make up your own association pairs. Look at this list of ten pairs first to get the idea.

Pair	*Rationale*
1. chicken and eggs	natural association
2. milk and coffee	both beverages
3. cheese and crackers	eaten together
4. bread and butter	logical pair
5. flour and sugar	baking ingredients
6. cookies and ice cream	desserts
7. cat food and paper towels	clean up after cat's feeding
8. ground beef and ketchup	eaten together
9. napkins and toilet tissue	both paper
10. tuna fish and rolls	possible sandwich

After looking at the paired items and their rationale, you may want to make up some of your own. Those of your own making will work best for you. Spend a few minutes going over your association pairs.

Cover the list and visualize the following single items. They will trigger the mates with which you paired them. Enter the mate alongside each of these items:

coffee	cat food
crackers	rolls
ice cream	ketchup
bread	chicken
sugar	napkins

If you try this tomorrow or even in a week you will notice that these image associations are still with you. After going through this exercise, you will find many useful applications of pairing image associations in your daily life.

Getting back to our shopping list, you can refine your associations even further. These ten pairs can then be clustered into five groups of two or three pairs. For example, try breaking them down as follows:

Meals: chicken/egg, beef/ketchup, tuna fish/rolls

Accompaniments: coffee/milk, cheese/crackers, bread/butter

Desserts: cake ingredients (flour/sugar), cookies/ice cream

Cat needs: cat food/paper towels

Other paper goods: napkins/toilet tissue

Your ten pairs are now reduced to five groups, which in turn trigger the 20 items. Try this with the pairs you chose.

HOW TO USE VISUAL AND VERBAL ELABORATION

The associations we make can be either visual or verbal. Visual associations use images or pictures. Verbal associations use words or sounds.

In school you learned to use shapes as visual association clues. On an outline map of the United States, Florida, Texas, and California were easy to identify because of their shapes. They became points of reference for states that bordered on them.

These are examples of visual elaboration. The "elaboration" creates a meaningful association between what is to be learned (the country or state) and what is already familiar (the shape).

Verbal elaboration includes such associations as rhymes, similar words, and spelling cues. Examples of popular rhymes include the following:

> If his face is red, raise his head.
> If his face is pale, raise his tail.
> (First aid for shock victims)

Some spelling clues:

> "Stationery" has an "e" as in "letter."
> "Stationary" has an "a" as in "place."

Exercise for Using Visual and Verbal Elaboration

Here are some everyday objects followed by their hiding places. Look at the list of pairs for about four minutes. Try to remember what's hidden where. Then cover the list and fill in the blanks that follow. In some cases the item will be listed; in other cases the hiding place is listed and you fill in the item that's hidden there. Use visual or verbal elaboration to make the association. For example, equate the marriage license with the bride and groom figures atop a wedding cake. Visualize the miniature couple locked up in a vault's safe deposit box.

pen/notebook	extra eyeglasses/sock drawer
stamps/file folder	bracelet/under sweaters
credit card/desk drawer	extra batteries/refrigerator
marriage license/vault	extra checks/bottom desk drawer
address book/kitchen drawer	photo album/TV cabinet

Cover the list and fill in these blanks:

stamps: _____	address book: _____
credit card: _____	sock drawer: _____
marriage license: _____	extra checks: _____
under sweaters: _____	extra batteries: _____
notebook: _____	TV cabinet: _____

GET GOOD RESULTS USING THE LINK SYSTEM

You now have experience in learning pairs of items and recalling them at will. There are many occasions when we need to recall a long list of items in a particular order, for example, lists of things to do, lists of customers, items to include in a speech or report, or course material.

A chain is a series of metal links or rings passing through one another. We've heard the adage that a chain is only as strong as its weakest link. In this memory system, we are going to link various individual items into a strong chain. It can be used in any situation where you want to remember a list of things. Each "thing" becomes a "link."

Learning the link system involves serial learning. You train yourself to go from one link to another to another and so on until you have mastered the list. This is different from the associations you made when you learned pairs of items.

There is a similarity because you will again be using visual and verbal elaboration. The major difference is that now instead of learning: A-B, C-D, E-F, and so on, you will be learning: A-B-C-D-E-F, and so on.

Recalling a List of Six Items

Assume you want to complete these six errands in this order on a given day:

Pick up a newspaper.

Make a dental appointment.

Get the car serviced.

Buy milk.

Take a tennis lesson.

Call the gardener.

The first step would be to reduce these errands into six basic words: newspaper, dentist, car, milk, tennis, and gardener. To use the link system in remembering these six items, you first form a visual association relating newspaper and dentist. You might picture opening the newspaper and seeing your dentist's face on page one. Next associate dentist and car. You might visualize your dentist driving your car, or you're running over your dentist. To associate car and milk, you might picture the service station filling your car's tank with milk instead of gas. To associate milk and tennis, you might picture a tennis racket and ball printed on the container of milk. To associate tennis and the gardener, you might imagine yourself playing tennis with your gardener, or think about your lawn at home and the fantasy of having your own tennis court installed by your gardener.

Of course, it might be just as easy for some people to remember six items without the need of a system. The procedure is, however, the same with six items or sixty.

The visual associations suggested for these six items are some possibilities that came from my mind. You will, undoubtedly, think of your own. Both visual and verbal elaborators tend to be more effective when you come up with your own. The choice of visual or verbal elaboration is also up to you.

More Suggestions for Using Links

Action scenes, exaggerated images, and distortions are important factors in making your associations. The more ridiculous, amusing, or outrageous the artificial association may seem, the more useful it can prove to be. Think of some of the outlandish images advertisers use on TV and print media to get your attention and to make sure you remember the product. Of the six associations I suggested, some are bizarre and some are plausible. The choice is always yours as long as the associations are vivid and interacting. It's a good idea to use the first association that comes into your head, because it will likely be the first one to come to mind when you want to recall the item.

In serial learning as we have here, you begin with the first item and proceed in order as each item leads to the next. For our example, you thought of newspaper, which reminded you of your dentist; dentist reminded you of car, which reminded you of milk; milk reminded you of tennis, which led to your gardener. Each item is cued by the previous one. The first item, newspaper, is the only one without a predecessor. You have to visualize this one yourself. Exaggerating its size is one way to do this.

Exercise for Using the Link System

Read the following list of eight items. Look at the list for about three minutes. Try to recall the eight items in this exact order. Write out your list and then check it for accuracy.

1. clock
2. piano
3. ladder
4. bed

5. briefcase
6. shoes
7. helicopter
8. video camera

If you had less than perfect recall go over your list and pay particular attention to those items you missed. What was your association cue? Was it vivid or easily forgotten? Your weakest link may be your weakest association. Make sure you actually "see" what you are visualizing, even if it is only for a few seconds.

Try this exercise again after you have patched up some of your weaker associations. Compare your ability to remember the eight items the second time around with your first attempt.

USING THE STORY SYSTEM
TO HELP YOU REMEMBER

There is a variation to the link system that lends itself to certain situations. It is called the story system, and here you weave the various items into a connecting story. It is actually an extension of the use of sentences as helpers in paired association tasks. You just continue with additional sentences to form a story based on the items you want to remember.

For example, let's go back to our six-word list: newspaper, dentist, car, milk, tennis, and gardener. You can string the six terms into one continuous story: "I took my newspaper with me to read in the dentist's office while waiting for my appointment. Driving there, I parked my car near the milk store so that I'd remember to pick up a quart on the way to my tennis lesson. I stored the milk in the tennis club's refrigerator. While playing, I hit a tennis ball over the fence into a neighboring garden. This reminded me to call the gardener as soon as I got home."

Four Differences Between the Link and Story Systems

The story system is similar to the link system in many ways, but there are some basic differences and advantages.

1. In the story system, you link the items in a continuous, logical sequence. This is an advantage for most people who find it easier to remember a story than a series of associations.

2. A little extra time is needed to make an association in the story system because you are concerned about the narrative. In the link system you merely use the first association that comes to mind.

3. The story system is limited to about 20 items. It's difficult to put together a story with a list longer than that. Using the link system, you may find it easier to associate even more items.

4. Items that you associate in the link system can be remembered backwards and forwards, as needed. Using the story system, you are locked into the logical, one-way story line.

People who are more comfortable with a verbal orientation may prefer the story system. Those who are basically visually dominant will prefer picturing the links rather than recalling the story with its dependency on words. The link system is effective for immediate recall but is less effective a week or two later. The story system may take a little more effort initially, but it is more likely to be recalled a week or two later. With practice, people using the link system were able to improve their performance so that they could soon remember 30 to 40 words.

Everyday Applications of the Link and Story Systems

Most of us do not have many occasions when we want to memorize 20 or 30 disparate items in a set order. When it comes to shopping lists, a simple written list is preferable. Many well-organized people write out a "To Do" list for each day's activities. There are times, of course, when such lists are left behind or not written. On those occasions, your ability to associate a variety of items will come in handy.

Factual material that we need to remember for work or school lends itself to these two systems, for example, a product line for a salesperson, a list of preferred customers, detailed information for the law or medical school student.

A popular example of this was provided by Dale Carnegie, the motivational speaker, when he suggested this story for remembering the names of the 13 original states in the order in which they entered the Union:

"A lady from *Delaware* bought a ticket on the *Pennsylvania* Railroad. She packed a *new jersey* sweater and went to visit her friend *Georgia* in *Connecticut*. The next morning they attended *mass* in a church on *Mary's land*. They then took the *South car line* home, and dined on a *new ham*, which had been roasted by *Virginia* (the cook from *New York*). After dinner they took the *North car line* and *rode to the island*."

This particular story system example has a high retention value. Students of mine, with little review, recall the 13 states months later. Obviously, the link and story systems are good for remembering lists of things.

Remembering classroom lectures is another application of this technique. You can link the points together in order as the speaker makes them. The trick here is to practice forming associations rapidly and to concentrate on what is being said so that you will be able to identify the key points. This doesn't have to be exclusively in a college classroom. It is a valuable technique to practice when listening to your boss, a customer, a family member, or a radio or TV broadcast.

How to Use These Techniques as a Speaker

The other side of the coin is to use this technique when you are the speaker. You won't be dependent on notes or other crutches when you use the link and/or story system. Begin by choosing a concrete key word to represent each point. Once you have your key words, you merely link them together in the order in which you want to discuss them in your talk.

Mark Twain spent the last years of his life giving speeches around the country. In his notes he wrote that he had a great deal of difficulty remembering what he wanted to say. At last he came up with the idea of creating pictures to represent the ideas he wanted to put across in his speeches. He created visual images. After that he was able to speak without notes. He merely drew a picture of each section of his speech and strung them out in a row. Then he would look at them and commit the images to memory. When he got up to speak, he had the row of images fresh and sharp in his mind. Each image stood for a topic, and he simply moved from one topic to another. This is another example of the link and story system. He "linked" the picture to an idea he wanted to get across. The row of images represented the "story."

Exercise for Using the Link and Story System

Pretend you have just returned from a cruise to the island of Bermuda. Several memorable events took place during your vacation. Now that you are back you want to tell your friends all about it. You don't want to leave out any of these experiences. Make a list of ten images or key words that you are going to use to employ the link and/or story system to tell of this adventure.

"Our car service arrived late and we barely arrived at the airport on time to get on our flight to Fort Lauderdale, Florida, where we had to board the ship by 4:00 P.M.

"The flight was fine but on the way from the airport to the ship our taxi had a flat tire. We made it to the cruise ship at 3:50 P.M.

"We went up to see our cabin but had trouble locating our luggage. It did not reach our cabin until 5:00 P.M. the next day! We had to stay in the same heavy clothing for 36 hours. Everyone else changed into fresh, light-colored cruise clothes.

"One of the passengers who shared our table had been a Hollywood reporter and columnist. She amused us with stories about many celebrities, such as Tom Cruise, Madonna, and Rosie O'Donnell.

"The second night out we were invited to sit at the captain's table. He was from Norway and told fascinating sea tales in a charming accent. By then we had appropriate clothing.

"Bermuda is beautiful, and we did quite a bit of shopping. I purchased a set of four coffee mugs made of bone china, with matching cake plates, for only $15. We enjoyed having high tea at one of the old world-hotels.

"The cruise back to Fort Lauderdale was very rocky. We met up with a surprise storm. Many passengers got seasick and stayed in their cabins. Fortunately, the two of us were fine and didn't miss a meal! We arrived home on time and really enjoyed our cruise—after its awkward start."

List your ten images or key words:

1. _____   2. _____   3. _____

4. _____   5. _____   6. _____

7. _____   8. _____   9. _____

10. _____

COMBINING THE LINK SYSTEM WITH ASSOCIATION PAIRS

There are many everyday learning tasks that involve both serial learning and paired-association learning. In such cases, you would combine the link system with the association pairs, for example, giving the sales manager's name when you are supplied with the company name. This is a paired association task. But how about being able to recall each company you deal with *and* the name of its sales manager? You could use the link system to link the company names together and the association pairs to associate the manager to the company.

In a school situation, students learn to give the capital-city name for each state mentioned or the name of the vice-president(s) when the president's name is mentioned. Foreign-language students frequently learn a nucleus of basic words with which to communicate in the new language. They then build chains of new words by linking them to the basic words until they become fluent in the language. You can probably think of other situations in which you can use this system.

Using the Alphabet to Link Items

One easy way to link separate items in a recognizable order is to make use of the alphabet. Alphabetical order is a simple way to implement the serial nature of disparate items. Let's assume that you sell residential real estate. At the present time you are trying to find houses for these six families: Rizzuto, Lucas, Petersen, Black, Lopez, and Cooper. This is the order in which they came into your real estate office. It does not have to remain the order in which you think of them or their home needs.

Each family has made clear to you that they will only consider a house that meets a particular need, such as four bedrooms, near a school, and so forth. Use the alphabet to link these names and make paired associations to match the family and their special needs, which are listed below.

Examples Using Links and Paired Associations

Study this list for two minutes and then cover the names and their needs.

Black	Must be near transportation. Only one car in the family.
Cooper	Must have a two-car garage.
Lopez	Must be near the elementary school.
Lucas	Needs large back yard.
Petersen	Wants a finished basement.
Rizzuto	Needs 4 bedrooms; they have 5 children.

Before you go any further, what are the names of the six families you are trying to find homes for?

_____ _____ _____ _____ _____ _____

Remember we were going to link them in alphabetical order. One cue to assist you here would be to remember that two of the names begin with the letter "L" and that these were the two middle names. Two names came before the "Ls" and two names came after. Then think of "BC" for the first two names and "PR" for the last two.

These cues should help you forge a chain of six links.

Now for the hard part—the needs of each family.

Black	Has only one car and so needs to be near transportation. Picture one very large BLACK car, perhaps a limo.
Cooper	Must have a two-car garage. Visualize the two Os in Cooper as two cars.
Lopez	Must be near the elementary school. Lopez and lower school begin with the same sound.

Lucas	Needs a large back yard.
	The Lucas kids need to run "loose" in the big yard.
Petersen	Wants a finished basement.
	Peter's son will live downstairs.
Rizzuto	Has 5 kids, needs 4 bedrooms.
	The Rizzuto house "resounds" with many voices.

These needs have been linked with images that come to my mind. You, of course, may come up with others that will work.

Exercise for Linking Associations and Names and Needs

Without looking at the earlier material, see how many of these questions you can now answer:

1. Which family needs a large back yard?
2. What is the Black family looking for?
3. What are the requirements of the Rizzuto family?
4. Which of your clients needs to be near the elementary school?
5. What did the Coopers say they wanted?
6. Who is looking for a house with a finished basement?
7. Which family wants to be near transportation?
8. Who is looking for four bedrooms?
9. Who must have a two-car garage?
10. What is the Lucas family looking for?

Whenever you try to link images you will find that exaggerations, similar sounds, and humor will enhance your ability to make the association.

PUTTING THE PEG SYSTEM TO WORK IN YOUR DAILY LIFE

The major failing of the link system is that it is difficult to recall an item in a specific position on the list. For example, you want to remember the fourth item, or the seventh item. With the link system, you would have to go through the entire list. A system that could

give you the ninth item if you just think of the number nine would
be helpful. That is what the peg system does.

The peg system substitutes something concrete and familiar for
each number. You then match that concrete item, or noun, with
what you want to remember. In the peg system you begin by memorizing a series of concrete nouns that in some way correspond
meaningfully with the numbers.

The use of pegs to remember items on a list goes back to the
seventeenth century and Henry Herson, who came up with a list of
ten objects that physically resembled the number itself. For example, the number 1 was represented by a candle, 3 was a trident, 8
was a pair of spectacles. Let's assume your list had as its first item a
paper, its third item a fish, and its eighth item a book.

Putting the fixed list of pegs to work: 1 = candle   3 = trident
and   8 = spectacles,   you would make these associations:

1 = candle = paper	(Don't let the paper get too close to the candle's flame.)
3 = trident = fish	(The fish is impaled on the trident.)
8 = spectacles = book	(The spectacles are needed to read the book.)

This list of number shapes, as they were called, were used
widely for about 200 years. In 1879, an Englishman, John Sambrook,
improved the peg system by using rhyming syllables and words to
represent the numbers. This made it easier to remember which
object represented each number. A popular version of that Peg system that is used today based on rhymes is:

one-bun	six-sticks
two-shoe	seven-heaven
three-tree	eight-gate
four-door	nine-wine
five-hive	ten-hen

It took little effort to learn these rhyming peg words. Recall was
enhanced when people recalled the nursery rhyme, "One-two buckle
my shoe, three-four shut the door. . . ." This may have worked well in
the past, but we have come up with a modern version that is concrete

and contemporary. Abstract terms like "heaven" and rarely seen objects such as "hive" make this list difficult to apply.

The concept of peg words is a good one. They become "hangers" or pegs on which you can hang different items you want to remember in a certain order. The hangers or pegs never change. The items you want to remember become the clothes that you change as often as you wish. Because the pegs are fixed, you can easily pull out the fifth item, the seventh item, and so on.

Recall of the items out of order is simple. For example, what was the fifth item? Since five = hive, you recall the item you associated with "hive." To come up with the seventh item, you would think back to the thing you associated with "heaven."

How to Use Familiar Items to Learn Pegs

The modern system that I propose you use is a combination of rhyming words, common coins, and obvious associations. We can easily take this to 30 objects. The older rhyme system ended at 10 because it is too difficult to rhyme words with numbers after 10.

We are familiar with pennies, nickels, dimes, and quarters. For that reason we use them as pegs for their corresponding numbers. That is,

1	=	a penny
5	=	a nickel
10	=	a dime
15	=	dime and nickel
20	=	two dimes
21	=	two dimes and a penny
22	=	two dimes and two pennies
23	=	two dimes and three pennies
24	=	two dimes and four pennies
25	=	a quarter
26	=	quarter and one penny
27	=	quarter and two pennies
28	=	quarter and three pennies
29	=	quarter and four pennies
30	=	quarter and nickel

We now insert a number of everyday rhyming words:

2 = shoe

3 = tree

4 = door

8 = skate

To this we add some obvious associations with numbers:

6 = a six-pack (of soda or beer)

7 = dice (lucky seven)

9 = a cat (nine lives)

11 = skis (ski poles look like an eleven)

12 = a dozen (eggs, donuts, bagels, etc.)

13 = unlucky number represented by witch's hat

14 = anything gold (ring, watch, pin) 14K

16 = candy or anything sweet; Sweet Sixteen

17 = a magazine—*Seventeen*

18 = voting booth or ballot box (Eighteen year olds can vote.)

19 = nineteenth hole on the golf course (mythical)

You now have 30 pegs for your peg system. This will not be any harder to learn than the 10 from the nineteenth century, and you will be able to access 30 items with their serial place number.

Let's try a few examples:

On your list, #5 is a golf ball, #9 are boots, #12 is a snowball, and #15 is a newspaper.

You know that according to the master peg word association 5 = nickel, 9 = cat, 12 = a dozen, and 15 = a dime and nickel.

You then make the associations between the object and the peg word:

#5 a GOLF BALL with an emblem of a NICKEL printed on it

#9 a CAT wearing BOOTS

#12 a DOZEN SNOWBALLS

#15 an old NEWSPAPER with a price of 15 cents on it, a DIME and a NICKEL

Again by using exaggeration, humor, and imagination you will come up with lasting associations. This is just what ad people do when they want you to remember an advertisement or TV commercial.

Exercise for Using Familiar Items as Pegs

The following list of ten items would not lend itself easily to a link or story system because the items are so varied and essentially different from one another. They can easily be remembered using the peg system by associating them with the peg words you already learned using coins, rhymes, and everyday items. The first one has been done for you.

1. symphony   PENNY—a symphony playing "Penny Serenade"
2. red ribbon _____
3. coffee cup _____
4. volcano   _____
5. bicycle_____
6. shovel   _____
7. jeans   _____
8. brown sugar _____
9. hamburger   _____
10. field of cotton _____

If you are confident of the peg words, it doesn't take much effort to go the next step and match the peg word to the item you want to remember.

Now that you have completed the exercise, let's see if these cues can help you recall any of the items you may have missed. If you had a perfect score, see how these associations compare with your own.

2. red ribbon   SHOE—   a shoe tied with a red ribbon instead of a shoelace

3. coffee cup   TREE—   a tree bearing coffee cups instead of leaves

4. volcano   DOOR—   a door cut into a volcano with lava pouring out

5. bicycle   NICKEL—   a bicycle with huge nickels for wheels
6. shovel   SIX-PACK—   a huge six-pack holding six shovels
7. jeans   DICE—   a pair of jeans with dice embroi-
                              dered on each pocket
8. brown sugar   SKATE—   skating on a rink of brown sugar
                              instead of ice
9. hamburger   CAT—   a cat with a huge hamburger in its
                              mouth
10. field of cotton   DIME—   a field of cotton with each cotton
                              ball displaying a dime in it

VISUALIZING A NUMBER-SHAPE SYSTEM

The seventeenth century number-shape system mentioned earlier used concrete objects shaped like the numbers. Unfortunately, many of those objects are no longer commonly seen, for example, 3 = a trident. Recent memory researchers and trainers have continued to use the number-shape system because it is so visual, and many people find it easier to remember than the more auditory story system. They recommend these shapes. We have added the rationale for their inclusion.

1	= pencil	A pencil has the shape of a 1.
2	= swan	The swan's neck resembles the number 2.
3	= heart	When turned on its side, a heart profile resembles the number 3.
4	= boat	A sailboat has the outline of number 4.
5	= hook	A fish hook looks like a 5.
6	= golf club	A golf club with a large face to the right resembles the number 6.
7	= fishing line	A fishing rod pointing to the left with a long line looks like a number 7.
8	= hourglass	The two glass bulbs are shaped like an 8.
9	= tennis racket	A tennis racket with its right side flattened looks like the number 9.
10	= bat and ball	The bat looks like the numeral 1 and the ball looks like the numeral zero.

Two Exercises for Using the Number-Shape System

EXERCISE 1: A salesman has taught himself to visualize some of his clients' telephone area codes with images that use the number-shape system.

For example, "Two swans separated by a pencil" tell him that the area code is 212. This happens to be the area code for New York City.

Here are three more of his number-shape images. Alongside each one write in the actual three-digit area code. For purposes of checking your answers these represent Chicago, New Orleans, and Puerto Rico area codes.

Heart, pencil, swan = _____

Hook, ball, boat = _____

Hourglass, ball, tennis racket = _____

EXERCISE 2: Make up an image using the number-shape system for each of these random numbers:

924 = _____

583 = _____

4765 = _____

HOW YOU CAN BENEFIT FROM HEARING AN ALPHABET PEG SYSTEM

This is the last of the peg systems. It gives you the ability to learn 26 items using the ABCs. Most people find it takes them little time to learn these pegs for the alphabet because they are based on simple sounds. Here they are:

A	Ace	J	Jay	S	Eskimo
B	Bee	K	Kay	T	T-Shirt
C	Sea	L	Elbow	U	Yew
D	Deed	M	MC	V	Visa
E	Easel	N	Enamel	W	W.C.
F	Efficient	O	Oboe	X	X-Ray

G	Jeans	P	Pea	Y	Wife
H	H-Bomb	Q	Cue	Z	Zebra
I	Eye	R	Arch		

Remember, this is an auditory system. For this reason it depends on the sound of the peg word and not its visual appearance, for example, Sea for C; Jeans for G; Eye for I. As with all the other systems, you must be comfortable with the pegs. Feel free to make changes in the preceding list. For example, you might want to use Okra or Oprah for the O.

Notice, because of the sound approach, these oddities: Arch for R, Yew for U, Wife for Y, and so on. When possible, it is good to use the letter itself, as in H-Bomb, MC, T-shirt, W.C.

On a piece of paper write the letters of the alphabet and make your own alphabet pegs. Feel free to use all or some of these. Now test yourself. Which ones eluded your memory? Identify these "hard" ones and practice them. Do so until you can come up with a peg for every letter of the alphabet.

Once you have mastered the ABCs, you merely peg the item you want to remember with the letter word. For example: you want to remember to take care of these chores tomorrow: dental appointment, library book, drugstore, video store, bakery, hardware store. You want to attend to these matters in the order listed. All you have to do is bond the peg word with the activity by visualizing scenes like these:

ACE—	The face of your dentist inside an ace of spades. Or, deal a poker hand to your dentist; you have four aces.
BEE—	As you approach the library, you see and hear bees buzzing.
SEA—	The drugstore is flooded by a break in the sea wall.
DEED—	You help an elderly customer cross the street from the video store.
EASEL—	The bakery window has an easel in the window with a picture of a birthday cake.
EFFICIENT—	The hardware-store owner is an efficiency expert. He helps you do an efficient job as a do-it-yourselfer.

Exercise for Using the Alphabet Peg System

Now that you have pegged these six chores, add the following nine items to your list, making a total of 15. Since we did the first six for you, start your list with the letter "G" or the peg word: jeans. Here are the nine items:

bank	dry cleaner	write letter
butcher	travel agent	gas station
call plumber	clean garage	pay insurance bill

Hint: Use all your senses, use humor, exaggerate and visualize.

By now you have developed a preference for visual or auditory systems. Your success is predicated on using the one with which you are most comfortable.

The peg system has several advantages over simple recall. You have a consistent and ordered learning strategy. You know exactly what to do with each item you want to remember. You have definite places or pegs to put them until you need to use them. There is no problem as to which item comes first because you know the sequence of the letters of the alphabet.

HOW TO USE PEGS TO KEEP TRACK
OF APPOINTMENTS

You can use the peg system to keep track of daily appointments. Begin by having a peg word for each of the seven days of the week. We suggest these peg words because they represent concrete, everyday objects. Also, they resemble the spelling of each weekday with a little imagination on your part.

Day	*Peg Word*	*Reason for Choice of Peg*
Mon.	Moon	Add an "o" to Mon.
Tues.	Toes	Change "u" to "o"
Wed.	Wedding	Double "d" and add "ing"
Thurs.	Nurse	Change the "Th" to "n" and add "e" to get rhyme

Day	Peg Word	Reason for Choice of Peg
Fri.	Frying pan	Change "i" to "y"
Sat.	Chair	Change verb to noun
Sun.	Sun	Keep as is

It will take you only a few minutes to master the pegs for these days of the week. The peg words for the hour you already learned when we did the everyday item peg system, for example, 1 = penny, 2 = shoe, 3 = tree, 4 = door, and so on.

Here are three examples of how you can put this to work:

Visit dentist Monday at 10	Picture a MOON with a DIME on its face.
Auto inspection Tuesday at 9	Picture a CAT licking your TOES.
Airport pickup Friday at 4	Picture a FRYING PAN hanging on the DOOR.

Exercise for Using Pegs to Remember Appointments

Think of a picture you can use to remember these items:

Sunday at 11 _____

Saturday at 6 _____

Thursday at 2   _____

Wednesday at 3   _____

What day and hour do these images bring to mind?

A shoe on the chair _____

A nurse shooting dice _____

A chair on skis _____

Moonlight on a tree _____

The use of paired associations, links, stories, and pegs will train your mind to better make associations that, in turn, will strengthen your memory.

MEMENTOS

1. Make associations between something new you want to remember and something you already know.

2. Elaborate these associations using visual and auditory cues.

3. Forge verbal links to make a chain of items you want to remember.

4. Put various items into a story to ease your recall.

5. Substitute something concrete and familiar to make a peg. Then match that noun to what you want to remember.

6. Use humor, rhyme, and exaggeration to enhance your memory.

7. Use the alphabet shape system when you want to remember up to 26 items.

8. Put the peg system to work when you want to remember appointments.

Chapter Three

Boosting Your Learning Potential

Your ability to learn new material, on the job or in your personal life, is dependent on simple, proven memory techniques. Research has demonstrated that it is not the amount of time spent in studying that brings results. Rather, it is the range of learning strategies used that ensures mastery. Good students, of any age, instinctively use their time more effectively and employ a variety of learning techniques.

This chapter gives you dozens of tips on how to maximize your learning potential in any area you choose. Specific hints are given on how to get more out of your reading; develop an effective study system; and master test-taking techniques. Even more important, you will acquire an arsenal of strategies to boost your learning in any area from stock-market quotations to card counting in the game of bridge.

HOW MOTIVATION ENHANCES MEMORY

If you wanted to teach your dog a trick, such as rolling over, you would reward him in some way for his efforts. The same is true for lion tamers, horse trainers, or an animal handler. In all aspects of learning, motivation is the first step.

People are usually cooperative and want to do well. They want to master the material, win approval from the teacher or boss, or please themselves.

We have all seen college students sitting in libraries for hours surrounded by open books. For many this is just a matter of "putting in time." They have no real desire or motivation to learn, and as a result they do not learn.

Some of their classmates cram for an examination the night before. They are extremely motivated because they've done little work all semester and now have to absorb all the course material in an "all-nighter." They can master the material because they want to and they have to. The motivation is there but the technique is not a good one because cramming produces poor long-term retention.

Strategies of Well-Motivated Individuals

Historically, well-motivated people have developed their learning potential to an amazing degree. Arturo Toscanini conducted long, complex symphonies without a written score. Napoleon Bonaparte learned the names of thousands of his loyal troops. General George Marshall committed to memory virtually every battle in World War II.

How did they do it? They used the same strategies for remembering that motivated people everywhere use. They were more successful because they intuitively knew the best way to learn what they wanted to learn, and they were motivated by their ambitions for themselves.

Motivation alone is not enough. You must have some proven strategies, whether from trial-and-error approaches or from this book.

If you are extremely motivated—you really want to enhance your memory so you can get ahead—but you don't master the techniques, you will be just another excited plodder. Similarly, people who expose themselves to a variety of techniques in great detail but are not motivated won't learn no matter how expensive the tapes, books, and courses they've purchased.

This chapter is structured with this in mind. Various learning situations are presented with exercises for you to do. As you gain skill in completing the exercises, your motivation will increase. By balancing your motivation and these techniques you will boost your learning potential.

TESTING YOUR SHORT-TERM MEMORY

Let's begin with a test of your short-term memory capacity. Variations of this exercise have been used by psychologists to measure memory ability. We are using it here so that you can have a reference point to use at the beginning and again at the end of this chapter.

Digit Span Test

1. You will be presented with a sequence of numbers or digits, and you will be asked to write them down in the same order.

2. The length of the span is steadily increased. You continue until you reach a point where you cannot get the sequence correct.

3. The longest sequence that you get right is considered to be your DIGIT SPAN, six digits, seven digits, and so forth.

4. Begin by looking at the first four-digit sequence—6975.

5. After reading the sequence, close the book and try to repeat it in the correct order.

6. On a piece of paper, jot down the letters from A to P. Alongside each letter write the appropriate sequence. Continue until you reach a span that you cannot recall correctly. At that point, stop.

Do the exercise now. Do NOT read on until you have tried the exercise.

A	6 9 7 5
B	4 3 8 2 5
C	5 6 5 1 4 7
D	3 9 4 3 1 2 8
E	2 6 8 2 5 7 4 8
F	8 7 9 4 1 9 2 4
G	7 9 1 3 8 2 5 7 8
H	6 8 4 3 6 7 1 9 7
I	9 5 8 7 4 6 3 9 8 1
J	6 7 9 8 5 2 3 6 8 9
K	4 5 3 1 6 8 4 2 9 8 6
L	5 9 7 1 8 5 9 4 3 2 6
M	9 8 6 9 5 1 3 7 2 5 4 3
N	4 6 8 9 7 6 3 7 1 8 3 9
O	3 2 1 6 8 3 9 4 8 1 5 7 4
P	7 6 4 8 3 9 8 6 4 8 2 3 5
Q	1 3 5 7 4 5 4 8 3 9 6 4 7 2

Most people can reach level C or D, six or seven digits. There is quite a wide spread in the general population. Some people barely get five and others get up to ten digits. After learning some of the hints we present in this chapter, you will be surprised at how many more digits you can span.

Try this exercise again after you apply these two techniques:

1. Reading aloud
2. Grouping the digits

Two Techniques for Increased Digit Span

1. *Reading Aloud.* In the first technique, read the numbers aloud: "6, 9, 7, 5." You will have better recall this way because hearing the digits registers them in your auditory memory. This will supplement your merely seeing the numbers.

2. *Group the Digits.* By breaking up the long string into more manageable chunks you will enhance their recall and also avoid transposing digits. For example, 98695137, is more easily remembered as 986 951 37.

Tomorrow, try this exercise again using these two techniques: read the numbers aloud and group the digits into clusters of two or three numbers.

Motivate yourself to continue with this exercise until you can reach your goal of digits. See if you can master two more digits than you started with.

HOW TO BOOST YOUR BRAIN POWER

Do smart people remember better? People with high IQs usually have good memories. Yet, some individuals with excellent memories seem to be intellectually disadvantaged. There are well-publicized cases of people with serious mental disabilities who have intense, accurate memories for specific types of information.

Superior memory for most people is a genetic endowment. For example, chess masters who can remember the moves of games played long ago as well as every move in a current game are uniformly born with high IQs. Although genes determine an individual's IQ, it is effort and training that increase intellectual efficiency.

Memory is certainly one of the building blocks of intelligence. Memory is a vital component of learning, as well. The ability to express yourself with precision and eloquence depends upon the extent of your vocabulary. The better your memory, the easier it is for you to learn new words and access them when you want to use them.

Although some superior memories are obviously built in at birth, with some training and effort on your part you can make a difference in reaching your full potential.

Certain myths about intelligence persist. One is that our brains grow rapidly in the first years of life and then begin a gradual slide into old age. Researchers now point out that, to the contrary, our nervous system, including our brain, continues to grow if we stimulate it by placing demands on it. The brain is designed to respond to prodding and will expand its powers to meet new challenges. This has been demonstrated in laboratory studies. The cerebral cortex remains structurally plastic throughout the life of the healthy organism.

If you want to maximize your intellectual potential or IQ, just keep it fit and active with provocative activities at work as well as stimulating recreational activities such as crossword puzzles, card games, discussion groups, book clubs, and a curiosity about the world around you.

Exercise for Boosting Your Brain Power

Books on games and puzzles will help keep your circuits open and your intelligence engaged. Here are a few samples:

EXERCISE #1:   The following sequences of letters contain letters that do not belong. Identify the superfluous letters and when you cross them out you will reveal a familiar word of at least seven letters:

1. I R N E C T S I E L N E T M E I S A O N

2. J A I F N S V E N I E L T G S O N H E T

3. A N M N L E R M E O N I C T

EXERCISE #2: What do these words: deft, burst, hijinks, nope, stupor, and coughing have in common?

EXERCISE #3: If you wrote out a list of all the numbers from 1 to 80, how many times would the digit "7" appear?

EXERCISE #4: A simple exercise you can do every day at home is to read your newspaper—upside down. Besides exercising your visual acuity, you are engaging your memory of words as you decode the first few letters.

EXERCISE #5: Construct your own game of anagrams. Each day, think of a word that will turn into a new word when its letters are transformed, for example, dial/laid; escort/corset; manila/animal.

Answers to these exercises appear at the end of this chapter.

HOW RHYTHM HELPS YOU LEARN

Did you ever wonder why poetry is easier to memorize than prose? Why memory drills emphasizing repetition seem to increase short-term memory? The answer is *rhythm*. Grouping the digits of a telephone number rhythmically into a jingle will reduce the tendency to recall them in the wrong order or not recall them at all.

Rhythm is an easy-to-apply memory aid that produces consistently good results. We have all heard the proud four year old recite the 26 letters of the alphabet—in order. She can probably do it only when using the rhythm of the pre-school song: "ABCD, EFG, HIJK, and so forth." The rhythms of the song establish the order of the letters.

As an adult, think how difficult it would be to memorize a number with 26 digits!

For example, try to remember this 26-digit number:

3 1 4 1 8 1 2 1 9 1 4 1 2 7 1 9 4 1 1 9 4 5 2 0 2 0

It seems somewhat daunting or impossible at first. It becomes quite simple when you break the number up into smaller chunks and sing them to yourself rhythmically. To do this, all you need remember are these few number clusters:

3.14 is the ratio for *pi*

1812 and 1914 are historic war dates.

12-7-1941 represents Pearl Harbor day, or the start of World War II.

1945 is the year that World War II ended.

20/20 represents perfect vision.

Now, sing these numbers to yourself. You will actually have trouble forgetting this string of digits once you have learned it. The average person can learn it after just three sing-alongs. While not every long number contains such neat clusters, you can make up your own "personalized" clusters.

Maximizing Your Body Rhythms

These are not the only rhythms that have a role in learning. Each of us has a mind rhythm. This is based on a body clock or circadian rhythm. Our internal or body clock wakes us each morning and helps us wind down at night. This clock regulates the flow of hormones that gets us through the day and prepares us for sleep at night. But every body clock is different.

During the day we each have a unique schedule or daily pattern. Some of us are like larks—birds that build their nests and do their best food hunting early in the day. Others are like owls—birds that are nocturnal—and do their best work at night.

In order to boost your learning potential, you must identify your peak performance or prime learning time. Many of your body's complex systems are regulated by an internal clock that is in sync with the daily pattern of darkness and light. These include body temperature, heart rate, blood pressure, and respiration rate. Most of us have our peak learning time a few hours after arising and lasting for several hours. And so, performing difficult mental work should be scheduled early in the day. Some people, however, learn best late in the day, and for them studying after dinner would be a better idea.

Learning While You Sleep

It would be wonderful if you could spend seven hours of your sleep time learning a foreign language or other material simply by turning on a tape deck. Unfortunately, university studies have shown that you cannot learn during deep sleep or dream sleep that makes up most of your sleeping time.

There is evidence, however, that people can learn while in the very light sleep that precedes deep sleep. There are certain conditions for such sleep learning to take place.

CONDITIONS NEEDED FOR SLEEP LEARNING

- The material presented must be limited to facts, dates, vocabulary, and other objective material.

- The level of sleep is light sleep, which lasts for just five minutes prior to the deeper sleep.

- For most material, reinforcement during waking hours is necessary to produce true learning.

So, it may be possible to learn some kinds of factual material in one level of sleep, but this is not an efficient way to learn. Complex material involving reasoning or understanding can't be learned while in this drowsy state.

HOW YOU CAN USE SLEEP TO ENHANCE LEARNING

There is some good news on the sleep-learning connection.

- Students who studied or reviewed previously learned material while in bed and ready to drop off did significantly better than those who spent the same time with identical material but then watched TV or read a magazine before dropping off to sleep.

- Students remembered less when they took a nap or went to sleep immediately before studying. It was found they did best when they were fully awake.

- A good night's sleep helped make them alert for memory tasks the next day. This had to be natural, restorative sleep. Taking sleeping pills, ingesting over-the-counter sleep aids, or drinking alcohol did not help them remember. The lingering effects of these drugs made them less able to register new memories the next day. Also, they were less responsive to stimulation that could help them remember previously learned material.

SIX STRATEGIES FOR BETTER LEARNING

In numerous controlled studies, researchers have found that there are six strategies that contribute significantly to the speed with which adults learn a variety of materials. They also contribute to a stronger retention of what is learned. They are as follows:

1. *Space learning.* Instead of cramming for six hours, you will achieve better results if you maintain three two-hour study sessions. Distributed or spaced learning is much more effective for efficiency of learning and rate of retention of what has been learned.

2. *"Take small bites."* It's usually best to break up the material you wish to learn into smaller parts and to study each section, verse, or paragraph separately. Don't go on to the second part until you have learned the first. Before studying part three, review the first two parts. This approach also makes the entire learning project less daunting. You bite off small pieces instead of trying to swallow the whole piece. You also get immediate feedback on how much you are learning, sooner.

3. *Recite material.* In this strategy, you recall as much of what you're trying to learn as you can, looking at the material only when necessary. Do this after you have read it once or twice. Reciting out loud is better than just repeating material in your mind because it forces you to pay more attention. Reciting can also give you feedback on how well you know the material so that you can concentrate your study time on what you don't know.

4. *Find relevance.* Whatever you want to learn should have some meaning in your life. Try to apply some practical use for every theoretical item you are required to learn. Make an association in your daily life or past experience to the new material presented for learning. Making what you want to learn relevant helps get you motivated and makes the material more memorable.

5. *Concentrate.* You can enhance your learning by narrowing your focus on the specifics you want to commit to memory. Put other matters out of your mind. Shut off the music and avoid answering the telephone. Pretend you are wearing blinders that narrow your field of concentration to the items at hand. Intense concentration is tiring and should be reserved for short periods of time when learning difficult material.

6. *Repeat.* A great booster of confidence is repetition. After you feel you have learned something you should continue repeating it a few more times. You may think you know it and might as well stop studying. You may reason that further studying would be inefficient. Wrong! Repetition or continued learning beyond the point of bare mastery or of mere recall is effective in two ways: It strengthens learning and it speeds retrieval time. This has been demonstrated many times.

Exercises for Applying Learning Strategies

Assume you want to apply these six strategies to learn the names of the 50 states in alphabetical order. This is a good exercise; it gives you a list of common, familiar items to use in practicing these strategies. Here are the 50 states, in alphabetical order:

1. Alabama	18. Louisiana	35. Ohio
2. Alaska	19. Maine	36. Oklahoma
3. Arizona	20. Maryland	37. Oregon
4. Arkansas	21. Massachusetts	38. Pennsylvania
5. California	22. Michigan	39. Rhode Island
6. Colorado	23. Minnesota	40. South Carolina
7. Connecticut	24. Mississippi	41. South Dakota
8. Delaware	25. Missouri	42. Tennessee
9. Florida	26. Montana	43. Texas
10. Georgia	27. Nebraska	44. Utah
11. Hawaii	28. Nevada	45. Vermont
12. Idaho	29. New Hampshire	46. Virginia
13. Illinois	30. New Jersey	47. Washington
14. Indiana	31. New Mexico	48. West Virginia
15. Iowa	32. New York	49. Wisconsin
16. Kansas	33. North Carolina	50. Wyoming
17. Kentucky	34. North Dakota	

These 50 state names can be memorized by applying the six learning strategies, as follows:

1. *Space learning.* Don't try to learn all 50 states in one sitting. That would be mass learning, or cramming, and not very efficient. It's likely to produce frustration and, ultimately, abandonment of the project. Instead, see how many state names you can master in one comfortable session. It may be limited to just the first four that begin with the initial "A." More likely, it will be six or seven. When you have accomplished this, divide that number into 50 to get the number of sessions most suitable for you to learn the list.

2. *Take small bites.* After you learn the first group of names, go on to the next group. Before attempting the third group, review to make sure you know the first group as well as you do the second. Each small bite has to be reviewed and absorbed before going on.

3. *Recite material.* Don't hesitate to say the names aloud. By doing this, you are rehearsing with your auditory sense as well as your visual. Try to get a rhythm to your recitation. Add a sing-song to states that begin with the same initial letter.

4. *Find relevance.* Learning the names of the 50 states in alphabetical order is merely an exercise, and there is probably no practical application of this list in your business or personal life. You can, however, apply relevance by thinking of personal associations or real-life links to each state name as you recite it. This kind of practice exercise will help you develop the skills needed to learn lists of your own.

5. *Concentrate.* By focusing on the group of names at hand, you can master this exercise with speed and accuracy. Don't think about anything else. Concentrate on these names by seeing the letters of the state name, its approximate location on the map, and your own patterns of memorization.

6. *Repeat.* When you feel comfortable with learning the entire list go over it again. Say the names aloud and then write them down. Just being able to say the list one time is not mastery. Only by repeated practice can you be sure you have truly learned the list.

This exercise may seem frivolous at first. But the strategies you apply to this learning task will assist you for the rest of your life. It is the direct application of these strategies, and others of your own, that makes the difference. It's one thing to read about six strategies, but it is something else to actually apply them to learning a series of 50 names.

HOW INTERFERENCE AFFECTS LEARNING

What we learn can easily be forgotten if similar events interfere. We pointed out earlier that students who go to sleep after studying are more likely to remember the material than do students who then go on to other cognitive activities, such as reading a magazine. One explanation is that memories are easily obscured or disrupted by similar actions or images.

For example, football players were asked to describe games they had played. Most could recount in great detail their last game no matter how much time had elapsed. Those who played another game in the interim had little recall of events in the earlier game. The elapsed time affected memory less than did the number of intervening games.

Recent memories interfere because new material pushes out old. You can remember where you parked your car today more easily than where you parked it a week ago today.

In one university study, volunteers memorized a long list of four-letter nonsense syllables. The equally matched volunteers were divided into two groups. Group A relaxed while Group B memorized a new list. Both groups were then retested on the original nonsense syllables. Group A was able to recall more than 55 percent of the first list. Group B, which had been busy with a new list, recalled only 26 percent of the original list.

The effect of interference on original learning is well documented. The more similar the interfering material, the greater the extent of forgetting. To help your newly learned material "gel," go on to a totally different activity if it is not practical to let it "set" as you sleep.

Exercise for Reducing Interference

Trying to learn material in which the items are similar to one another is difficult. The similar items tend to cause interference with your memory processing. For example, the memory confuses similar terms. We see this in such commonly misused words as affect/effect, discreet/discrete, and precede/proceed.

Because of similarity in meaning or spelling we confuse such words or have trouble learning them in the first place. We do the same thing with people. For example, two potential customers you have just met have black mustaches and eyeglasses. They are harder to tell apart in your memory than two other men you just met with totally different appearances.

This exercise consists of two lists, A and B. On both lists are five occupations, each followed by a descriptive adjective.

Start with list A, trying to memorize the adjective associated with each occupation. When you are finished, cover the list and test yourself on the test list that follows it.

If necessary, repeat the procedure until you get all five correct. Write down how many times you needed to do the exercise before getting all five correct. Then go to list B and repeat the process.

List A	*List B*
doctor—compassionate	minister—warm
lawyer—ambitious	pastor—friendly
accountant—careful	rector—jovial
engineer—creative	priest—cheerful
teacher—dedicated	bishop—caring

Test List A	*Test List B*
engineer— _____	priest— _____
lawyer— _____	rector— _____
teacher— _____	minister— _____
doctor— _____	bishop— _____
accountant— _____	pastor— _____

You will find it is much easier to learn list A. Here the occupations and their associated adjectives are dissimilar. In list B the occupations are similar and the adjectives are almost synonymous.

We conclude that if you learn one item and then try to learn something else that is similar you will have more trouble with the second item. You will also tend to forget the first item to a greater degree than would be the case if the two items were unrelated. For example, the compassionate doctor and the ambitious lawyer are quite different from each other and so are easier to memorize. The warm minister and the friendly pastor are similar and so are harder to learn.

If you have a great deal of material to master, break it up into small parts, or bites. Vary the type of material studied to ensure less interference.

HOW TO BETTER RETAIN WHAT YOU READ

If you want to increase your learning potential, you must master ways of holding on to what you get from your reading. Whether you read quickly or slowly, the important outcome is how well you retain what you read.

To increase your retention rate, you have to involve yourself in the reading process. Most people who report an inability to remember what they read are guilty of not getting actively involved in what they read.

Getting Involved in the Reading Process

- Reading is an active, not a passive activity. It doesn't happen to you. You have to make it happen.

- Before picking up a book or other reading material, ask yourself questions as to your purpose in doing the reading. What do you hope to find out?

- Ask yourself questions while you are reading. Are there any diversions or contradictions in the writing? Is the author consistent?

- After you finish reading, ask yourself questions about details in what you have read. Did the book contribute to your understanding of the topic? Did you learn anything new?

- Make comments to yourself, aloud, about things that you find appealing or worthy of quoting.

- Summarize one section at a time. How can you reduce this section or chapter to a single sentence? Review previous sections you have read.

Using Your Imagination to Improve Reading Retention

As you read, keep your imagination active. Place yourself in the situation being described. The more vividly you place yourself in the scene, the better you will remember what you are reading.

This goes for fiction as well as for nonfiction. When you need to recall what you have read, you will find it easier and more exact because you have actually participated in the action or thinking.

You will need to use a different technique if you have to remember numbers, but you will get specific help on that area in Chapter Seven.

USING YOUR EXTRINSIC MEMORY

Extrinsic memory employs materials outside your "head," or intrinsic memory. Learning the multiplication tables is an example of using intrinsic memory. Taking notes is an example of using extrinsic memory.

- Notes can be on a separate piece of paper or on index cards.
- Label your notes or cards with the title, author, and page number if you want to go back at some future time for more detailed information.
- Underline key passages if this is your book. Make notes in the margins or place checks and asterisks to signal important points.
- Use a highlighter pen to emphasize key words, phrases, or lines. You may want to use different colors to highlight facts versus opinions or different areas of interest.
- Before closing the book or periodical, review your notes.

The important point to remember is that time taken to underline, highlight, or make notes is justified only if you take time to review your notations to cement retention.

Research indicates that by reviewing immediately after reading, the individual remembers 70% of what she or he read 24 hours later. Reading without review produces just 30 percent retention 24 hours later.

MEMENTOS

Every day we are exposed to more and more information that we need to learn. Your memory can improve your ability to learn more effectively and so improve your earning and satisfaction levels.

Some memory tools specific to developing your learning potential were presented in this chapter.

- The first step to effective learning is *motivation*.

- Although your IQ is basically determined at birth, there are many things you can do to keep your intelligence working at maximum.

- Adding rhythm to what we want to memorize will make the task easier. We must also recognize our own body rhythms of peak and down times.

- Sleep and learning are connected in some ways. There is some evidence that we can learn during the first few minutes of sleep

- There are six learning strategies that can make a difference in the way you absorb information: Space learning, take small bites, recite material, find relevance, concentrate, and repeat learning.

- The effect of interference on learning is well documented. You can ensure less interference in your learning if you vary the types of material studied.

- Getting actively involved in what you are reading will enhance retention.

- Participate in situations you are reading about. The more vividly you imagine what the words describe the better will you remember what you read.

- Taking notes on what you read will help you remember what you have read. It is necessary, however, to review your notes or underlined material after reading in order to gain this benefit.

ANSWER KEY

Answers to *How to Boost Your Brain Power* Puzzles

1. a. retention
   b. insight
   c. mnemonic

2. They each contain three consecutive letters of the alphabet: *deft, burst, hijinks, nope, stupor,* and *coughing*.

3. There are 18 sevens: 7, 17, 27, 37, 47, 57, 67, 70, 71, 72, 73, 74, 75, 76, 77, 78, and 79.

Chapter Four

Remembering What You Hear and Read

So much of your daily life is spent trying to remember all the information we hear and read. At first these appear to be passive activities. Someone else has spoken or written. All *we* have to do is take in the information but that is not as easy as it seems.

When we direct our attention to hearing or reading the words of others, we are actively engaged. We actually raise our pulse rate and body temperature when we are in deep concentration trying to remember what we hear or read. Directing our attention to what someone else has put together means putting aside our own interests, preoccupations, and problems for the moment.

In order to remember, we have to focus 100 percent on what the other person has said or written.

In this chapter, we examine memory techniques that we can use to remember better what we hear and read. These techniques will make your memory skills sharper while helping you to remember the oral and printed word.

REMEMBERING WHAT YOU HEAR

Hearing is the sense by which sound is perceived. *Listening* is paying attention to what we hear. These two terms are often used interchangeably. We make a distinction between the two later on in this section.

The Art of Listening

Adults spend 70 percent of their waking time communicating. Each type of communication has been broken down as follows:

Writing 14%   Speaking 14%   Reading 17%   Listening 53%

Besides being the most often-used form of communication—more than the other three combined—*listening* has been identified as the most important on-the-job communication skill. A study examining the link between listening and career success revealed that better listeners rose to higher levels in their organizations.

There is more to listening than sitting quietly while someone else talks. Research reveals that people remember only half of what they hear immediately after hearing it. Within two months, half of this information is lost unless it is repeated or put to use. This high rate of forgetfulness isn't so bad when you consider how much listening we do each day.

Effective listening depends on four factors: hearing, attending, understanding, and responding.

Hearing and listening are not the same. Hearing is a physical process that can be stopped only by injury, age, illness, or ear plugs. Listening is not automatic. Many people hear but don't listen. We stop listening to a car alarm or when we find a subject unimportant or uninteresting. Commercials and complaints are examples of messages we hear but don't listen to. True listening involves more than mere hearing.

Attending is a psychological process. Our needs, wants, and desires determine what we attend to. We couldn't possibly attend to every sound we hear and so we consciously filter out some messages and focus on others. The level of attention depends on the degree of payoff. If you're trying to make a sale, you'll attend carefully to your prospect's objections. We listen best when we attend carefully. We attend carefully when we see some tangible or intangible reward for doing so.

Understanding depends on the listener's insight and intelligence. First of all, you must understand the language, jargon, or shop talk of the speaker. Then, you must be able to make sense of the message even if the speaker rambles or is not clear in his presentation. You will need insight in order to understand disorganized speech or mixed messages. Feeling and empathy also affect understanding of what is said.

Responding is giving feedback to the speaker. Responding—answering questions and exchanging ideas—can take place only after careful listening.

Selective listeners respond only to part of what the speaker is saying—the part that interests them. Everything else is shut off. We all do that at times, such as when we tune out TV commercials. At other times, when a topic comes up that we would rather not deal with, we fail to hear or acknowledge it. If you remind an adolescent about an incomplete job, poor grades, and the like, he or she may nod or answer briefly and then promptly forget what you just said.

GUIDELINES FOR EFFECTIVE LISTENING

You can become a more effective listener by following these do's and don'ts:

1. *Do search for key ideas.* You can think faster than the average speaker can make her point. Listen for the central idea and supporting points from the many words and details you are hearing.

2. *Do ask questions.* If you can't figure out what the speaker is driving at, ask tactful questions. These will make sure you are receiving his message accurately.

3. *Do restate the speaker's message in your own words.* Such paraphrasing will tell you whether you understand what is being said before you ask additional questions. By restating what you think the speaker is saying in your own words, you are checking on your understanding.

4. *Don't talk too much.* Some feedback is necessary to clarify what the speaker is saying. But most of us shift the conversation to our ideas when we should be trying to understand others'.

5. *Don't jump to conclusions based on first impressions or snap judgments.* Examine criticism to see if it contains any valuable truths. Listen first; be sure you understand; then evaluate.

Barriers to Effective Listening

It is important to recognize certain barriers to good listening that make it difficult to remember what was said, or may give the wrong interpretation of what was said. These include the following:

1. *The setting.* Is the room too noisy? Is it too cold, or too hot? Are you both standing for a long time? Suggest changes to remove these barriers: "Could we sit down in the quiet corner?" "Do you mind if I close that window?"

2. *The speaker.* Does he create barriers with his mannerisms— jingling keys, gesturing with his eyeglasses, pointing his finger? Does he punctuate every remark with, "you know" or "see"? Force yourself to cut through these gestures and mannerisms and focus on what he's saying. Visualize his main ideas as if they were in print.

3. *The listener.* Are you creating barriers because you're absorbed in your own thoughts, problems, or ideas? Put these thoughts out of mind by promising to think about them at some fixed time. For example, "I'll solve the problem of next week's meeting conflict when I get to the office tomorrow. Right now I want to find out what this woman is saying about downsizing."

4. *The culture.* In the multicultural workplace, it is important to recognize and respect certain cultural differences in communication. Lack of eye contact on the part of an Asian colleague may be wrongly viewed as "insecurity" or "avoidance." On the other hand, some cultures interpret eye contact as "domineering, invasive, and controlling." Cultivating a sensitivity to the diverse ways of communicating is an important element of strategic listening and remembering.

Four Hints for Practicing Effective Listening

Very often we listen to the radio or a speaker and we feel the rate of speech is too fast for us to comprehend. Or, we find the speaker's message to be vague and abstract. Later, we have trouble understanding or recalling what has been said. The fault may or may not be with the speaker. We may not have been listening effectively.

The following four hints will help you become a more effective listener:

1. *Picture what you want to remember.* Visualize what the speaker is saying. Use your mind's eye as well as your ears. If the speaker says he has four reasons for his position, count them off in your mind as he addresses them. "See" the four reasons, reduced to one or two words each, on a large screen in your mind.

2. *Use humor or exaggeration.* If the radio announcer is describing a low-fat, reduced-calorie food product you will remember it better if you think of the product's name as being written in very thin, stringy letters.

3. *Make the images vivid with color and action.* A friend tells you she has purchased a new car. You may not remember that the next time you see her. But if you ask for a description of the car, you will have a more vivid, easier-to-remember image, for example, a red Ford cruising on a local highway with your friend behind the wheel.

4. *Compare and contrast the information you heard.* When you hear a great deal of information on a single topic, it is helpful if you compare and contrast the data you have received. For example, two physicians spoke at your service club on health issues. You have trouble remembering which speaker said what. By using comparison and contrast you will remember them more effectively. One talked about common stimulants to avoid and the other emphasized a calmer approach in our emotional life.

You compared their names with their suggestions and came up with

Dr. Coffey (sounds like coffee) spoke about stimulants.

Dr. Blanding (sounds like bland) spoke about being calm (bland).

Exercises for Effective Listening

1. Listen to radio commercials and visualize the phone number or product name as it is given. Test your recall of the number or the spelling of the product name after the commercial has ended.

2. As you are introduced to a new person, silently use humor or exaggeration to help you effectively recall the name, for example, "fat" Matt or Mr. Bush has a thick, bushlike head of hair.

3. When attending a lecture, add your own vivid images to what the speaker is saying. For example, a speaker is talking about an impending fuel shortage and you see the gas gauge on your car pointing to "Empty."

4. Instead of static figures, place your mental images in action situations. For example, a candidate is "running" for office. The office door of the office he is running for says "City Council."

5. Compare numerical statistics with the aid of an imaginary graph or chart. For example, your employer has given sales and cost figures for the past three years. You see them as they would appear on a line graph or in a pie chart.

A REMEMBERING-WHAT-YOU-HEAR WORKOUT

The single biggest mistake made by people who can't remember what they hear is their tendency to rush ahead of themselves. They rush to speak before making an effort to hear what the speaker is saying or they jump to conclusions before the speaker has finished.

This exercise, or workout, will train you to practice good listening habits.

For the next week, follow these rules exactly as they appear here. Don't make any compromises. Apply these rules in the workplace and at home.

Rule 1: *Don't interrupt.* To interrupt a speaker is not only rude but it diminishes your ability to remember what the speaker is saying. You are concentrating on what you want to say and so miss part of what the speaker is saying.

Rule 2: *Count to three.* Pausing for three seconds when the speaker has finished will help your mind absorb what the speaker has told you. This is vital to long-term memory storage. Also, pausing before you speak may serve as a cue for the speaker to recap or sum up. This is another memory aid that will help you recall what you have heard.

Rule 3: *Keep pace with the speaker.* Don't jump to conclusions or anticipate her next point. Keeping pace will help your memory access the information being presented.

Rule 4: *Focus on what is being said.* Avoid daydreaming by imagining the speaker's main point written out in a few words.

TAKING NOTES TO HELP YOU REMEMBER
WHAT YOU HEAR

The written word is an invaluable memory aid when you try to recall what you heard when listening to lectures, radio, TV, or any oral presentation. Taking notes is a skill that can be easily mastered. The following techniques will help you take good notes—painlessly.

1. *Use a tape recorder when practical.* For detailed lectures with many facts and figures, a cassette recorder is ideal. You must have the speaker's permission ahead of time. When you play back the lecture you can "pause" and "play back" at will with the flick of a finger.

2. *Take written notes for an immediate record of the highlights.* Pretend the speaker is talking to you alone. Such intimacy will force you to concentrate and reduce distractions. As far as you are concerned, no one else is in the room. Your attention is riveted on the speaker and on no one else.

3. *Rephrase what the speaker is saying into language that you are familiar with.* As you rephrase, you are processing the information.

4. *Use a minimum number of words.* Note taking is not a stenographic exercise. You want to get down the main ideas and not a word-for-word replay.

5. *Draw symbols, arrows, or lines to connect, visualize, or illustrate the points you want to remember.*

6. *Use initials if there is more than one speaker.* For example, "MC:"—these are the speaker's initials followed by a colon. This will help you recall who said what.

7. *Review your notes at the end of the day for clarification and elaboration.* Don't let notes get cold for several days before going over them. By that time you won't remember what the reference stood for.

Exercises for Taking Notes While You Listen

1. *Watch the evening news on TV or listen to the news for thirty minutes on radio.* Jot down notes on two international news stories,

two national stories, and two local stories. After the broadcast, shut off the TV or radio. From your notes reconstruct each of the six stories.

2. *Listen to a radio or TV commercial.* Take notes on the product or service described. Get all the specific information given, such as price, phone number, business hours, address, and so on. See if you can get all of this down with just one listening session.

3. *Listen to the lyrics of a popular song.* Jot down the lyrics as they are sung by the recording artist. See how close you get to recalling the complete lyrics with just one playing.

4. *Keep a notebook near your telephone.* The next time a friend calls, use the notebook to record the major topics the two of you discussed. Wait until you are off the phone before you fill in the details. Think back to see if there are any topics you missed.

5. *Use a cassette recorder to make a note-taking training tape of your own.* Use the "record" function as you read an editorial from the daily newspaper. Then, record some technical material from the newspaper, such as stock quotations, high and low temperatures in major cities, and so forth. Take notes when you play this back. Then, replay the tape to see how effective your note taking is.

THREE SUCCESSFUL TECHNIQUES FOR REMEMBERING WHAT YOU HEAR

We often hear a speaker in person or on the radio or TV who sounds interesting. A few minutes later, however, we have trouble remembering exactly what she said. We have a general feeling of what as said but we are lacking factual material when we try to tell someone else what we heard.

These three techniques will enable you to accurately remember what you hear:

1. *Put the speaker's message into your own words.* As you listen to a lecturer, employer, or colleague tell you something you want to remember, in your mind's eye imagine you are passing this information on to another person. Pretend you are going to tell a friend or colleague what you have just heard in your own words.

This is a two-pronged approach. One, you can't daydream or wander off the subject if you are paraphrasing the speaker. Two, by putting the speaker's message into your own words, you are reinforcing what you heard.

2. *Separate fact from opinion.* Pay close attention to what others are telling you. Decide for yourself if what they are saying is factual or merely their opinion. You want to remember what you hear, but you don't want to automatically make someone else's opinion your own.

Listen closely to separate facts and opinion. Speakers routinely mix the two. A *fact* can be verified or supported by outside sources. An *opinion* is a belief that rests on the individual's impression, sentiment, or view.

If we say water freezes at 32 degrees Fahrenheit, we are stating a fact. A fact is a generally accepted statement. If we say rain is better than snow, this is an opinion. A skier may have another opinion.

It is important for you to put what you hear to the fact/opinion test lest you remember what is not necessarily true.

3. *Ask a question to clarify what you hear.* It is flattering to the speaker, whether he's at a lectern in a large auditorium or standing right next to you, if you ask a question in order to clarify your understanding. Asking questions also deposits what was said into your memory bank because you participated in the learning experience. By asking a question you made it interactive.

Begin your question with phrases such as these and you will be on the road to remembering what you hear because you help to clarify it:

"Did you say that . . .?"

"What do you think will happen if . . .?"

"Why do you think this is so?"

"What can we expect to gain from . . .?"

By confirming the speaker's main points and conclusions with a question, you are ensuring your recall of these important facets of his presentation.

FIVE WAYS TO SHARPEN YOUR LISTENING SKILLS IN A ONE-TO-ONE SITUATION

Very often, at a social occasion or in a relaxed business situation, you tend to drop your attention level. As a result, you can't remember details later, when you need to.

You don't have to be on the alert every waking minute of the day. But there are certain techniques you can develop that will sharpen your listening skills and help you recall information when it is needed in the future. These include the following:

1. *Don't pick sides.* You don't have to dwell on whether you agree or disagree with what the speaker is saying. Hear what the speaker is saying and don't label it good or bad, right or wrong. Merely listen. This will help you remember what was said. Taking sides encourages you to forget what you didn't agree with.

2. *Learn something new.* Be open to conversations that break new ground. Your dinner partner may be talking enthusiastically about an African safari or cyberspace—two topics about which you know little. Open your ears and try to follow what she is saying. Ask questions for clarification. Listen to learn. Your speaker will appreciate your interest as you exercise your "Remember-What-You-Hear" muscles. This introduction to a topic unfamiliar to you may lead to a greater curiosity and further study on your part.

3. *Forge memory links.* Mentally link new data to familiar ideas. Think of your mind as a notepad jotting down what you hear. As soon as you've heard what the other person has said, file it away with similar data in your head. This kind if mental linkage will not only make you a more polite listener but will help you retain more of what others say.

4. *Don't judge the speaker.* Work hard at *not* making snap judgments about other people based on their physical appearance, dress, or speech. Such judgments make it harder to listen with an open mind, which diminishes your ability to remember what others say.

5. *Don't be a "know-it-all."* Remembering what you hear will be impossible if you think you know more than the person talking to you. If you are convinced you have nothing left to learn on the subject, you

will lose out. Everyone has something unique in his or her experiences to contribute. Only by opening your ears will you hear it.

Diagnostic Self-Help/Test: Do You Hear to Remember?

Adlai Stevenson once began a speech with "My job is to speak. Your job is to listen. Let's hope we finish our jobs at the same time."

This self-help/test will help you identify warning signs that you may be easily distracted. In order to remember what you hear, you have to begin listening at the same moment the other person starts speaking.

These questions help you assess whether you allow past or future anxieties to cloud your ability to focus in the present:

1. Are you easily rattled by "little things"—such as a misplaced personal item—for many hours after it happens? _____
2. Do you have recurring daydreams that interfere with your listening? _____
3. Do you have trouble listening after a disappointment at work or at home? _____
4. Do upcoming events, such as an annual meeting, upset you days before they are scheduled? _____
5. Is time management a problem that keeps you looking at your watch when you should be listening? _____

If you answered yes to any of these questions, you need to change your thinking if you want to open yourself up to better listening.

Your energies are better used listening to what a speaker says now than in mulling over past or future activities. Concentrate on the here and now if you want to remember.

HOW TO HANDLE THE REPETITIVE SPEAKER

On occasion, we all come in contact with the "Broken Record." This is the insecure speaker who repeats, rehashes, and restates the same point, over and over. Repetitive speakers want to make themselves perfectly clear, so they speak in loops to convince themselves their message is getting through.

You can tactfully get such a speaker to move along with any one of these remarks:

"OK, I get it. What else?"

"That's good, go on."

"What should we do next?"

"What do you make of that?"

"I never thought of that. What else would you recommend?"

Restate or paraphrase what they say to assure them their message is clear and then push the conversation forward.

SEVEN WAYS TO REMEMBER CONVERSATIONS BETTER

Conversation is a basic human activity. Yet speakers and listeners are easily disturbed by the behavior of the other person. Paying attention to the following items will keep extraneous factors from interfering with your ability to remember what you hear.

1. *Face the speaker and make eye contact.* This will keep you from being distracted by other people in the room.

2. *Use occasional nods and sounds that show you are listening.* This will encourage the speaker to move on and will furnish you with mental "punctuation marks" in your memory bank.

3. *Learn to listen to what you may not want to hear without losing your temper.* You may need to remember what was said so that you can refute it later on when you have cooled down.

4. *If you hear something unbelievable, check the facts rather than accept everything the speaker says.* You want to remember only those items that are accurate and unbiased.

5. *Don't give advice unless asked to do so.* Just keep quiet and listen. You want to remember what the other person has to say without injecting your thoughts.

6. *Avoid giving examples from your own experiences.* Instead, ask follow-up questions. You won't forget your own experiences.

However, the distraction will keep you from remembering what else was being said.

7. *Don't interrupt the speaker early on.* Let him get into his presentation. Save questions for after he has made his major points. He may clear things up by then. By interrupting with a question early in the talk, you may throw both you and the speaker off the train of thought.

A Personal Listening Analysis

Now that you have read about a variety of techniques and strategies for remembering what you hear, it's time to reflect on just how well *you* listen. Take a moment to answer these questions.

The listening situations that I find most difficult are:

1. _____
2. _____
3. _____

The single technique that would help me in such a situation next time is _____
_____

I find I am most comfortable listening to people who project these traits:

1. _____
2. _____
3. _____

The one area in which I am going to concentrate improving my listening skills is: _____
_____

HOW TO REMEMBER WHAT YOU READ

Reading can be an enjoyable as well as a frustrating experience. We all know how much pleasure great literature, popular novels, or nonfiction books can give us.

Sadly, you also recognize how frustrating it is to read a paragraph or even a whole page and then realize that you have no idea of what you have been reading. The eye has seen the words but has not grasped the meaning. A lack of concentration is the villain here. You were not focusing on what you were reading. Your eyes were scanning the page without processing the material.

While your eyes are moving across the words, your mind drifts to something else. You're not paying attention to the words, just as you didn't pay attention when you placed the checkbook on top of the TV and searched for it an hour later.

Diagnostic Self-Test: Do You Read to Remember?

Reading involves your active participation. It is not a spectator sport in which you merely watch the words go by. In order to remember what you read, you must get involved with the written material by feeling the emotions described, seeing the main points, questioning the author's views, and following the progression of ideas.

This takes work, but the rewards make it worthwhile. Don't sabotage your ability to remember what you have read. These questions help you assess whether you set yourself up for success or failure when you sit down to read:

1. Do you put aside a sufficiently long enough period of time to read? _____

2. Have you taken care of your basic needs before beginning to read? Are you going to become distracted because you are hungry, thirsty, or need to use the bathroom? _____

3. Have your eyes been checked recently? Are your glasses, if you use them, up to date? _____

4. Do you keep a notepad or highlight pen nearby when you read? Is note taking part of your nonfiction reading routine? _____

5. Do you leave time to reflect or review what you have read before moving on to another activity? _____

If you answered no to any of these questions you need to change your reading habits if you want to be able to remember what you read.

IMPROVING YOUR LEVEL OF CONCENTRATION

Why does your mind wander occasionally while you read? You allow your mind to focus on something other than what you are reading for a variety of reasons, including the following:

1. The meaning of the words don't register because the vocabulary is unfamiliar.
2. The material is complicated, and so it is hard to follow.
3. The book is not well-written, and so your mind is not engaged.
4. You are tired or upset and have trouble focusing your attention.
5. The physical conditions are not conducive to reading. The lighting, ventilation, or room temperature keeps you from concentrating.

In this section, we are going to look at ways in which we can focus our attention on what we take in with our eyes as well as our ears. We are going to pick up techniques for remembering what we read.

How to Get Rid of Distractions

The solution involves getting rid of all possible distractions. Obviously, you need a quiet place with good lighting and ventilation if you are to see clearly what is on the page and if you are to stay awake in the process. You can't concentrate if you must squint at every word or fight sleep because of stale air.

In most cases, lack of concentration is due to mental distractions. If you're reading a book and thinking about what you can get to eat or whom you should call on the telephone, you cannot concentrate on what you are reading.

The best way to eliminate mental distractions is to bury yourself in the author's thought process instead of in your own. When you make the decision to sit down and read, make another commitment to concentrate on the author's message. You may not agree with everything the author has to say, but get involved in what he or she is saying.

It's important to pause occasionally to think through what point the author is making. This pause will help your brain absorb the author's point of view. Some readers actually close their eyes for a minute and "see" the author's main points inscribed by their mind's eye. Others look away from the printed page and in their imagination see the main idea lettered on the wall.

Comprehension is dependent on concentration. If you want to remember what you read, you must understand it. This is accomplished by focusing on the author's words and pausing from time to time to consolidate the main ideas.

GUIDELINES FOR IMPROVING READING RECALL

If you are reading this book, you obviously know how to read. These suggestions are to help you remember better what it is that you do read.

1. *Do you read efficiently?* Do you sound out words or subvocalize as you read? This will slow down your reading speed and also interrupt the flow of comprehension. Practice reading without subvocalizing by placing your fingertips on your throat as you read. You can feel your subvocalizing and can practice eliminating it.

2. *Are you a slow reader?* Your mind may become slowed down by your reading slowly. Pick up your reading speed and read more in the same amount of time by taking in phrases and groups of words, instead of individual words. This is a skill that you can acquire by practicing. Every time you read a page of print try to cluster groups of words instead of scanning each individual word. At the beginning, you can use a piece of paper or even your finger to help you go across each line of print at few phrases at a time. Reading this way will do a great deal for your comprehension as well as your speed.

3. *Do you skim occasionally?* Not every word or even every page has to be read in a nonfiction book. In a novel you are caught up in the author's style and the beauty of the language and you may not want to skim. In reading nonfiction, you are reading for information. As you come across some information that does not meet your needs, by all means skim over it.

4. *Do you summarize as you go along?* Some nonfiction books have a summary at the end of each chapter. Many do not. Make it a habit to pause at the end of every chapter and summarize what the author has said in your own words. In some books you may have to do this several times within each chapter. There is no point in moving on to the next chapter if you do not remember enough about this chapter to be able to distill the main ideas by summarizing it.

5. *Do you test yourself?* At the end of each chapter, pretend you are a college instructor and you are going to test the reader on the contents of the chapter. What kinds of questions will you make up? Include a balance of thought and fact questions. See how well you can answer them.

6. *Do you cram your reading into a short period of time?* If you are preparing for an exam or any kind of reading deadline, it's best to space your reading over an extended period of time. Although intensive cramming may get you through for the short term, it is better for long-term memory if you space and pace your reading.

7. *Do you share what you have read?* An effective way to remember what you have read is to tell someone else about it. The skills you need to paraphrase and recall what the book is about are the same skills that will help you remember what you read over an extended period of time.

How to Read a Book Like a Newspaper

We are living at a time when we are bombarded with new books virtually every day on a topic that interests us or is in our field of work. It's not possible for the average reader to keep up to date with all that is being published in his or her business or professional field.

Although some nonfiction books are a "must read" if we want to stay current, many others are merely of marginal interest. How can we keep up? I'm going to describe a simple technique for you now that will capitalize on the reading time you now have. By using the same amount of time, you will be able to get the essence of many more books.

Few people read a newspaper in sequential order, page by page. We usually read the first few pages in some detail and then skim the others looking for something that captures our interest. You're now going to learn how to do the same with nonfiction books.

For some reason, we are taught in elementary school to begin on page 3 and plod through every book one page at a time. It was implied that something bad would happen to us if we skipped anything. This was before the information explosion. It was also before the explosion of electronic competition for our reading time.

Let's begin by looking at some of the helps we can get before we even start on page 3:

The book jacket: The publisher sets forth the most important points of the book on the jacket. This helps sell the book. It also gives the publisher's perspective on what this book is about. It gives you an idea of what you are likely to find inside.

The author's biography: This tells you something about the author—his credentials for writing the book and what he is doing now. By reading "between the lines," you can get an idea of the particular point of view of the author.

The frontmatter: This may include a preface, or foreword, or introduction. In any case, the frontmatter tells you what this book has as its goal—its mission statement. Read this before you go any further. See if this book seems to meet your particular needs.

The table of contents: This is really the outline of the book. The author uses each chapter topic as a hook on which she hangs her text. How many chapters are there? Are there any clusters of chapters, such as Part I, Part II? Read the table of contents carefully to see if these are the topics you are interested in.

The index: Scan the index in the back of the book. See if there is an entry that interests you. Look it up and see how the author develops it.

The chapters: Go back to the table of contents. Find a chapter that interests you more than any other. Read the heads. Is there a chapter summary? Do you like the way the chapter is organized? Does this chapter offer you any information that you consider valuable? Did you like the way the author presented it?

You should do all this before you begin to read the book itself. Once you start reading the book, you should feel free to skim through material you are already familiar with. Skip those pages that have no application for you. Glean what you can from this book. There may be some parts of it that you will want to read twice. Perhaps you will want to take notes on some of the material presented by the author.

Make use of the illustrations, charts, graphs, or other visual material. Use the headings and subheads as markers for specific information you may find valuable.

After scanning the book, you may decide you don't want to read it. You have not invested a great deal of time. You have also avoided the frustration of plodding through a book you're not sure is what you need to read.

Even if you reject the book, make a few notes on a 3 × 5 inch index card regarding it. List some of its strong points and perhaps some specific pages you might want to refer to in the future.

With all the books published annually, it's difficult to keep up with what is new and current. Some readers report that reading every word of a technical book gives them so much detailed information that they can't glean the important concepts. By reading a book the way you read a newspaper you will be geared to the main ideas and concepts.

Whether you buy these books, get them from the library, or scan them in a bookstore, you will expose yourself to many more books and many more ideas than if you read fewer books and read every word.

Four Ways to Remember the Main Idea

Most of the magazines, periodicals, letters, and so forth, that cross our desk each day do not require meticulous reading. If you habitually plod along at a snail's pace, you can easily miss the forest for the trees. You will recall some interesting detail or oddity and miss the main idea or concept. Here are four ways to remember what you read, especially the major points.

1. *Read with a highlighter pen.* These are colored markers you can use to highlight what you want to remember. Yellow seems to be a popular color along with light blue, green, and pink. This will force you to analyze what is a main thought and what is there to support the main idea. Highlight the main ideas as you encounter

them. Later, review what you have highlighted. These are the points you want to commit to memory.

2. *Recognize topic sentences.* A well-written paragraph should contain one important sentence that sums up the content of the entire paragraph. Usually the topic sentence is the first sentence of the paragraph, but not always. Practice finding the topic sentence in your daily reading.

3. *Notice subtitles and subheads.* The writer puts them there to alert you to the fact that a new topic is going to follow. Ask yourself what points should be covered in these articles, chapters, and subsections. Read on to see if they are covered. Write your own subheads if you think they are missing. These, and the author's, then become your main ideas.

4. *Cut the length without rewriting.* Do what newspaper reporters do. They are taught to put the most important facts first, then to include items of gradually diminishing significance. You won't have the luxury of cutting only from the end. As you read, skip the parts that do not contain material you need or want.

How to Increase Your Comprehension Level

You can remember only what you understand. You can understand only what you truly comprehend. Some rapid-reading systems imply that if you increase your reading speed you will automatically improve your comprehension, but this is not necessarily true. It is possible to read too fast and sacrifice comprehension in the process. Unless you comprehend what you are reading you won't *remember* what you have read. Some of the ways reading comprehension can be increased are as follows:

1. *Get inside the author's head.* What is he trying to say? The sooner you discover the theme, the intent, the focal point of the material, the better your comprehension and memory of it will be.

2. *Avoid word-by-word reading.* Try to grab a group of words with your eye at one time. This will not just speed your reading, it will also keep you from getting bogged down. The author's ideas will be grasped more easily if you don't read haltingly.

3. *Previewing will increase your comprehension.* Go through the entire letter, chapter, or article searching for headings, illustrations, visuals such as graphs, and so on. If you know the overall scheme of the book or article before you begin reading, your understanding of it will be improved and made more memorable.

4. *Look at the title of the book or the topic sentence of the letter.* Does the writer go on to develop this idea or is it misleading? Be more analytical as you read. The author is telling you something, but is this the something she promised to tell you in the topic sentence or in the title of the piece?

5. *Summarize as you go along.* If there are no chapter summaries, make them up as you finish each chapter. If this article were in a newspaper, what would you write as the headline? What would you include in the first paragraph, the one that is never cut out?

6. *Compare this piece of writing with other things you have read on this subject.* How is this different? What does it contribute to your understanding? Did you learn something new? What was the most important thing you learned from reading this?

7. *Act as an editor.* How could you improve this piece of writing? How could it have been made more clear? What parts of this piece do you not understand?

8. *Take notes.* Your memory of what you read will be enhanced if you write comments as you go along. By writing down some key ideas on a separate piece of paper, you are consolidating what you have just read. The physical act of writing combines motor and visual memory cues. Having the notes to refer to at a future time further enhances your understanding of the material.

TWELVE WAYS TO INCREASE YOUR READING EFFICIENCY

1. *Select your reading material carefully.* Don't waste your time on books of questionable value. Preview what you are considering reading before you start a book.

2. *Eliminate poor habits.* Don't sound out words in silent reading or read each word separately. Avoid distractions.

3. *Make a conscious effort to broaden your reading.* Don't confine your reading to one narrow area. Become aware of best-seller lists, fiction and nonfiction, to see what the rest of the country is reading.

4. *Watch for changes in the author's trend of thought.* Be on the lookout for words such as, for example, but, therefore, however, despite, yet. They indicate the author is going to present a contrary idea.

5. *Look at headings, subheads, and visual material that may be inserted within the text.* Scan these before you begin to read the chapter or article. They will set the tone for your reading and get you thinking appropriately.

6. *Know exactly what information you are looking for when you read factual material.* Prepare questions in advance. Pretend you are going to interview the author when you finish reading the book or article. What are you going to ask her?

7. *Try to understand the big picture.* Read for main ideas. Don't get bogged down in a morass of details in what you read.

8. *Don't sacrifice comprehension for speed.* Make sure you understand what you are reading before you go ahead.

9. *Concentrate on what you are reading.* Get rid of distractions. Focus on the author's message.

10. *Ask yourself questions as you read.* Test your own understanding of the author's words and ideas.

11. *Visualize the author's main points as you read them.* Reduce them to short headlines. Actually "see" them in your mind's eye.

12. *Keep your notes on what you read.* Organize them so that you can retrieve them in the future. Review them from time to time to better remember them.

Exercises for Remembering What You Read

1. Turn to the editorial page of your daily newspaper. Read the lead editorial. What is the major point the editor is making? Is this reflected in the title of the piece? Rewrite the title to better reflect the writer's point of view.

2. Read two different letters to the editor in your newspaper. Have the writers made their points of view clear? Are there any parts of these letters that are not clear to you? What questions would you ask these letter writers, to clarify what they have written?

3. For this exercise, you will need a nonfiction book on any subject. Examine the table of contents. On a piece of paper list the three chapters that interest you the most. List them in order of importance or interest. Paraphrase the chapter titles in your own words.

4. Read the book jacket. Write down the two major selling points the publisher gives for buying this book.

5. Read the author's introduction or foreword or preface. Reduce this piece of writing to one sentence.

6. Assume you are writing a book review on this book. Your editor tells you to devote one paragraph to your recommendation for buying or not buying this book. Write a short paragraph with your recommendation.

7. Now let's see how much of this you can remember:
   • What was the editorial about?
   • What were the subjects and points of view of the two letters to the editor?
   • Which were the three chapters you thought were the most important in the book?
   • What are the two selling points made on the book's jacket?
   • What was your one-sentence summary of the front material of the book?
   • Why should the reader of your review buy or pass up this book?

By applying these kinds of questions to all of your technical or nonfiction reading, you will find that not only do you understand it better, but you also retain the information longer and with more accuracy.

Recalling a Business Memo

Paying attention to the six question words: Who, What, Why, Where, When, and How (or How much) will help you when you want to remember a piece of business correspondence. People don't write in direct response to these questions. But the trick is for you to have these questions in mind as you read what others have written. You will find this technique helpful as a check of your own correspondence to see if you are covering all of the bases.

Here is a sample business memo. As you read it, pay attention to these six questions.

EVERYMAN DISCOUNT STORES, INC.

TO: Marion Count
              Controller

FROM: C. P. Aize
              Staff Accountant

DATE: October 28, 199_

SUBJECT: Suggested Software Purchase

When you mentioned at the last staff meeting that you wished we would automate some of the functions now performed by staff accountants, I looked into the cost and effectiveness of new software.

The result of my search is the recommendation that we purchase Phase-II, a software package produced by Misso, Inc. The package will cost $4,725 and we will have to pay a semiannual maintenance fee of $100, which includes all updates.

Enclosed is a description of Phase-II and its capabilities, along with a list of firms currently using it. Jack Smith and I visited one installation (Mano Manufacturing), and we both think the system will be just what we need.

Enclosure

cc: Jack Smith

Now, without looking back, answer these ten questions based on the memo.

1. What was the name of the company involved in sending and receiving the memo?
2. Who wrote it and what was his or her title?
3. To whom was it sent and what was his or her title?
4. In what month of the year was this memo sent?
5. What was the subject of the memo?
6. What kind of item was suggested for purchase?
7. How much does it cost to purchase and maintain?
8. Where was this item seen in use?
9. Who else went to see it?
10. What is the goal in using such an item?

TAKING NOTES TO HELP YOU REMEMBER WHAT YOU READ

You will remember much more of what you see on the printed page if you take notes as you read. Any nonfiction reading material will stay with you longer if you follow these simple techniques.

1. Use a dictionary as you encounter unfamiliar words or terms. By ensuring you understand every word you read, you will produce better notes and better recall.
2. Include in your note taking the material the author considered important enough to underline, italicize, and print in bold type.
3. Take cues from headings, maps, graphs, photo captions, and other graphics used in the book or periodical. They are there to illustrate an important point and so should appear in some form in your notes.
4. Use your own words as you take notes. Rephrase what the author has said into more familiar language.
5. Keep each note short but long enough to trigger your memory when you go back to it.

6. Cite page numbers when taking notes. This will make it easier for you if you want to go back to the text for more details or explanation.

7. Mark your copy if the book is yours. Using pastel highlighters or writing marginal notes is helpful for many readers. It also ensures you will not misplace your notes; they will be in the book itself.

Exercises for Taking Notes While You Read

1. *Read the first few pages of your daily newspaper.* Choose three stories that interest you. Pretend you are a radio or TV newscaster. Using the newspaper as your source, take notes on how you will present this story on your broadcast. Construct your news show from your notes.

2. *Take notes on some large-print advertisement that appears in a magazine or a newspaper.* Jot down what you consider to be the essential information. Now close the magazine or newspaper and try to reconstruct the ad. Is your final copy complete? Check with the original to see how good your notes were.

3. *Read a movie or book review.* Take notes on the main characters, plot, mood, locale, and so on. From your notes, try to reconstruct a review of your own. Compare what you have written with the original for completeness of details.

4. *Read some technical material relating to your work or interest.* This can be an annual report, balance sheet, stock-performance chart, team averages, and the like. Take notes on this. Now, looking only at your notes, write a summary. Compare your summary with the original.

5. *Select a topic that interests you in any field.* It can be, for example, something from plant or animal life, transportation, computers, or another country. Look up this topic in a general encyclopedia. Take notes. The next day see how well you can develop this topic from your notes. Compare your written piece with the original.

A Personal Reading Analysis

You have read a great many techniques and hints for improving your reading comprehension.

Take a few minutes to answer these questions. Put down the first response that comes to your mind. This analysis will help you reflect on how well you are reading to remember.

The kinds of reading material I find most difficult are:

1. _____

2. _____

3. _____

The reading technique(s) that I am going to use in the future that I haven't used in the past is (are) _____

_____

The kind of reading that I enjoy and that I remember by category or author is:

1. _____

2. _____

3. _____

The area in which I am going to concentrate on improving my reading-to-remember skills is _____

_____

My peak time of day for reading with understanding and retention is _____

MEMENTOS

1. Focus your attention to get meaning from what has been said or written. Both listening and reading require us to concentrate.

2. Look for key ideas when you listen or read. Mentally search for the central or main idea of the speaker or writer. Ask yourself how these ideas are supported.

3. Learn to overcome barriers to listening or reading. Avoid distracting thoughts of your own. Bury yourself in the speaker's or writer's thought processes and not your own thoughts.

4. Ask yourself questions as you listen or read. These questions will help clarify the information being presented.

5. Take notes as you listen and when you read. As you write these notes, you are gleaning the main idea from the speaker's or writer's words.

6. Listen carefully and pretend you are going to paraphrase the speaker's thoughts when you tell a friend what you heard. This will force you to listen actively.

7. Help the repetitive speaker along with prompts.

8. Read a nonfiction book with better recall by using some of the techniques you use when reading your daily newspaper.

9. Use a variety of techniques as you read in order to increase your reading efficiency.

10. Look for visuals to help your reading comprehension. Cues such as headings, graphs, charts, pictures, and maps will help you remember what you have read.

Chapter Five

Making Others Remember What You Say and Write

There are many occasions when you may feel that you are not making an impression on others. They don't seem to remember what you have said or written. The techniques presented in this chapter will help you change that.

Using these tested memory techniques, you can improve the impact your speaking and writing has on your listeners and readers.

MAKING SURE WHAT YOU SAY IS REMEMBERED

A basic rule for ensuring what you say will be remembered is "Overstate and bore; understate and score."

People are more likely to remember what you say if you are brief and to the point. You can further ensure your message will be remembered if you follow these steps.

Six Guidelines for Memorable Speaking

1. *Be literal and direct.* Until you get to know your listener, avoid jargon, idiomatic expressions, or sarcasm. These may be lost on a listener, or worse, may cause misunderstanding.

2. *Repeat your main idea.* Listeners are easily distracted no matter how fascinating your subject. Give them a chance to catch up on your main points. You need more repetition in oral communication than in writing. Repetition allows readers to retrace their steps if they lose their way.

3. *Pause for questions or responses.* Don't make every speaking opportunity a lecture. If your audience of one, or one hundred, appears attentive but not responsive, ask the audience a question.

This will help you understand how much of your message they are getting.

4. *Use visuals when appropriate.* These can be photos, charts, or a mnemonic the listener(s) can refer to as you speak. This is especially helpful if you are presenting difficult or technical information.

5. *Tell them the benefits.* People are busy and have many tugs at their time. Emphasize why what you are saying is of interest or importance to them. Motivate them to listen—with a purpose in mind. Give examples or ask questions to personalize your approach. This will ensure their attention, understanding, and retention.

6. *Summarize by telling your listener(s) what you want them to remember.* For example, you might say, "These are the three main reasons for . . ."

How to Structure What You Say So It Will Be Remembered

As far back as the great Roman orator, Cicero, speakers have looked for a magic outline or formula that would help them give memorable speeches.

Audiences want to come away from a speech or presentation with some information. They frequently want to be amused. This means you have to make the factual material more palatable with an anecdote or other humorous device.

A simple and proven format for delivering a message that is likely to be remembered is this one:

1. Open with a short story or anecdote.
2. Tell them what you are going to tell them in the body of your talk.
3. Interject a bit of humor or another anecdote.
4. Deliver your message.
5. Interject another bit of humor.
6. Tell them what you have told them.

In this format, the odd-numbered items are the lubrication that smoothes the delivery of information. Number 5 can be eliminated if necessary.

Number 2 is vital. Audiences want to know, early on, what you are going to talk about.

Number 4 is the core of your speech. This should take up most of your time and effort.

Number 6 is the close that summarizes the main points you have made. In this part, you are doing the audience's homework for them. In essence, you are saying, "These are the main points of my talk. This is what I want you to remember.

It works! Audiences love it. You have helped make their memories work better.

Eight Strategies for Speaking Effectively

When we speak, the measure of our effectiveness is how well people remember what we say. Putting these effective devices or strategies to work will help you get your oral message across and remembered.

1. *Use concrete terms to engage the listener.* Clear, everyday terms are remembered better than such abstract terms as, for example, factors, areas, aspects.

2. *Include adjectives and adverbs.* These modifiers paint a picture for your listener. They add color and texture to your painting. Don't tell them about a "steak," tell them instead about a "juicy, tender steak."

3. *Be careful with pronouns such as he, she, they and their.* If you are talking about several people, make sure there is no question about which woman you are referring to when you say "she" or "her."

4. *Use vivid verbs.* These words describe action or movement. They create a picture in the mind of the listener. "He came into the room" is a bland picture unlikely to be remembered. "He bounded, lumbered, loped, rumbled, ran . . ." all convey a more vivid picture that is easier to recall because it was stored better.

5. *Choose active, not passive, voices.* "All the managers met" is better than "The meeting was attended by all the managers." In the first, active-voice sentence, the listener hears about something the

subject (managers) did. In the second, passive-voice sentence, the managers (concrete term) are subordinated to the object—the meeting (abstract term). The active voice suggests energy and so is remembered better.

6. *Reduce verbiage; don't use words that obscure content and add nothing to memory.* "Because" is stronger than "due to the fact that . . ." which is weak. "If" is better than "in the event that." Some trite phrases need no substitute at all. They should just be dropped from your speech, for example, "at this point in time." Hearing too many words is a distraction for the listener, something you don't need if you want to be remembered.

7. *Vary your use of words for emphasis.* Feel free to use contractions as you engage in informal speech—words such as can't, won't, shouldn't, and so forth. In formal speech, your key points will be remembered better when you add emphasis by using two words instead of the contraction: use can not, will not, should not.

8. *Distinguish among the three types of speaking: tough talk, sweet talk, and stuffy talk.* The key to each kind of talk is the pronoun you use: "I," "you," or "it." Tough talk hammers away with an authority. We see that in, "*I* want to get . . ." Sweet talk is "you" talk. This is the language of sales talks and advertising copy. "If *you* want *your* career to take off . . ." Stuffy talk is "it" talk. This is impersonal and official sounding: "*It* has come to my attention that . . ." Decide on your goal and use the appropriate talk. Sweet talk flatters the listener and hooks her into the message. This invites memory. There are occasions, however, when you may want to use either tough or even stuffy talk.

How to Make Sure You Speak Effectively

The way you deliver your message can be a big factor in how well it is remembered. Review this list to see how many of these techniques you use when you speak.

1. *Look your listener in the eye.* This rivets his attention and helps ensure he will remember what you say. If you are talking to a large group, "choose" three people in different parts of the room and talk to them.

2. *Eliminate hedges from your speech, such as "kind of," "sort of," "quite a few."* They confuse the listener and become a distraction as the listener tries to figure out just how many or what kind of item you are talking about.

3. *Watch your mannerisms.* You want your listener or audience to focus on *what* you are saying, not on how many times you push your glasses up your nose.

4. *Engage the listener by alluding to her.* For example, "As a teacher, I'm sure you've . . ." or "No doubt, Joan, you have seen this in your practice."

5. *Avoid offensive gender or ethnic terms.* They may alienate your audience and turn them off from listening. Say "flight attendant" rather than "stewardess." Use "Asian" rather than "Oriental."

6. *Assess your listener's knowledge of the subject and gear your speaking to this level of understanding.* We can't remember something if we don't understand it.

7. *Seek feedback.* Pause frequently to ask or answer a question. This will guide you as to how much of your message is being assimilated.

Putting Your Thoughts Across in Public

If you want people to remember what you have said during your speech, you must master the secrets of platform professionals. Just looking and sounding good might make the experience pleasurable for you and your listeners but nobody will take away your important message.

Good speakers "spoon-feed" their audience. They present their messages in "bite-sized portions" that the audience can ingest and chew on with ease. They give an overview at the beginning of the talk. This alerts the audience as to what to expect. They then "dish out" the material in suitable portions. They sum up by reminding the audience of what they told them. Such speakers not only entertain, they inform.

To determine how well you can put your thoughts across in public, take a look at these statements. After reading each one, decide if the response should be yes or no.

Public Speaking Test

	YES	NO
1. To get the audience's attention and support I should insert one or two jokes.	_____	_____
2. I should memorize my speech so that it will flow smoothly and be easily remembered.	_____	_____
3. Visual aids are hard to handle and may confuse my audience.	_____	_____
4. The part of my speech the audience will remember best is the ending.	_____	_____
5. Audiences are turned off by repetition. I'd better make my point just once.	_____	_____
6. My appearance has little to do with my message. The audience couldn't care less.	_____	_____
7. It's important for my audience to hear my credentials from me if they are to remember what I say.	_____	_____
8. It's best that I hand out a written summary of my major points at the end of my speech.	_____	_____

Eight Ways to Make Your Speeches Remembered

These eight suggestions for helping your audience remember what you said follow the eight questions in the Public Speaking Test. Incidentally, except for numbers 4 and 8, all your answers should have been no.

You will see why as we go over these eight points.

1. *Humor is a valuable adjunct to every speech.* It helps the audience see you as a real person and reduces tension—both yours and theirs. Humor can take the form of a funny remark, a play on words, a personal reference, and the like. This is not necessarily joke telling. Telling a joke can easily backfire. It may be a joke the audience has heard before, and you will bore them. The topic may be offensive to some members of the audience: minorities, women, senior citizens, and so forth. Joke telling takes a special skill, includ-

ing masterful timing, which many excellent speakers lack. It's best to leave jokes to comedians. Use humor instead.

2. *Rehearse, don't memorize your speech.* You may want to memorize a few key phrases or statistics to make sure you have them right. To memorize all of your speech invites disaster. If you lose your place, you're dead! Instead, move smoothly and logically from one idea to the next. Use index cards on which you write your main points and detailed, factual information.

3. *Visual aids have no place in delivering a eulogy or when you want to sustain a mood in an emotional talk.* Everywhere else they are valuable assets. They help the audience follow your remarks. They illustrate your points. They're worth their weight in gold if you're talking about numbers or graphs. Use them to illustrate major points and not details. Stay away from electrical visuals that can break down and require you to shut the lights and put your audience in the dark. These are needed for travel films and the like. If your is not an actual film or video cassette, stick to charts and other visuals that you can put up on an easel and refer to in your talk. People remember what they hear and see better than they do the things they hear but do not see.

4. *The end of your speech is the part the audience takes home with them.* It is also your last chance to highlight what you want them to remember. Power your ending by reprising the main ideas. Tell them what you want them to remember.

5. *Your audience can't go back to read and reread what you have said.* You have to anticipate what is important and what you want them to remember. Tell them what you are going to talk about. Talk about those things. Illustrate those points. Then, close by telling them what you told them. This will help your audience remember your speech.

6. *Your audience will size you up in the first 30 seconds that you stand in front of them.* Your manner, appearance, diction, posture, and voice quality will either impress them or turn them off. If you give the impression that you didn't care enough about your audience to pay attention to your appearance, they won't think enough about you to pay attention to your words. Without attention there can be no memory.

7. *Let the introducer briefly allude to your credentials for speaking on this topic; don't you provide them.* It comes across as either immodest if lengthy, or marginal if too short. Your first few sentences will convince them of your authority if you look and sound the part.

8. *Printed handouts are relished by audiences.* They may read them and then leave them behind, but they certainly like getting them. Giving them out at the start will encourage them to read while you open with a grabber they will miss. Giving them out in midtalk is to court inattention and an interruption of your flow of ideas. You may want to tell them about it, so they'll look forward to it. But don't distribute any material until you're finished and you have summed up orally.

Twelve Ways to Add Chemistry to Your Presentation

Audiences are more likely to remember what a speaker says if there is a positive emotional climate between the presenter and the audience. We call this "chemistry," or rapport. It is a kind of bond that must be initiated by the speaker.

Once this chemistry is in place, the speaker can sense it. The audience is now on her side and wants her to succeed. More importantly, they will listen attentively and take her message seriously. In short, they will remember the speaker and the message.

You can add this important ingredient to your presentation if you make sure to do the following:

1. *When you're introduced, walk to the microphone with energy and enthusiasm.* The audience feels a positive flow.

2. *Vary the pace of your delivery.* A slow, deliberate manner can degenerate into boredom. A faster pace, from time to time, bespeaks urgency, importance, and emphasis.

3. *Outline the important points you plan to cover.* This helps your audience anticipate what comes next. It helps clarify their thinking.

4. *Seek out individuals in your audience to engage with your eyes.* Make friends as your eyes roam from one section to another. Once you make contact and detect signs of agreement, smile and move on.

5. *Ask your audience a question.* People remember what they participate in actively. Keep their minds engaged as you move along. Don't let them assume a passive mode for your entire presentation.

6. *Check out your audience's eyes.* They may listen with their ears, but their eyes tell you when they're bored or when they're alert. Use their eyes as a barometer of their memory reception. Adjust your material accordingly. Wake them up with a question.

7. *Don't depend solely on your material to make a memorable impression.* Your audience is not reading it. They're looking at you and listening to your words. Make them something they'd want to remember.

8. *Think twice about using electronic audio-visual equipment.* Your credibility often declines with AV aids. They came to see and hear you. Otherwise, they could have watched a video tape in the comfort of their own home.

9. *What would you like your audience to say about you after you have made your presentation?* Interesting, informative, enjoyable, knowledgeable, exciting? Your answer will provide you with a goal to work toward when you prepare.

10. *Focus on the audience's concerns, needs, problems, and desires.* Your presentation must be all about *them.* Your knowledge and material must relate directly to the self-interest of your audience.

11. *Never underestimate the sensitivity of an audience.* From your delivery they can tell

- how you feel that day.
- if you like them or if you wish you were somewhere else.
- if you've memorized your speech.
- when you're bluffing or making up an answer.

12. *Watch your language.* What may be colorful to you may be offensive to certain members of your audience. Instead of recalling your main message some will remember only your use of an offensive word or expression.

Following these suggestions will separate you from the mediocre speaker who loses half of his audience. Integrate these suggestions into your next presentation and watch the retention rate of what you say soar.

How to Develop a Voice That Makes You Memorable

The text of what you say is important. It is your message. However, the voice of the messenger has the ability to turn listeners off or to gain their attention. Their attention is necessary if there is to be any retention.

Your tone of voice, projection, and volume will reach your listener before you complete your first sentence. A thin, whiny mumble will not hold the attention of your audience. You need a vocal tone that enhances your message and your image. If you want what you say to be remembered, your voice needs to grasp and hold the listener's attention.

You can work with a voice coach or modify your voice by yourself. These proven suggestions will give you the voice you want.

1. *Gather samples of your speaking voice.* Place a small tape recorder near your telephone. Turn it on each time you use the phone. After three or four calls play the tape back to get an idea as to how you sound to callers.

- Before making a presentation or giving a talk, go through it once by speaking into the recorder.
- Read something into the recorder. It can be some business correspondence or a newspaper article.

2. *Play these samples back.* Take notes on what you like and what you'd like to see improved.

3. *Use your tape recorder to get samples of voices that have the qualities you are looking for:* modulation, diction, timing, timbre, and so forth. Get these samples from radio or TV, video tapes, or audio tapes.

4. *Take notes on the qualities of these professional speaking voices that you want to emulate.* Replay these tapes frequently.

5. *Write out some lines you heard the professionals say.* Make a tape with you reciting these lines; then play it back. Do this enough times until you notice a difference in your recorded speech. Continue until you see you are internalizing some of the good speech you heard.

6. *Do not try to impersonate your model.* You want your listener to remember *you.* Your goal is to change your voice tone and quality gradually so that you are pleased with it. Then your listeners are sure to follow.

How Body Language Helps to Get Your Message Across

Body language determines how well people remember you and your message. Your audience (of one or one hundred) interprets the meaning of your words through your body movements and gestures.

Your eye contact, facial expressions, posture, and gestures are power tools in getting your message across and stored in the minds of your listeners.

Here's how you can supplement what you say with body language that makes your message memorable.

Eye Contact

- Maintain a relaxed gaze for about half the time. In small groups focus on one eye of the person you are talking to. To stare into both eyes is intimidating.
- Avoid a steady stare. If your eye contact is rigid and fixed you will come across as aggressive.
- Lack of eye contact suggests you are bored, lack confidence, or are untrustworthy.

Facial Expression

- Maintain a pleasant expression. Look as if you are happy to be in their presence.
- Smile when appropriate—when first introduced, upon leaving, and when your listener smiles.
- Avoid a fixed smile. Your listener can spot an insincere grin.

Posture

- The way you stand reflects your self-image. It also shows how you feel about your listener(s).

- Stand with your feet firmly planted and slightly apart. Do not drape yourself on the lectern or lean on a chair for support. Standing up without support helps you project a command posture that indicates that what you are saying is important.

- Be aware of your spine and keep it straight. Hold your head erect. Good posture lends authenticity to what you are saying.

Gestures

- Punctuate your main points with a confident, natural use of your hand.

- Take up space. The more space you take up with your body and hand gestures the more powerful you appear. This makes what you are saying worthy of remembering.

With a little practice you will master these body-language hints; then you will project yourself as having something important to say that is worth remembering.

How to Leave Your Audience with a Memorable Happy Ending

You want your audience to remember your message and the messenger as well. As you near the end of your talk, don't feel nervous and grope for a closing line. Sitting down and getting out of sight may seem attractive to you after going through most of your speech. But the ending is important and can't be left to chance.

You want to leave a strong positive impression on your listeners. Your concluding comments must do the following:

1. Recap your speech and give your audience the main ideas you covered.
2. Show you to be a prepared, polished, and memorable speaker.

You can't wind down at the end of your presentation like a child's wind-up toy. You've got to make your listener feel good about the speech and the speaker before she gets out of her seat.

Tie your ending to your opening. If you opened with a question, then answer the question as part of your conclusion. If you began with a statistic or startling statement that caught their attention, then end with a direct reference to that statement.

Do not rush your conclusion; be as calm and forthright as you were in the opening. Audiences want closure; don't let them down.

You can add drama to your ending if you finish with a "call for action." Urge your listeners to do something: take a stand on some issue, write letters, buy a product, or improve themselves in some way. The thrust of your speech will stay with them as they head for home.

The appropriate ending will have them remember you and your message just as the opening captured their attention.

MAKING YOUR WRITING MEMORABLE

In business, professional, and personal situations, we are called upon to write letters, reports, notes, and memos. When we do this, our major goal is to communicate. We want our readers to understand our message and to remember it. We also want them to remember who wrote it.

To do this well and to be remembered, we must consider three things: we need to identify our purpose; imagine the reader of the message; and choose the form for delivering the message.

Your purpose may be simply to *record* information as in the minutes of a club or corporation. It may be to *inform,* as in a price list, annual report, memo, or invitation. It may be to *persuade,* as in a sales letter, position paper, or charity solicitation. Before you begin to write, you have to identify your purpose. Just what do you want the reader to remember?

The reader won't remember anything unless you first engage her attention. This can be done with a strong opening sentence that grabs the reader's attention. After that you have to demonstrate that this piece of correspondence has some benefit for her. If you don't do this she won't continue reading and, of course, won't remember anything.

The length of your message, along with its tone, will dictate the form your message should take. Should this be a personal or more formal letter? Should it be a short memo or a longer report? Choose the format that you think will be remembered.

Not until you answer these questions are you ready to actually write your first word.

When we use the term "memorable," we are not thinking in terms of great literature. We are talking about writing that is direct and clear enough for the reader to remember what you have said long enough to take the requested action.

The cardinal rule for writing in a way that the reader will remember is good conversation in print.

People remember certain conversations they have had even when they took place many years ago. These conversations have the following things in common:

- They were pleasant.
- The other people were easy to talk to.
- The language used was familiar and not difficult to understand.
- The other people did not put on airs or in any way make the listener feel intimidated.
- The speakers came to the point and did not beat around the bush.
- They ended on a positive note.

These are precisely the qualities you want to include in your business and personal writing. This is not as easy as it seems. For a variety of reasons many people feel that their writing has to be overblown. Most of the writing we receive is read and then tossed out. If it is not tossed out, it is filed. This is virtually the same thing because most pieces of filed correspondence are never looked at again. If you aim for some high-powered, erudite prose when you write a simple note or memo, you are asking for trouble. The reader will feel somewhat insulted and is not likely to remember what you wrote.

Aim for a natural, conversational style in your writing. The reader will show his appreciation by remembering what it is you wrote. He will also remember the writer—with affection and gratitude. No one likes to be talked down to, in person or in writing. Many people make the mistake of thinking that professional or business writing must be formal and must demonstrate the advanced education of the writer. Readers don't want that. They want clear, simple writing that conveys its message and has no hidden agenda. This is the kind of writing they remember.

Test Your Ability to Write So That You Will Be Remembered

Following are ten brief statements. Some are true, others are false. After reading each, make a choice. Check the response that, in your judgment, is the better approach.

Statement	*TRUE*	*FALSE*

1. Your opening sentence has two purposes. The first is to grab the reader's attention. The second is to provide the reader with a benefit.

2. A good way to make sure that what you write is easy to read is to use language taken from a thesaurus rather than from everyday speech.

3. Check the ways your ideas flow. Make sure they are easy to read.

4. Cross out words, sentences, even paragraphs if they don't add meaning to your writing.

5. Mentally picture the results you want before you begin writing.

6. Mentally picture the person you are writing to before you begin.

7. A good way to show your interest in the person who will be reading your writing is to make your points from your own perspective.

8. People like reading business letters that are written on a higher level than their newspapers.

9. The form you use in business writing is dependent on the length of the message as well as the tone.

10. People resent reading business correspondence that is conversational in tone.

When you complete the test, compare your answers with this list:

Answers: 1. T, 2. F, 3. T, 4. T, 5. T, 6. T, 7. F, 8. F, 9. T, 10. F

A score of seven or fewer correct answers suggests an urgent need to improve your ability to put your thoughts down on paper. As you read on, you will find suggestions that will help you write so that your message is both understood and remembered.

Guidelines for Making Your Writing Remembered

Before you put your writing into its final form you should consult this list.

1. *Analyze your readership.* Who is going to read what you write? Is it likely to be passed on to others? What are they looking for?

2. *Begin with an outline.* This will help you organize your information and your document.

3. *Pick out your main points.* Just what is it you want your readers to remember? Identify three or four major points.

4. *Begin with a strong opening.* Your initial sentence or paragraph should hook your readers and make them want to continue.

5. *Use memory aids.* Make it easy for your readers to remember your written message. Use illustrations, charts, and a summary to emphasize your main points.

6. *Define your terms.* Your readers are more likely to remember your writing if you use the vocabulary they are familiar with. Any new terms should be fully defined and explained.

7. *Tell them what they should remember.* Mention what your main points are in the beginning. Proceed to develop each one. End your writing with a wrap-up of your main ideas.

8. *Make associations.* Help your readers understand your writing by relating your new information to material they already know.

9. *Use verbal pictures.* Help your readers visualize the ideas you are presenting. Use vivid images to illustrate your main points. Give concrete examples to help them remember.

10. *Tie it up.* Be sure to provide a summary paragraph at the end of your writing. This should highlight the main ideas you promised to discuss in your opening paragraph.

Analyze Your Own Writing

Find a letter, report, or memo that you have written during the past year. Reread it objectively. What general impression do you get? Now, read it again as you answer these questions. How many "yes" responses do you come up with?

1. Does my title or lead sentence make the reader want to continue?
2. Do I offer the reader a benefit for continuing?
3. After reading what I wrote does my reader know what my main points were?
4. Is my language clear and easily understood by my reader?
5. Do I sum up at the end of my writing?
6. Do *I* remember what this piece of writing is all about?

If you come up with fewer than 5 "yes" responses, you need some more help. Reread this chapter before you attempt any major writing task.

How to Grab Your Readers' Attention

The lead, hook, or opener of your written piece has to grab the readers' attention. If they don't read on, they're not going to remember you or the article.

Many writers struggle to get just the right opening sentence before they proceed. If you don't think of a hook right away, it's best to just begin writing. The lead will come to you after you have gotten something down on paper.

This applies to all business and professional writing, regardless of length. In short texts, such as memos and notes, the brevity of the material will focus more on the theme and tone than it will on the lead. In longer texts, such as reports, directives, policy statements, and correspondence, the lead or opening will be more important.

A good lead has four basic functions:

1. The lead has to command attention. Readers must be drawn in by your lead and want to read on. Example: "We want to save jobs and increase productivity this year. The following procedures will help accomplish both goals."

2. The lead or introduction has to describe the subject and general theme of the text. It has to point the way to what is to follow. This is also a memory aid. Example: "There are four ways in which you can reduce absenteeism in your department."

3. The lead paragraph should establish the tone of the text. Is it going to be serious or lighthearted? Is it a thoughtful policy statement, a report on an accident, or a holiday greeting? This, too, helps the memory get ready. Example: "By this time you have, no doubt, heard about the accident at our Springfield plant."

4. The lead or introduction must accurately describe what the rest of the writing is about. Don't write a lead that promises more than it delivers. Example: "We are prepared to offer three incentives to those who opt for the Early Retirement Package."

CHOOSE ONE OF THESE OPENERS FOR LONGER TEXTS

1. *Everyone likes a story.* Start your longer piece with an anecdote, action scene, or narrative description. It's best to put your readers into the driver's seat early on. Drag the readers right into the action. Put the readers in a position to identify with the argument you are making. For example, describe the kind of client that is being served by your medical provider or pharmaceutical manufacturer account.

2. *Begin with somebody talking.* We love to eavesdrop on other people. Quotation marks promise something lively and informal to get the readers' interest. The bit of conversation you start with should be engaging and show promise of what lies ahead. For example, "The fire department was gone just a few minutes when my Acme Insurance agent called to see what he could do to help me file my claim."

3. *Open with a statement.* It can be a controversial opinion or a startling statistic. Either will make your readers continue to see how you back it up. For example, "One out of three of our customers leaves town." This could be a lead into an office moving company's sales letters.

Any one of these approaches will work. A lead that catches the reader's attention and lures them into reading what you've written is a good one.

How to Help Your Reader Remember More of What You Write

Readers appreciate anything you can do to help them remember what you put down on paper. You can do this without talking down to your readers or sounding pedantic. Make use of these "write-to-remember" devices:

- Use a variety of sentence lengths, but emphasize short sentences.
- Do the same with paragraph length.
- Include boldly lettered section headings and subheadings in appropriate places.
- Highlight key words in italics.
- Define new terms the first time you use them.
- Include illustrations and graphics to clarify the points you are making.
- Begin with an introduction that mentions the main points you plan to make.
- Check to see that you've answered any questions you posed in the introduction.
- Tie in new material with information your readers are likely to have already.

How to Make Your Readers Want to Read What You Write

You've got to make your readers feel that what you've written is important and worth remembering. A quick scan of your writing will tell the business reader whether or not it's worth reading, based on the following:

- A good opening or lead
- The length of the article
- The length of most paragraphs
- The use of graphics: charts, graphs, photos, tables, and so forth
- The vocabulary as gleaned from skimming
- A tidy closing (many readers peek at the ending)

ZERO IN ON THE BUSINESS PROBLEM

Readers are looking for answers to questions or problems that they have in the workplace or their professions. If you want to make others remember what you write, you have to meet their needs. You can reach your readers and have them remember your written message if you ask yourself these questions:

- What is the problem I want to solve or the information gap I want to fill?
- What angle will I take on this subject?
- What main points will I make?
- How will I illustrate these main points?
- How will I summarize what I have written?
- How does my ending tie in with my lead?

Ten Ways to Make Your Reader Remember You and Your Writing

These writing suggestions are not listed in any particular order of importance. They are all important if you want your readers to remember your name as the author and what you have written.

1. *Never put on paper anything you wouldn't feel comfortable saying in front of a group.* When speaking, you try not to seem stuffy or dull. Yet, many writers don't take pains to see to it that they don't "read" that way.

2. *Don't use big words, unless they're the only way to make your point.* Everyday words will make your memos, letters, and reports easier to read. Avoid the "corporate" voice in favor of the "direct" voice. For example:

Corporate Voice	*Direct Voice*
In regard to the matter above	Concerning X
Please be advised by this correspondence	I'm writing to
We wish to advise you that	(Omit. Just begin.)

Corporate Voice	*Direct Voice*
Thanking you in advance for your kindness and attention to this matter I remain,	Thank you.
Your recent communication relative to	Your letter about

3. *Reduce the number of words you use to make your point.* "Now" will do better than "at this point in time." The fewer words you use the easier it will be for your readers to remember your message.

4. *Check to see that what you write is perfectly clear.* If what you write *can* be misunderstood, it will be. People remember only what they can understand without a great deal of effort.

5. *Be entertaining.* No matter how important your information may be, it should be presented in an interesting way if you want it to be remembered. Readers remember best what appeals to their emotions.

6. *Tell them what you're going to tell them, tell them, and then end by telling them what you've just told them.* Such emphasis reinforces memory.

7. *Show, don't tell.* "Show" the readers why your material is important. Let the readers reach their own conclusions. Don't "tell" them what to think. Use graphics, such as graphs, charts, pictures, and so forth, to help the readers visualize what you want to be remembered.

8. *Give your article a title that also provides a theme.* It helps the readers focus on your main idea. It also helps them remember what the piece was about. For example, How Jim Jones Turns Cold Calls into Gold

9. *Let the readers know what your qualifications are to write this material.* Relate your own experiences and successes. The authenticity they add to your text will provide additional memory cues. These cues will help the readers remember you and your writing better.

10. *Include a teaser near the end of your longer written pieces*— reports, motivational articles. Hint at other areas you are exploring. This will alert the reader to look for other reports, studies, sales pieces, and so forth, with your name on them.

Four Examples of Memorable Business Writing

1. In a memo to advise employees of new safety procedures begin by stating the need for new procedures and then list them in logical order with a sensible reason for compliance. Your employees should understand the rationale for the memo in the first place. Each procedure should be clear enough to be easily remembered.

2. In a written policy statement, which is likely to be a longer text, you should break the material up into smaller sections that can then be converted into short memory bites. These may include personnel issues (for example, hiring, firing, promotion, compensation packages), corporate social or community responsibilities, advertising and promotion standards, and so on. Your readers will need these global policies broken down if they are to remember them.

3. In a letter to employees concerning the adoption of a new logo and instructions for its use, you will need a memory-friendly approach if the employee-readers are to comply with the wishes of the writer. To facilitate remembering the contents of the company letter, certain graphics should be included such as reproductions of the old and new logos, with comments as to the differences. The reason for the change and the source of the new design should be included for the readers to comprehend the entire picture. The letter should inform and persuade the readers as to the benefit of a change in logo if the readers are to remember what is to be done.

4. In a facsimile transmission (FAX) to a branch office, you want to convey sales and inventory data. To assist the readers in remembering the major points you wish to make, be sure to begin and end with a general statement making a comparison to last year's figures or this year's projections. This kind of summary statement is needed to give the readers a "handle" on what you want remembered. Your FAX must convey a summary of the big picture you want remembered as well as the details.

How Your Writing Will Benefit Your Reader

When you implement these suggestions your reports and memos will be more meaningful and memorable.

One of the benefits that your readers will gain will be a comfortable feeling when reading your material, whether short texts—

memos, notes, and so on—or longer texts—correspondence, reports, studies, and the like. Your language and sentence structure will be reader-friendly and less likely to threaten the readers.

Another benefit for your readers will be that your writing style will not only get your message across, but will assist them in remembering what you write. Your clarity, repetition, and style will feed into the readers' ability to recall the material you are presenting. Most readers are lazy when it comes to memory enhancement of what they read. By making your message easier to read, and repeating points when necessary, you are breaking up your message into manageable morsels that can easily be committed to memory.

How to End Your Writing with a Bang

Some dinner guests, after spending a lovely evening, don't know how to say goodbye. As a result, they postpone it and in so doing overextend their welcome.

The same is true for many writers. They don't have the ability to close with a short, snappy, memorable ending.

Your ending of a written piece is the last chance your reader will have to remember what you want them to remember. It's also the last chance for them to remember you.

A good ending can compensate for a lot of sins. The final thought with which you leave the readers will determine how well you or your writing are remembered.

Guidelines for a Memorable Close

- A good ending is satisfying to the readers. Their expectations have been met.

- All the promises made in the introduction have been kept by the author.

- The major points have been developed and are easy to remember.

- Check to see that the lead and ending are compatible and complement each other.

- Try to end sooner rather than later. The readers shouldn't feel their memory is overloaded with new information.

MEMENTOS

1. Start with a good opening statement when speaking or writing. You need to grab your listeners' or readers' attention right away. Unless they attend carefully they won't remember.

2. Organize your speech or writing in a way that is logical and clear to those you want to reach. This is the only way you can inform or persuade them. People need an orderly arrangement of thoughts if they are to remember them.

3. Provide your audience or readers with memory aids such as visuals or graphics. People remember what they can see in a vivid way. Flip charts on stage or graphs in a report help clarify your message.

4. End your oral presentation or written text with a neat ending. Tie up any loose ends. Refer back to your opening statement. Reinforce your main points to assist the listeners/readers to remember more easily and accurately.

5. Help your listeners/readers out by breaking up your message into small bites. Explain each point clearly before moving on to the next one.

6. Use body language to supplement what you say. Eye contact, facial expression, posture, and gestures all add to your impact on the listeners.

7. Use vivid language in your writing. Get your readers involved in what you are writing about. Show, don't tell the readers how your message is important to them.

Chapter Six

Conquering Absentmindedness

In school, students either attend class or are absent from class. As adults, we are either "attend"-minded or "absent"-minded. When handling our car keys, eyeglasses, important papers, and so on, our minds are frequently absent when we put down the item.

Actually, you didn't forget where you placed it. You forget things you once learned. You never attended to or learned where you placed the item in the first place, so you can't forget what you don't learn. If you never really registered where you placed the item, how can you recall its location minutes or hours later?

It's perfectly normal for you not to pay attention to things that appear to be unimportant at the moment. With all the things you have on your mind when you put down something such as a pen, watch, or letter, it may not seem important at that time.

As you go from one activity to another, you are not always "attending" to what you are doing. Thoughts of the next task distract you just when you should pause and reflect on what is taking place. For example, you've paid for a purchase with a credit card and are now thinking of how quickly you can exit the crowded store. In your haste, you absentmindedly leave without retrieving your credit card.

This chapter helps you erase absentmindedness by showing you how to avoid misplacing papers, jewelry, keys, notes, glasses, and the like. You will enjoy these benefits:

1. You will be able to save time and duplication of effort.
2. You will reduce the frustration of retracing your steps to check up on routine actions.
3. You will gain confidence in yourself when you "know" that you locked the door or shut off the appliance.

Before we go any further, let's evaluate your level of absentmindedness with this test.

Testing Your Absentmindedness

This self-scoring exercise tests a variety of memory lapses. These happen to all of us from time to time. The test points out those aspects of absentmindedness involved in daily life.

Give yourself 2 points for each occurrence that took place in your life this past week. Give yourself 1 point for each occurrence that took place in the last month but not in the last week.

1. Repeating a joke or story to the same person
2. Forgetting where things are normally kept or looking for them in the wrong place
3. Repeating a routine thing by mistake, for example starting to comb your hair when you have just done so
4. Losing items around the house
5. Forgetting to give someone an important message
6. While talking to someone, pausing and asking, "What was I talking about?"
7. Forgetting to do things you said you would do, even things you were looking forward to doing
8. Starting a book or video tape that you have already read or watched
9. Leaving things behind and wasting time going back to get them
10. Going back to check on yourself about, for example, locking the door, shutting off an appliance
11. Not remembering changes in routine, following your old routine by mistake
12. Failing to recognize places you have been to before

A total score of 9 or less indicates a degree of absentmindedness less than that of the general population. A score of 10 to 15 is average. If your score is 16 or more, it represents a high degree of absentmindedness.

Don't be alarmed if your score is higher than 16. This could be a function of a very busy lifestyle. Being busy or rushed all the time puts great demands on your memory. Logically, the more situations in which lapses are possible, the greater the number of lapses you will report. Older people often report fewer memory lapses because they are generally more dependent on routine and extrinsic memory aids such as calendars that remember for them. Receptionists in physicians' offices report that retired people are less likely to forget an appointment than are younger ones. The older patient has fewer distractions in his life and more time to remember with (in spite of scientific evidence that most memory functions decline with age). Retired people are more selective when it comes to memory. They exceed the average person in some respects and lag behind in others.

EIGHT WAYS TO REDUCE FORGETFULNESS

Here are eight techniques you can use to improve the quality of your registration and bid a fond farewell to absentmindedness:

1. Talk to yourself to help memory.
2. Use your mental cross-index file.
3. Develop attend-minded habits.
4. Use visual reminders.
5. Fine-tune your powers of observation.
6. Use mechanical devices.
7. Learn to handle distractions and interruptions.
8. Master automatic gestures.

How Talking to Yourself Improves Memory

Of our five senses, our sense of hearing, or auditory sense, is one of the strongest. Experiments have demonstrated that hearing a string of nine numbers will register them in our memory for a longer period of time than merely looking at the nine numbers for the same period of time.

We've all had the experience of trying to remember a phone number we have looked up and not having pencil or paper to write it down. We repeat it aloud over and over until we have the materials to write the number. Hearing our own voice repeat the number assists us in holding on to it. (Before dialing it, you should write it down. A busy signal or no answer might add enough delay time for you to forget the number.) But our auditory sense frequently comes to the rescue, especially if it is asked to remember items in our own voice.

If you merely observe yourself putting your keys on the shelf, you are using a visual cue. However, if you say to yourself, or preferably aloud, "I am now putting these car keys on the shelf," you are adding a powerful second dimension. Besides just seeing the words "keys" and "shelf," you are hearing the connection.

A busy attorney I know describes herself as having "several irons in the fire." For her, "verbalizing aloud what I am doing is a must. Very often, "she continues, "I announce to myself what I want to do next. As I complete one task I ask aloud, 'What should I do next?' In this way, I don't forget assignments I have given myself."

By talking to yourself, you are preventing absentmindedness that keeps you from remembering. Instead of being "absent" when you put your keys down, you "attend" to the task. You actually reinforce the image three ways:

- By talking to yourself you *hear* where the keys were placed.
- You *think* about where you put the keys.
- You *see* exactly where you placed the keys.

This multisensory cueing makes so-called "forgetting" less likely to occur. By utilizing this multisensory approach, you are *registering* what you are doing. Each time you add another sensory dimension, you increase the ease of recall.

Be sure to describe to yourself what you are doing. "I'm putting my keys on the wooden shelf. I see them there. I hear them as they are placed on the shelf. I hear my voice record the deed." Actually talk to the object for emphasis or further reinforcement. "Now stay here, keys. Don't drive away." This kind of verbal elaboration, using humor and/or exaggeration, further intensifies the image and enhances your memory skills. The more often you practice a variety of memory skills the less often you will be absentminded.

Talking to yourself is so simple that many people do not include it in their mental arsenal of memory aids. Don't ignore it because it seems silly. Wearing glasses may seem silly at first. But after you become aware of the vast improvement in vision you wear the "silly" glasses regularly.

Reviewing your shopping list out loud on a crowded commuter bus or train may cause raised eyebrows and certainly is not appropriate. But in the privacy of your own home or office, such subvocalization or low-voiced reminders work wonders. This simple, proven method requires no practice or study—it just works.

Exercise for Talking to Yourself

Here are two lists of random items. Read the first list silently, then close the book and write down as many items as you can recall.

For the second list, read the items *aloud,* then close the book and write down as many items as you can recall. You will be seeing *and* hearing what you want to remember.

Notice the difference in the number of items recalled.

List One	*List Two*
paper	book
tree	house
pencil	watch
dish	cup
fork	spoon
table	chair
sofa	rug
ball	toy
car	truck
wall	roof

How to Use Your Mental Cross-Index File

In an office, when we file an item under more than one heading we are said to be "cross-indexing." This same system can be used to reinforce items that we want to store in our memory bank.

The more associations you attach to a fact you want to remember, the more retrieval cues you have to recall that fact. Strengthen your attentiveness by not only thinking or talking to yourself but by cross-indexing the facts or items you want to remember.

The time you take to attach a web of associations and meaning to the fact or item will enhance its transfer to your long-term memory. This buys insurance that you will be able to retrieve what you stored when any one of these cues comes to mind in the future.

Examples of Retrieval Cues

Occasionally. a smell, sound, taste, sight, or feel will bring back an experience we had years before. At the time we think of them as "reminders" of the past. For example:

- A stranger walks by wearing a certain fragrance. This reminds you of an old friend who wore the same scent.
- In a public place, a child's voice or laugh reminds you of your own child or grandchild.
- A taste of some exotic or ethnic food recalls a similar dish prepared by your grandmother years before.
- The sight of a stranger who looks so much like a now-deceased friend.
- The feel of a certain fabric brings back the feel of a favorite garment worn years before.

The ability to remember experiences from the past can help you produce retrieval cues in the present. Capitalize on this by using your senses to cross-index associations. For example, in putting down your car keys at home be aware of the following:

- The sound of the keys making contact with the surface as you place them down: wood, metal, glass, and so on.
- The sight of the keys in place.

We can apply cross-indexing to some of the items listed at the beginning of this chapter.

Example 1:   "The pen is next to the phone."
Some cross-index cues might include:
While on the phone, I doodled with the pen.
I take phone messages with this pen.
Both the phone and the pen are made of plastic.
I tucked part of the pen under the phone.

Example 2:   "The glasses are on the kitchen table.
              Better to see the stains on the table top.
              I placed the lens side facing up.
              My glasses are next to a glass of water.
              I need my glasses to see what I am eating.

Cross-indexing is an antidote for absentmindedness in every-day situations. In addition to mental images, I recommend conducting an attention scan also. It is a cross-index of items and images. This is a check that you perform routinely throughout the day.

For example, it may include a brief pat of your wallet in your pocket or purse, a reach for your earring after a phone call, a visual sighting of your bracelet or watch after putting on your coat. Such scans compensate for the absence of mind that may take place when you remove your wallet for a purchase, take off an earring to use the telephone, or wrestle with a heavy garment. Combined with stress, anxiety, and/or fatigue, such absentmindedness can lead to disaster. Scanning, when established, together with cross-indexing of mental images, helps fight absentmindedness.

It is important to note that the images and scans you come up with yourself are the most effective. Those I cited are merely suggestions. These came from my head and obviously will work for me. They are no better or no worse than anyone else's. Begin now to make up your own cross-index system for things you want or need to remember.

DEVELOPING ATTEND-MINDED HABITS

With a little practice these easy-to-learn habits will become second nature to you and will eliminate your predisposition to absent-mindedness.

1. *Stay on track.* You are sitting in the living room and want to get the book you were reading in bed last night. You start walking to your bedroom and notice that someone left a drinking glass on the end table. You return it to the kitchen. While there you see the cat's food dish is empty and you fill it. Upon reaching the bedroom you wonder why you went there. The book has left your mind. You allowed the drinking glass and cat dish to edge it out of your mind. The book absented itself.

Next time, make a conscious effort to stay on track. As you get out of your chair, visualize the book, see its cover, recall the precise place you left it, feel its weight as you pick it up. Think of just where you left off when reading last night. This will keep your mind filled with the image of the book. Your brain will be so filled with this image it will not be side-tracked or derailed by the stop in the kitchen. When you reach the bedroom, you will know why you went there because you will remain on track.

2. *Do it now!* Absentmindedness can occur at any time. It is especially prevalent when we postpone an action. For example, you are concerned about your credit-card bill; you don't want any interest charges this month. Pay it now. Train yourself by habitually doing things when you think about them, doing them while they are present in your mind. Telephone friends while you are thinking about them. Lose the self-defeating habit of procrastination—through action.

You will feel better about not being absentminded as you take the step. Of course, there are times when we must postpone action. You need to have a deposit clear or have access to a telephone. In such cases, plant as many cues as you can so that your cross index file will help you do it right away. Put a check on your calendar when the deposit has cleared so you will know you can now pay that bill. Or, visualize yourself getting home and walking straight to the phone to call your friends.

3. *Use regular fixed places.* Your greatest weapon in fighting absentmindedness is order. If you spend time needlessly looking for your car keys, decide once and for all on one place to rest them when you arrive home each day. When you are out of the house, but not in the car, develop the reflex of always putting them in one special pocket of your jacket, pants, or purse. Pick a regular, fixed place and stick with it. Place them there consciously until it becomes a conditioned reflex. Use the same habit for your glasses, gloves, checkbook, tools, and so on. A place for everything and everything in its place.

Make a decision to find a regular fixed place for all the household or office items you have ever misplaced. Reinforce these places by making a mental sketch or cartoon drawing to help you. You needn't possess any artistic skills to do this, just a fertile imagination.

For example, in the past few weeks you have spent time searching for each of these items: eyeglasses, gloves, checkbook, screwdriver. After a few seconds of thought you come up with these convenient resting places for each item: eyeglasses in top drawer of desk, leather gloves in dress-coat pocket, wool gloves in pocket of ski parka, checkbook in righthand desk drawer, screwdriver in kitchen "junk" drawer. Now, all you have to do is make a mental sketch or cartoon of each item in its place. The eyeglasses are in the desk drawer, but in your cartoon they are oversized and barely fit in the drawer. This exaggerated sketch helps to reinforce the connection. In a similar manner, you sketch the gloves in the appropriate pocket with just one or two fingers handing out to reinforce the location. The checkbook is in the top drawer, but you have left the drawer ajar to help you remember the location. The screwdriver is in the junk drawer atop all the miscellaneous items in there.

These mental pictures will appear on your memory screen each time you look for the item. Because you "drew" these cartoons yourself they will be easy to recall. Adding humor or exaggeration will make them even easier to bring to mind. This is still another way to keep them from being absent of mind.

4. *Change a pattern.* One of the most vexing kinds of absentmindedness is when you want to make a change in your regular routine. Your brain seems stuck in the rut of established patterns and resists remembering that today you want to do something differently. For example, you want to take a different train to work, you must report to a different office, or it's your turn to pick up breakfast for your co-workers before reporting for work.

To help you stay attendminded or focused on the change, you should alter a simple item of attire or jewelry. This will serve as a red alert that a change is taking place in your regular routine today. This could be placing your watch on your other wrist, carrying your purse on your other shoulder or your wallet in another pocket, or wearing a pair of shoes that you don't ordinarily wear to work. Making these changes before you start your day will serve to keep you from being absentminded when you want to remember these more complex changes in routine.

Exercise for Developing Attendminded Habits

The following five objects are frequently misplaced. Assume that you own each of them. Assign each one a fixed place in your home. Use visual reminders such as those just described.

Object	*Fixed Place*
Checkbook	_____
Car keys	_____
Eye glasses	_____
Pen	_____
Wallet	_____

Refer to this list in a day or two. See if you can recall *all* the locations.

Using Visual Reminders

Absentmindedly leaving something on the stove or your keys in a locked car brings frustration and misfortune. This can be avoided if you use visual reminders. For example, after you put a pot of rice on the stove to cook, take the box of remaining rice with you to the table or counter as you prepare the next course. Each time you look up the box of rice will remind you that you have rice cooking on the stove.

Similarly, when you park your car "see" the keys leave the ignition and go into your right hand. See this as a smooth movement as automatic as engaging the parking brake. Look at the empty ignition slot as you get out of your car. Such a visual reminder will preclude your absentmindedly leaving the keys in the car as you leave and engage the door lock. Seeing the keys in your hand is a backup visual reminder. You can't have too many.

This is *not* a waste of time. When we are busy, distracted, or in a hurry, we tend to do routine things without thinking. Our minds are on what we have to do next. We don't attend to an action we somehow already consider to be in the past. Although there is a reason for such behavior, you must recognize how inefficient it is. More time is wasted looking for absentmindedly misplaced objects than in recording the action properly. It's amazing how a few seconds of attention can make a big difference in avoiding daily calamities.

Visual reminders can help keep you from misplacing ideas as well. Retracing your steps and looking for visual cues will help you find a lost thought or idea. If you were reading, reread the previous page. If you were walking, go back to where you were or retrace your steps mentally. If you were talking, backtrack to what was said. Going from one topic to another frequently triggers new ideas with loose logic. Such scattered digressions are the chief cause of lost ideas. Visualize the conversation, recall who said what, and reconstruct the chain of thoughts. Asking questions will also actively assist recall. Be observant and you will find more visual cues. As you develop good observational skills, your recording will be more precise and the recall will follow suit.

Here is an example of a visual reminder. A salesman used to absently leave his sample case behind when making a call. He spent a great deal of time retracing his steps. I suggested that he associate the sample case with the passenger seat of his car. He made a conscious effort to visualize it as his passenger. He also developed the reflex of looking for his sample case in his left hand as he extended his right hand in a farewell shake. He made a point of staring at his case as he placed it on the passenger seat.

FINE-TUNING YOUR POWERS OF OBSERVATION

Memory researchers have concluded that people who are observant of the world around them are less absentminded than people who are oblivious to their surroundings. People who develop powers of observation for their job performance, such as detectives, security personnel, and FBI agents, are also less likely to be forgetful about everyday matters.

Each day our mind is bombarded with millions of images. Just a ten-minute walk through the aisles of a supermarket requires us to block out 95 percent of what we see. We'd go mad if we were aware of every message our brain received, such as products on shelves or people on a crowded street.

Sadly, most of us block out *more* than we should. In order to be more observant and thus reduce absentmindedness, we must block out less. Much of what we see everyday goes unnoticed. Your job is to start noticing more, that is, become more observant. In the beginning, it will be a conscious effort. After a short time you will do it automatically.

You can begin sharpening your sense of awareness by paying closer attention to the things that surround you. Look at things in more detail than you have in the past. By doing this, you will enhance your awareness and then your memory.

How observant are you? This evaluation is also a prescription for things you should do in the future to hone and develop your powers of observation. Best of all, you can perform this exercise during your spare time and without anyone noticing what you are doing.

Exercise for Developing Your Powers of Observation

1. Describe the front doors of each of your neighbors.
2. How many of your male friends have beards or mustaches?
3. What kind of car or cars does each of your neighbors own?
4. How many of your co-workers wear glasses?
5. What color eyes does each of your relatives, neighbors, or friends have?

Get the idea? Many commonplace objects go unnoticed— unless we work at seeing them. No wonder so many matters become absent of mind if we are not in the habit of attending to what we are doing or seeing.

One of the most commonly seen and held objects is the copper penny. Take a moment to visualize the "head" side of this one-cent coin. In the circle below, sketch in Lincoln's profile from memory. While this is merely a sketch, be sure the profile is facing in the correct direction.

This will all be done from memory. Include these items that you recall seeing on the penny:

Lincoln profile	Liberty
One Cent	In God We Trust
United States of America	date

Just to make this a little more interesting, we have included two items above that do *not* actually appear on the head side of the penny.

Decide which four items do belong and place them in the correct location within the circle.

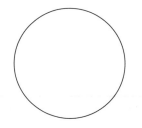

Compare your completed sketch to an actual penny. The purpose of this exercise is not to make you a coin collector. Rather, its aim is to point out how observant you are about everyday objects. The more observant you become, the better able you will be to recall where you place items, park your car, and whether or not you turn off appliances. By tuning up your powers of observation you will be lowering your instances of absentmindedness.

Using Mechanical Devices

Traditionally, people tied a string around their finger to serve as a reminder and defeat absentmindedness. The problem was that sometimes they forgot what the string represented.
Here are examples of five specific, user-friendly devices you can use to defeat absentmindedness and still not look silly.

1. *Place an inch of transparent tape on your watch crystal.* Use the kind of matte-finish tape that allows you to write on it with a ballpoint pen. Jot down a reminder on the tape. Use just one or two key words or numbers. It could be a person to call or a phone number. Each time you look at your watch, which is several times a day, you will see your reminder stare back at you. Once you have completed the task, remove the tape and discard it.

2. *Leave messages on your answering machine.* Before leaving work, call home and leave a message on your answering machine such as "Defrost dinner entree," "Attend PTA meeting." This way as soon as you get in you will have a reminder to help keep you from forgetting what you need to do.

3. *Select a "memory pocket."* Devote one pocket of your jacket, coat, or pants to house reminders of things you may forget. The memory pocket might hold a laundry or dry-cleaning ticket, a phone number, a list of calls to make, a recipe with needed ingredients underlined, or a bill to pay.

4. *Use a timer with a bell.* This will keep you from forgetting to disconnect the iron, make a phone call one hour from now, or get out of the house on time for your carpool pickup. A timer will help you remember to redial someone whose line is busy, or remind you to view a special TV broadcast.

5. *Make use of voice mail.* Over the weekend, you may come up with a great idea that will make your job easier, increase productivity, or save the company a lot of money. By the time Monday morning comes around, you're likely to forget the concept and major details. To avoid this, dial your work extension and leave yourself a message at work. This way you can follow up when you arrive on Monday.

These simple mechanical devices are external aids to memory. They help relieve the internal memory overload that may be increasing your degree of absentmindedness.

LEARNING TO HANDLE DISTRACTIONS AND INTERRUPTIONS

Even when we have the best intentions to avoid absentmindedness we are assaulted by interruptions and distractions that take us off track. These digressions lead to attention deficits that make us feel frustrated and lower our sense of self-esteem because we seem so absent of mind. Here are five tested and proven methods for overcoming this.

1. *Get your act together.* In the workplace you can eliminate these deficits by getting better organized. We've all heard the occupants of messy desks brag: "Oh, I know where everything is. Please don't straighten out my mess." Of course, occasionally, they can amaze co-workers by extracting a needed document from a tall pile of miscellaneous papers. This is definitely the exception.

Well-organized people are more attendminded than are disorganized people. As we have seen earlier, the nature of our brain's storage capacity gives the well organized a decided advantage. We carry too much information in our brains to ever hope to recall or retrieve what we need without a systematic, organized approach.

The well organized supplement their natural or intrinsic memories with external pencil-and-paper devices. These are in addition to the mechanical devices we just read about. All are available in stationery stores and all are inexpensive. Here are some examples, along with suggestions for using them.

- *A wall calendar.* This helps you see, at a glance, the major activities of the month. Deadlines will not creep up on you as a surprise when you scan your month's entries. Use different colors to highlight different activities or responsibilities. They will help you attend better.

- *A pocket calendar.* Be sure to carry this with you at all times. Coordinate entries with the wall calendar that you or your spouse have made. Be sure those dates are reflected in your pocket calendar. Pencil in prospective appointments or projects. Write them in ink when they are confirmed.

- *Post-it™ Notes.* Use these slips of paper, usually yellow, with a gummy strip on the back. They are excellent reminders when applied to your telephone, file cabinet, pocket calendar, wallet or car dashboard. They are easily removed and discarded when the task has been completed. At home they can be temporarily affixed to shaving mirrors, refrigerators, and the inside of your front door to help you remember things that might otherwise be lost to absentmindedness.

- *To-do lists.* On a small piece of paper, jot down all the things you want to accomplish today. List them in order of importance. Cross out each listing as you accomplish it. Write down the phone number alongside the name when needed. This saves time later on. As you plan your list, include the names of key people and phone numbers that you may need later. On the back of the paper, list the same items in chronological order. You may have to do the most important task "third" because of time zone differences or office hours. You will now have two lists with the same entries—one, in order of importance and the other in the order that you will perform them. These two different approaches will double your chances of doing all that you planned in spite of interruptions or digressions.

2. *Sustain your concentration.* It is essential that you develop an awareness of what you are doing and why it is important. This is a distraction buster. I call it "total immersion." When approaching an activity, don't do it tentatively. Jump right in and sustain focus on what you are doing. Lose yourself in the task at hand. Don't think about what you are going to do next until this task is completed. Once you get totally involved and immersed, your commitment to the activity will help block out distractions and you are less likely to be absent of mind. This will also contribute to your sense of satisfaction and increase your success rate.

3. *Do the obvious.* There are many obvious attention-wasters that we must distance ourselves from if we want to avoid absent-mindedness. Idle chatter and extraneous sounds are two of them. Avoid chatting with a co-worker or family member as you approach a demanding task. Also, turn off the radio or taped music. Part of your brain will be attending to these other sounds. Teenagers claim they can study for an exam and listen to rock music at the same time. These are not usually the best students—*they* know better. As we get older, we become more sensitive to distractions that interfere with attention. (Interestingly, researchers have found one exception: Baroque music, with its unusual cadences, enhances memory and on-task thinking. If this kind of music is not to your taste, work in silence. In this way your mental images and focused attention will help walk you through the project.)

4. *Master the telephone.* The greatest villain when it comes to interruption is the telephone. Few of us can tolerate ignoring the ringing as we continue to work. Use an answering machine if you are totally absorbed in what you are doing. If this is not practical, get in the habit of giving yourself an extra minute before you pick up. Let it ring two or three times. By answering on the third or fourth ring you will have time to finish the sentence you are writing and not lose the thought, make a note to yourself, turn off the household appliance, or plant some other cue so you can pick up the thread after the call. Your caller won't notice the difference, but you will be better able to master the situation and not give in to interruptions.

5. *Keep the thread.* In your conversations at home or at work, it is important that you avoid tangents. Tangents are when you change suddenly from one thought to another. This reduces your listener's comprehension of what you are talking about. Even more important, breaking the thread of the conversation leads you to becoming absentminded. People who go off on tangents frequently pepper their conversation with remarks such as, "What was I saying?" or, "What were we talking about before I mentioned . . .?" Such digressions from your main idea sidetrack you and contribute to absentmindedness. By darting from one topic to another you confuse your listener and yourself. For most of us this is a habit, and like all habits it can be broken.

Exercise to Help You Keep the Thread

In your everyday conversation it is important to stay on track. When you go off on a tangent your listener can't follow your thought. Sometimes you have trouble keeping the thread yourself.

This exercise will help you keep on track. Choose one of these subjects and then pretend you are telling a friend about it. Be careful to emphasize the main idea, follow along logically, and avoid tangents or extraneous thoughts.

- *Describe a film or TV program you saw.* Give an outline of the plot and set the story in time and place.

- *Give a review of a book you read.* Emphasize the main idea or plot. Tell about the tone or mood and something about the author.

- *Give travel directions to your home.* In simple, clear language tell a friend how to reach your home by car or public transportation. Assume they have never been there before.

MASTERING AUTOMATIC GESTURES

A frequent question is, "How come I can't remember if I shut off the coffeemaker of if I locked my front door, yet I can remember lots of complex data?" The answer involves an understanding of the conscious learning of the complex data as opposed to habitual routines that bypass consciousness and therefore are never registered.

These habitual routines that go unnoticed and unregistered are called automatic gestures. If you are in a hurry, stressed, or preoccupied you are even more likely to perform these routines without registration.

In this condition, a kind of light sleep or self-hypnosis, we easily forget whether we performed the routine or where we parked the car. Fortunately, ordinary daily events do not stand out in our mind—unless we command them to. If they did we'd never be able to learn all the new material that comes our way each day. Can you imagine what it would be like to tie your shoelaces if you had to concentrate on and visualize each step?

In order to become aware of automatic gestures you must pay attention to what you are doing—even if it is a fleeting awareness. Here are six ways to increase your awareness of routines:

1. *Reduce haste by employing the pause.* The more hurried we are the more likely we are *not* to remember. No matter what your schedule—master the pause. Practice looking around and register visual cues before you go into or leave a room. Pause and ask yourself: Where am I going? What do I need to take? Do I have to turn anything on or off? No matter how rushed you feel, do this slowly to make sure it is done right. You will save time in the long run because you won't have to go back and check on yourself.

2. *Leave a marker.* No matter how hard we try to concentrate or focus on what we are doing, there will inevitably be distractions. This is always true. It is especially destructive to memory in the area of automatic gestures. If a mate or co-worker speaks to you or the doorbell rings, continue the action long enough to leave a marker or cue so that you'll know where to pick up and continue. This can be just a word or two on scrap paper. It can be continuing to hold the key in your hand in an exaggerated posture. Leaving a marker shows you are present of mind.

3. *Record your gesture with a picture.* Know what steps you take each day getting ready and leaving your house or shutting down the office or plant. Anticipate them. Take a mental snapshot of yourself as you complete the action, for example, shutting lights and closing windows. Take a "photo" of yourself locking your front door. What color was the sleeve of the jacket as you turned the key in the door? Was it brown tweed? That's the jacket I wore today, so I must have locked the door this morning.

4. *Organize your routines.* Anticipate what can go wrong and review your routines to minimize "glitches." Write down your routines and refer to them the first few times. Then throw the paper away. Once it is gone, you will be forced to remember the list. Many elderly people are afraid that they'll forget to take their medication—or that they'll take it twice in one day. A little organization can make this routine foolproof. Do what an older student of mine, who lives alone, does. She must take three prescription medications each day. Some are two-capsule doses plus three therapeutic vitamins her doctor ordered. Each morning upon entering the kitchen she gets them out of their containers, counts them, and puts them on her breakfast plate. As she swallows each one, she thinks about today's date and the day of the week. If she didn't consciously organize this

routine she might forget. By concentrating on the day and date she reinforces the fact that she took today's pills and there is no danger of a double dose. This is also reinforced by the routine of taking them at the same time each day. By counting them out in advance she assures herself of the correct dosage.

5. *Strike when the iron is hot.* Take immediate action while you are thinking about it. Don't say, "It looks like rain; I'll take my umbrella when I leave the house." Instead, as soon as you think about the umbrella, take it out of the closet and put it in front of the door where you are sure to see it when you leave. Now, you can have your breakfast and know you won't forget your umbrella.

6. *Review promptly.* We know that to learn anything we have to review it. Review has many synonyms: rehearse, repeat, recite by rote, practice, reinforce, and so on. As soon as you have attended to some new data, review them. On the way home from a party, review with your spouse or companion the names of the new people you met and their mates. Trying to do this tomorrow will leave many blank spaces. Check the door to see if it's locked immediately upon locking it. When you park your car, immediately look around for parking lot markers. When you're about to leave the kitchen, pause and immediately check to see that all appliances are disconnected. I call this the "Pause-Swivel" motion. Before leaving a room for an extended period of time, pause, swivel your head in each direction to check on switches, faucets, and so on, and then continue your exit.

Exercise for Organizing Routines

Many of the routine tasks we perform each day become automatic. In the early stages of mastery, however, we don't always remember the steps in sequential order. That's why writing things down is such a memory help.

Choose one of these activities and write out the steps that have to be taken to complete the task. Be sure to list them sequentially. Make your directions short and simple.

1. Program your VCR or some other appliance.
2. Bake a cake. Use any recipe.
3. Plan a wedding for a niece.

Exercise for Remembering Some Everyday Items

Early in this chapter, we referred to a variety of household items that frequently get misplaced because of absentmindedness. Now that you have learned some strategies for conquering this, we are ready for an exercise.

It's perfectly normal for us not to pay attention to things that appear to be unimportant at the moment. With all the things you have on your mind when you put down something such as a pen, watch, or letter, it may not seem very important at that time. When you are looking for one of these commonplace items and it is not where you thought you left it, however, you sense a feeling of frustration and incompetence.

This next paragraph contains ten items and their locations. Read the paragraph once and slowly. Then see how many items you can recall, in any order.

You put your keys on the shelf, the book on the bed, the pen next to the phone, your glasses on the kitchen table, the shopping list on the hall table, your wallet on the piano, your watch on the sink, the letter on the sofa, the discount coupon on the counter, and the phone bill on the TV.

The ten items are:

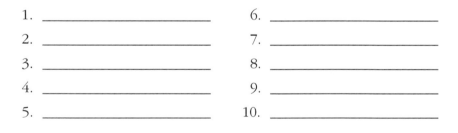

1. _____   6. _____

2. _____   7. _____

3. _____   8. _____

4. _____   9. _____

5. _____   10. _____

Here are the ten locations. As you look at each one, try to recall the name of the item placed there.

1. shelf _____   6. piano _____

2. bed _____   7. sink _____

3. phone _____   8. sofa _____

4. kitchen table _____   9. counter _____

5. hall table _____   10. TV _____

This is not easy. It's difficult because of the casual way in which these items and locations were read. This casual approach is sadly similar to the way people put things down without attending to what they are doing. They are "absentmindedly" performing the action.

Go back and reread the paragraph listing the items and their locations. Put into practice some of the techniques described in this chapter. Utilize the eight ways to reduce forgetfulness. Now, see how much better you are able to recall both the items and their locations.

You can remember only what you register. And you can register data only if you attend at the time of registration. Apply this principle in your daily activities and you will see a steady decline in incidences of absentmindedness.

FOLLOW-UP EVALUATION

How prepared are you to conquer your absentmindedness? How many of the suggestions made are you ready to implement? This test will help you assess your ability to become attendminded instead of absentminded.

See how many of these questions you can answer without turning back to the book for your answer.

1. Why does talking to yourself improve memory?
2. Give an example of how you can use your mental cross-index file.
3. Give an example of a change in pattern that helps you remember a change in your regular routine.
4. Describe a visual reminder you can use to help you remember to perform a routine task.
5. Describe the hair of each of your co-workers or family members. Include color, length, and/or degree of baldness.
6. Choose one mechanical device that can serve as a memory aid. Describe how you could use it.
7. Choose one paper-and-pencil device you can use to remember an upcoming event. Describe it.
8. Give an example of how prompt review reduces absentmindedness.

MEMENTOS

The eight ways to avoid misplacing things and thoughts are as follows:

1. Talk to yourself. This will add another dimension to your remembering: auditory cues. What you see will be enhanced by what you hear.

2. Use your mental cross-index file. Attach a web of associations to those items you want to remember. The more retrieval cues you employ, the less likely you are to be absent of mind.

3. Develop attendminded habits: stay-on-track, do it now, use fixed places, and change patterns as reminders.

4. Use visual reminders. "See" what you are doing and retrace steps to capture lost thoughts.

5. Fine-tune your organizational skills. Look at your surroundings and your customers more carefully. Pay attention to distinguishing marks or changes in appearance.

6. Use mechanical devices. Use the simple, everyday tools around your home or office, for example, timers and answering machines to reduce absentmindedness.

7. Handle distractions and interruptions so that they do not reduce your efficiency or productivity. Train yourself to make use of stationery-store items that can enhance your memory and reduce absentmindedness.

8. Master automatic gestures by concentrating on what you are doing. Employ the pause-and-review techniques.

Chapter Seven

Recalling Numbers with Speed and Accuracy

I'm embarrassed to admit that I have to carry my Social Security and bank account numbers in my wallet. I just can't get them straight in my mind.

It's awkward asking my spouse for our daughter's phone number.

People who have average or better-than-average memories frequently forget Personal Identification Numbers, auto license plate or model numbers, along with street addresses, ZIP codes, shirt sizes, room dimensions, and other numerical data.

Number retention has been an acknowledged problem for ages. As early as the seventeenth century in Cambridge, England mathematicians were coming up with mnemonic systems for remembering numbers. Most of these employed "pegs." These are words or letters that you commit to memory so that they stand in for numbers. They become a prelearned mental structure that provides hooks on which you hang more difficult material such as numbers. These pegs or hooks usually employ the first ten numbers of our numerical system.

In the following pages you will learn a variety of systems using visual and auditory cues to recall numbers, including the following:

- A system for recalling telephone numbers
- Relating shapes to numbers
- Using the letter-count system
- Rhyming numbers for ease of recall
- Associating numbers with what you already know
- Recognizing number patterns
- Converting numbers into sentences
- Mastering the number-consonant system
- Using the number-consonant system in business applications

143

HOW YOU CAN REMEMBER TELEPHONE
NUMBERS MORE EASILY

The main problem with numbers is that by themselves they have little meaning until they refer to specific information. Without meaning there is no interest, and without interest no impression is made. Because there is no interest, meaning, or impression there can't be any recall.

Also, numbers by themselves are abstract, and our brains do better remembering concrete objects. The number "four" has little meaning but "four quarters" are more tangible, and as we can associate them with a dollar, they are more memorable.

It is much easier to remember a sequence of words with meaning than it is to remember a sequence of numbers with no particular meaning. Words strung together form meaningful thoughts and sentences. Numbers strung together don't necessarily have meaning unless they refer to something specific.

Converting Numbers into Letters
to Help You Remember

This is a good technique to learn before we go on to more elaborate systems involving shapes, sounds, words, and sentences. In this technique, we make up word combinations from a phone number as it appears on the dial or push-buttons.

The telephone dial has numbers 1 to 0, but there are letters only with the eight numbers 2 through 9. There are three letters for each number. That makes a total of 24 letters. The letters Q and Z do not appear on the dial.

To make our system more universal and to make it easier to associate words with numbers, we have eliminated most of the vowels, except for O and I. The letters A, E, U, Q, and Z are not used in this technique. We have also moved two letters. We have moved the O from its customary place alongside the 6 and put it near its look-alike, the O for operator. Likewise, we've moved the letter I from its usual position near the 4 and put it near its look-alike, the 1.

With these changes in mind, our telephone dial will look like this:

1	2	3	4	5	6	7	8	9	0
I	B	D	G	J	M	P	T	W	O
	C	F	H	K	N	R	V	X	
			L		S				

Assume you want to recall this phone number: 287-6679.

Looking at your dial, and it's always right in front of you when you use the telephone, there are letter choices for you to use to make up words.

For example:

2	8	7	–	6	6	7	9
B	T	P	–	M	M	P	W
C	V	R	–	N	N	R	X
		S	–			S	Y

A brief scan of the letter combinations available to you will suggest word combinations that are easier to remember than a meaningless number. Remember, we have eliminated most of the vowels so that you can insert those of your choice when the consonants appear. In the previous example, I thought of BTR-MMRY, which I read as "better memory." You may come up with other consonant combinations of your own, each number offers you two (2, 8, 6) or three (7, 9). The vowels are wild cards.

What city does this number suggest?

974-6486

9	7	4	–	6	4	8	6
W	P	G	–	M	G	T	M
X	R	H	–	N	R	V	N
Y	S						

Remember, you supply the vowels and you select the consonant you wish to use from among the two or three associated with each number. In the previous example, you can select W, X, or Y for the number 9. For 7 you can use P, R, or S. The number 4 offers you a choice of either G or H. Just by scanning with your eye the choices for these three numbers you come up with WSH. WASH or WISH would be words using these three consonants with a variety of vowels. We gave you a hint by suggesting a city. A quick look at the 6 and 4 offers you M or N followed by a G or H. Finishing the number letter substitutions you come up with WSHNGTN. Putting in vowels of your choice gives you WASHINGTON.

PRACTICE CHANGING TELEPHONE NUMBERS INTO WORDS

With a little practice you will find yourself quite adept at substituting letters for numbers and selecting those letters that lend themselves to words. The words are much easier to remember than are abstract numbers. There is a good reason why we shifted the letter "O" from the letters M and N alongside the 6 and moved it to the "O" for Operator. It is because many numbers end with two or three zeros. Rather than look for a word that ends with two or three letters that are the same, we offer you this shortcut.

For example, when you try to encode this number: 216-4000 you can use BINGO. This seven-digit number is reduced to a five-letter word because the last number "O" is repeated twice. A final number when repeated can be dropped. So, 216-40 stands for 216-4000; 896-9800 can be shortened to 896980 or 896-980.

This will become easier for you to do when you practice changing these three numbers into words or names:

245-1600 _____

476-6000 _____

275-5000 _____

The following phone number can be encoded to spell out a city and its state abbreviation, or it can become a silly phrase of your choice. Try it:

242-4015 _____ or _____

This works both ways. You need practice and speed in changing the letter phrase, city, name, or brand name into a phone number.

Practice changing HOME FRIES into a phone number.

The first step is to separate the letters into the phone-number format. So, HOME FRIES becomes HOM-EFRIES. The next step is to eliminate the E's (the only vowels we use are the I and O). You now have HOM-FRIS.

Which becomes 406-3717.

Notice that while the R and S are different letters, they both stand for the number 7.

A SPECIAL TECHNIQUE FOR THE TOUCH-TONE TELEPHONE

On push-button or touch-tone phones you can "see the numbers in sequence and develop a motor or kinesthetic memory pattern. Look at the touch-tone pad and you will see that 258 is a straight line, as are 741 and 369. The four digits 5896 form a square. Frequent dialing of these and dozens of other number combinations will become a kind of familiar gesture to you. Motor memory is easier for most people to learn and use.

Some memorable patterns are suggested by numbers such as:

951-2369

852-3698

321-4789

Trying these on a touch-tone dial will illustrate what is meant by visualization and kinesthetic memory. With practice, any frequently dialed number will give you a "motor memory" that will help you remember it.

USING LETTER ASSOCIATION RECALL IN TELEPHONE NUMBERS

1. What numbers do these phrases suggest?

    CRY LOST

    SIR GEORGE

    WARM KITTEN

2. What word combinations can you use to remember these phone numbers?

    214-2257

    741-6206

    207-3955

SHARPEN YOUR MEMORY BY SEEING
SHAPES IN NUMBERS

For people who prefer to "see" or visualize their cues as pictures, this may be the system of choice. Here, objects resembling numbers provide the pegs that are the basis of this time-tested system. Pictures are adapted to look like the actual numbers from 0 to 9, inclusive.

Most memory researchers refer to this as the number-shape system. The following list represents those pictures or forms that are generally used to stand in for numbers. As always, you are encouraged to use your own images as they will have more meaning and will speed recall. These will serve to give you the general idea behind this popular system.

0 =	EGG	The oval or egg-shape looks like a zero.
1 =	CANDLE	A tall, thin candle resembles the number 1.
2 =	SWAN	A swan with curved neck facing left looks like a 2.
3 =	PITCHFORK	Positioned horizontally with prongs to left, it looks like the number 3.
4 =	SAILBOAT	A small boat with just the left sail up bears a close resemblance to the number 4.
5 =	HAND	A spread hand with fingers apart symbolizes the number 5.
6 =	GOLF CLUB	An erect golf club with its head on the ground facing right suggests the number 6.
7 =	SEMAPHORE	A railway signal with its arm raised and pointing left looks like the number 7.
8 =	HOURGLASS	Its classic shape suggests the number 8.
9 =	TENNIS RACQUET	With its handle somewhat askew resembles the number 9.

How to Create Vivid Number Pictures

Your own pictures may strengthen these number-shapes even more. You may prefer a pennant for 4 or a snake for 6 or a snail for 9. Use whatever association comes to mind for you. As a general rule, it is best to see vivid action figures. Once pegged, they tend to stay in your mind more so than do static images.

You can develop your own system for a shorthand area code/picture association.

For example, here are some area codes for major cities in the United States and Canada:

Baltimore	410	Miami	305
Chicago	312	Montreal	514
San Diego	619	Raleigh	919
El Paso	915	Seattle	206
Houston	713	Toronto	416

Most telephone area codes have either a 0 or a 1 as the middle number. Since it is unlikely that you frequently call cities that have exactly the same first and third number, you can drop the middle number from your area code picture.

In order to make our pictures vivid and memorable, we are going to exaggerate some of our images.

Baltimore	A boat filled with eggs: 4 _ 0
Chicago	A pitchfork in the mouth of a swan: 3 _ 2
San Diego	A golf club and tennis racquet crossed as an X: 6 _ 9
El Paso	A golf club with a large hand wrapped around it: 9 _ 5

Now you write in your images for each city's telephone area codes: (Be sure the two images interact.)

Houston	_____
Miami	_____
Montreal	_____

Raleigh   _____

Seattle   _____

Toronto   _____

Two Exercises for Using the Number-Shape System

1. Write a friend's telephone number in these blanks:

— — — ‐ — — — —

Transpose each number into a shape. Wherever possible, have the pictures interact with one another. For example, the swan has a candle in its mouth. Or the pitchfork has an egg impaled on it.

Example: 7 6 1 – 8 0 2 3

For the prefix, or 761, you could envision an unusual semaphore. The vertical post has a candle painted on it and the horizontal arm is a golf club. In this way, one image is recalling three different numbers.

Instead of trying to remember the four digits 8 0 2 3, you can substitute two pictures or images. The first is an hourglass. In the glass bulb instead of the usual sand you imagine an egg. This gives you 8 0.

For the 2 3, you picture a swimming swan pulling a floating pitchfork across the pond. Because the swan is pulling the pitchfork you know the 2 comes before the 3.

2. In this exercise, I am going to give you the pictures and you will practice figuring out the phone number. Although they are my pictures and not yours, it is the practice that counts and not the precise images. You can have them interact in any way that makes sense to you.

Hand-sailboat-hand.   _____

Candle-golf club-egg-egg.   _____

Tennis racquet-swan-semaphore.   _____

Egg-hand-hourglass-swan.   _____

HOW THE LETTER-COUNT SYSTEM
HELPS YOU REMEMBER

Every word in our language is made up of letters. Each word has a fixed number of letters in it. This simple concept is the basis of the letter-count system for remembering numbers. It uses phrases in which the letters of each word are counted, thus giving you the number needed. The actual words, or their letter count, serve as the memory aid.

For example, you want to remember the numerical value of pi to eight decimal places, which is

3.14159265

This is not an easy task. But using the letter-count system you construct a phrase or sentence in which each word, when its letters are counted, would supply you with the correct number:

MAY I HAVE A LARGE CONTAINER OF COFFEE, CHEAP?
 3   1   4   1   5   9   2   6   5

In this easy-to-master system, each number (date, address, statistic, phone) is identified by a word containing the exact number of letters as the figure itself. They run from 1 to 10, with the 10 standing for zero.

For example, you want to recall the year of the Battle of Hastings (1066) when William the Conqueror defeated Harold.

I, CONQUERING, KILLED HAROLD
1   0   6   6

Notice that a ten-letter word stands for zero. "Conquering" is ten letters and becomes the 0 of 1066.

Or, 11/22/63 the tragic day when JFK was assassinated becomes:

Pres. Kennedy - is in - Dallas, Tex.
    11   - 2 2 -   6   3

Or, a five-digit street address 14467 on the outskirts of town becomes:

A VERY LONG TIRING JOURNEY
1   4   4   6   7

Two Exercises for Using the Letter-Count System

1. Decode these phone numbers by counting the letters in each word:

Every girl on line was as tall.   __ __ __ - __ __ __ __

The lady said it was not delineated.   __ __ __ - __ __ __ __

2. Make up your own sentences for each of these phone numbers:

478-2355   _____

293-4610   _____

3. Since most telephone area codes have a one or zero as their middle number you can use your own shorthand system. If your area code is just two words, assume the middle number is a zero. Example: Denver's area code is 303. You can think of it as "Fat man." Because you encoded a three-digit number into just two words, we know the middle number is a zero.

Quebec is 514, or "Catch a cold." The 1 becomes "a." Convert these telephone area codes into letter codes:

517	313
616	096

HOW TO USE RHYME TO RECALL NUMBERS

This phonetic number system pegs the first ten numbers, plus zero, with words that rhyme with each number name:

Zero	=	zero	Six	=	sticks
One	=	bun	Seven	=	heaven
Two	=	shoe	Eight	=	skate
Three	=	tree	Nine	=	wine
Four	=	door	Ten	=	pen
Five	=	hive			

Notice that all the rhyming words are nouns. That's because you will have a picture that you can visualize when you recall the rhyme word. For example, let's take an automobile license plate that we want to remember: 328JK4

You can enhance your memory of these diverse items if you join them in some coordinated way. For example: 328JK4 becomes

three-shoe-skate-J-K-door

This can be linked or joined into this amusing picture: "A tree with a shoe hanging from one of its branches and a skate hanging from it. You see the letters JK carved into a door, which is cut into the trunk."

The rhyming word system works well for people with strong visual imaginations.

Using Rhyme to Remember a Shopping List

Not only do these rhyming words stand for numbers but you can also match them to a list of items you want to recall in a particular order.

Let's go back to a shopping list we used as a link story in Chapter 1.

snow shovel	talcum
six wine glasses	toothpaste
six oranges	thirteen bagels
bar of soap	head of lettuce
dozen eggs	bunch of flowers

In order to recall each of these items, in numerical order, you would make these number-rhyme associations:

1. A snow shovel lifting a bun
2. A shoe resting on six wine glasses, or, a huge shoe holding six wine glasses
3. An orange tree bearing six oranges
4. A bar of soap with a door cut into it

5. A beehive containing a dozen eggs

6. Sticks in the shape of cans of talcum powder

7. A tube of toothpaste resting on a cloud

8. A skate with a logo of thirteen bagels

9. A wine bottle with a picture of lettuce on it

10. A trick pen; when you remove the cap a bunch of flowers springs forth

Rhyming is a fast and efficient mental holding device and retrieval cue. Again, you should use whatever associations you feel most comfortable with.

A LIST OF SUGGESTED NUMBER RHYMES

The following list suggests other rhyme words that may suit your needs better than those given earlier.

     0 = hero, Nero, De Niro
     1 = sun, gun, run
     2 = glue, blue, Sue
     3 = ski, bee, tea, tee
     4 = store, boar, floor
     5 = chive, jive, dive
     6 = bricks, chicks, ticks
     7 = Kevin, leaven
     8 = gate, plate, mate
     9 = vine, pine, stein
    10 = den, men, Zen

Putting the Number-Rhyme System to Work for You

1. Put the number-rhyme system to work and match these stationery items to your own ten rhyme words:

1. a calendar

2. a dozen pens

3. typewriter ribbon

6. an appointment book

7. a seat cushion

8. a date stamp

4. a computer disk   9. a desk blotter

5. computer paper   10. cellophane tape

2. See how quickly you can recall these same items in the random order given below:

9. _____   5. _____

8. _____   3. _____

1. _____   6. _____

7. _____   2. _____

4. _____   10. _____

3. Encode each of these three automobile license plates:

403F7   RS2115   580B9

MAKING OBVIOUS NUMBER ASSOCIATIONS

Associations make it possible for you to remember a familiar number in a different context. A PIN or phone number containing 1492 or 1776 is an obvious example.

We have already given shapes or rhymes to the first ten numbers. Here are numbers that suggest their own meanings because of some obvious association:

0 = doughnut or wheel

1 = penny or dollar bill

2 = twins or eyes or ears

3 = triangle or 3M corporation

4 = car (4 wheels) or chair (4 legs)

5 = nickel, or $5

6 = six-pack, 6 cylinders

7 = week, 7-Up drink

8 = octopus, octagon

9 = cat (9 lives), baseball (innings)

10 = dime, $10

Most of these associations are based on visual images. Still others include:

12	dozen	49	Forty-niners
13	baker's dozen	50	golden wedding anniversary
14	14K gold	52	deck of cards
16	sweet birthday	54	Car 54, where are you?
18	voter's age	55	speed limit
20	score	57	Heinz varieties
21	Blackjack	62	Social Security
23	skidoo	64	$64 question
24	hours in a day	65	senior citizen
25	silver wedding	66	Route 66
28	February	007	James Bond
30	September	180	degrees in a straight line
31	January	212	boiling point of water
32	freezing point of water	360	full circle
35	eligible to be President	711	dice; store
36	yard	747	jet plane
39	Jack Benny's age	911	police emergency
40	life begins at	1812	overture

You may be able to add many of your own that are special to you, such as birth years, addresses, phone numbers, significant numbers of any kind.

Just as in other number systems we have learned, it will be helpful if you can connect two or more number associations.

For example: a cat dragging a six-pack = 96.

Whereas a six-pack of cats would be 69.

Two Exercises for Using Number Associations

1. Uncode these number associations:

A cat with a huge nickel in its mouth followed by a triangle and a wheel. _____

A car with an octopus driving with twins in the back seat. __

On the ground, you see the following objects lined up: a yard-stick, a dime, a dollar bill, and a baseball. _____

2. Chunking or clustering the numbers into small bites of meaningful associations is a big help.

For example: The number 392112007 is somewhat difficult to retrieve even if you add commas. By breaking this nine-digit number into obvious associations it becomes easy:

39 21 12 007   Jack Benny+blackjack+dozen+James Bond

Try these two:

57194114   _____
2420747212   _____

USING PATTERN RECOGNITION
TO INCREASE YOUR MEMORY

The number-pattern system is based on the fact that you may notice another kind of meaning in a number you encounter. It could be an obvious numerical pattern such as 2, 4, 6, 8; or 5 10 15 20. These are hardly commonplace, but they illustrate how sequences can be memory aids.

More interesting, and much more applicable, are patterns you use including time, dates, addresses, money, or measures.

Numbers express amounts and measures, whether they apply to distance, age, weight, or anything else. That's their job. The best part of this system is that it is personalized and you can use it in a variety of situations for easy recall. You see with your eye but you observe with your brain.

There are endless ways this system can be used. All make meaningless numbers meaningful. You may want to combine some parts of this system with parts of other systems we have presented.

1. *Time.* Here you code an abstract number into a time of day that is concrete and meaningful. The number 615 quickly becomes 6:15. Neither A.M. nor P.M. are needed here. Those readers familiar with the military or 24-hour clock will have even more applications available to them.

2. *Dates.* Using the numerical designation for months (January = 1; February = 2, and so on), any date you already know and recognize can be coded. For example, 214 is a valentine (February), 1225 is Christmas, and so on. If you have trouble remembering 415, think of it as April 15th. Family birthdays and special events lend themselves well to this system.

3. *Addresses.* The numbers you already know such as your house or business address or ZIP code can be found in difficult-to-remember numbers, if you look for them. Likewise familiar street or avenue numbers as well as route numbers can be helpful as you transfer the familiar to the less familiar.

4. *Money.* Virtually any number can be thought of as a price, profit, loss, or cost. For example, 1875 becomes $18.75 and 20563 is more meaningful when thought of as $20,563 or $205.63.

5. *Measures.* Age, height, weight, and other familiar measures lend themselves to associations with complex numbers. The four-digit 3965 can be Jack Benny collecting Social Security; 986 can be remembered as normal body temperature, 98.6.

The more whimsical you make the phrase, the easier it will be to remember. For example, the number 12741 could be coded in at least two ways. One is silly and one serious. You decide which is more likely to provide ease of recall.

Silly:	I drank a dozen 7-Ups on April Fool's Day (4/1). 12 - 7 - 4 1
Serious:	Pearl Harbor Day, 12/7/41
Example:	257 - 4952 becomes
	2 ketchup bottles - Panning for gold with a deck of cards
	2 57 (Heinz) - 49 (forty-niners) 52 (deck of cards)

Two Exercises for Using the Number-Pattern System

1. Encode these phone numbers using any pattern of your choice:

761-8007 _____

224-4023 _____

538-1250 _____

2. Try these eight-digit bank-account numbers as pattern codes:

10361213_____

4011 0315 _____

IMPROVE YOUR MEMORY BY CHANGING
NUMBERS INTO PHRASES

Long numbers with seven or more digits are best learned by this system of phrase-and-sentence associations. In this system called phrase/number we observe two basic rules:

1. Chunk or break up the long number into small bites.
2. Join the word associations into a memorable phrase.

The idea is to code the numbers into a phrase or sentence that is a lot easier to remember than a long number. This example will make the system clear to you:

Number: 2455507115

In its present form it represents ten distinct units or numbers that need to be memorized. After looking at it briefly, you may recognize some number associations. Try for two- or three-digit chunks in order to reduce the units needed to remember.

One suggested breakup of this number would be:

24   55   50   711   5

These are recognizable number associations you can easily recall:

24   hours in a day

55   miles-an-hour speed limit

50   golden wedding anniversary

711   chain store

5   nickel or fifth

These five chunks can be strung together to form a sentence, or in the case of long numbers, a group of sentences.

"I drove *24* hours at *55* miles an hour to get to the *Golden Wedding Anniversary* party. I made a right turn at the *7-11* store. Theirs was the *fifth* house from the corner."

How to Recall the Exact Sequence of Unrelated Numbers

Have you ever been frustrated by combination locks or other number series where you have to recall the exact sequence of unrelated numbers? For example, at the health club you use a combination lock on your locker. To open it, you need to remember 28 right, 8 left, and 14 right. You have no trouble with the directions but can't always come up with the number sequence. By utilizing this phrase/number system you'll never have trouble again. Just make these, or any other appropriate associations:

28 = February (only month with 28 days)

 8 = octopus has 8 tentacles

14 = gold, as in 14K gold

Now, you construct your simple, easy-to-recall sentence:

In *February* I saw an *octopus* wearing a *gold* ring.

       28   8   14

By making the three images (February, octopus, and gold) interactive, the sentence is easier to remember. The sentence format also makes it more foolproof as to the order or sequence of numbers. You might wonder "Is it 28-14-8 or is it 28-8-14?"

The wording "an octopus wearing a ring" tells you which number comes first after the 28. If it were, "a ring with an octopus carved on it" then the sequence would be 28-14-8. The order of the words in the sentence determines the order of the numbers.

Two Exercises for Using the Number/Phrase System

1. Encode these seven-digit numbers by making up a phrase or sentence:

6635212 _____

7473913 _____

2. From these sentences come up with the correct number:

A full-circle gold pin was given to the girl at her Sweet Sixteen party. _____

The twins bought a baker's dozen at the senior citizen's price.
_____

The Blackjack players listened to the overture while the dealer opened a fresh deck of cards._____

PUTTING THE NUMBER-CONSONANT SYSTEM TO WORK FOR YOU

This technique of matching numbers with letters is usually referred to as the figure-alphabet system. I think a more accurate designation would be the number-consonant system because the word "figure" has meanings other than numbers. Also, the system uses only consonants, omitting all the vowels, and so does not utilize a complete alphabet.

The concept of this system is more than 300 years old, and its present form was refined by Gregor von Feinagle in 1813. In his system, the numbers were represented by consonants that are similar in some way to the digits they represent. Their similarity is based on both appearance and sound. It is the most sophisticated and most versatile of all the mnemonic systems, and I have saved it for last. If you learn just one system, this should be it.

This code does take some effort to learn at the beginning. You will need at least 30 minutes to master the number-letter pairings. Because they emphasize the sound, many of the numbers can be represented by more than one letter. This other letter is easily remembered because it has a similar sound, such as T or D for number 1 or F or V for number 8. This will be more clear in a moment.

Here are the codes for the numbers 1 through 5. Alongside each letter is a rationale to help you remember it.

      1 = t or d   t has one vertical stroke when writing it.

      2 = n   n has two vertical strokes.

      3 = m   m has three vertical strokes.

      4 = r   r is the final sound for *four.*

      5 = l   l is the Roman numeral for 50.

Examples of the Number-Consonant System

In this system, vowels are used as wild cards or fillers to make words from the consonants. The letters W, H, and Y are treated as vowels and omitted unless they are attached to another letter to make a sound, as in WH, CH, SH.

Let's review. The consonants stand for numbers. The vowels are merely "wild cards" or fillers to make familiar words. For example, the word TaiL or TaLe would both stand for the same number because they have the identical consonant combination: T followed by L. The vowels: a, i, and e were used to make a word out of the T and L.

Both TaiL and TaLe represent the number 15 because the T is a 1 and the L is a 5. In order to make this more visual for you, we have capitalized the consonants and kept the vowels in lowercase letters.

Using the five number-consonants that were just presented, come up with the four-digit numbers that these word pairs represent:

      Example: TiNy TiM   =   1213

                 ReaL LioN   =   _____

                 TaMe MaLe   =   _____

                 NoSy MaTe   =   _____

                 RaRe MeaT   =   _____

You have now learned half the code. The second half is more difficult because all the numbers have two or more letters representing them. The good news is that only like-sounding letters are used for each number.

6 = J   J in script looks like a backward 6.
               Ch, sh, and the soft g also stand for 6.
               You can remember all these sound-alikes with the sentence: "The *j*eweler *sh*owed me a *ch*oice 6-karat *g*em."

7 = K   K looks as if it was constructed of two small 7's.
               ck, Q, hard c, and hard g, also stand for 7.
               Remember them as "7 *k*ings and *q*ueens *c*ount *g*old qui*ck*ly."

8 = F   F in lowercase script looks like an 8.
               V also stands for 8.
               Remember: "An 8-day *f*un *v*acation."

9 = P   P is a mirror image of 9.
               B also stands for 9.
               As in "*P*retty *b*aby born on 9/9."

0 − Z   Z as in *z*ero.
               S and soft C also stand for 0.
               As in "A new *c*entury ends in *z*ero*s*, such as A.D. 2000."

Using alternate letters for each number increases your range of possible words. For example, 67 could be "jug," "jack," "shock," or "check," among others. The choice is always yours. The variety makes it easier for you to encode once you learn the 10-Number-Consonant System.

Remember, it's the *sound* of the consonant that counts. Silent letters are omitted, as in 28 = NiFe instead of KNiFe. The silent "gh" is also omitted as in RighT = 41.

If a word has two of the same consonants they still make just one sound. So, whether you encode the number as CaFe or CoFFee, it has only one "F" sound and stands for 78 with either word.

Also, you'll find that four-digit numbers are usually best encoded into two-word combinations instead of one long word.

For example, 2179 could be NeaT CaB or NighT (or NiTe) CaP.

Two Exercises for Using the Number-Consonant System

1. Encode these numbers:

654	_____	315	_____
420	_____	6161	_____
1777	_____	5963	_____

2. What numbers do these word combinations represent?

NiTe SHow	_____
No ToP	_____
LooSe SHoe	_____
BeeF RaRe	_____
MeaT PieS	_____
FaT PayMeNT	_____

Using the Number-Consonant System for Daily Applications

1. *Remembering telephone area codes.* Frequently, we know a number but can't recall the area code or else come up with an incorrect three-digit code. It's good to remember that most area codes in the United States and Canada have 0 or 1 as the second number, for example, 212 for New York City and 604 for British Columbia.

Using the number-consonant system, it's easy to remember a catch word for the area code. For example, 201 is needed to call Newark, New Jersey. Those letters can be exchanged for the consonants NST and so the word NeST becomes the association for the Newark area code.

Following are two lists of area codes and words that I would like you to match up. List A contains the cities an their telephone area codes. List B has the suggested word associations for the codes. We have jumbled up List B. Your job will be to match the city with the word. You may want to cover list B first and figure out your own word associations for List A. You can then compare them.

Because most of the telephone area codes have a 0 or 1 in the middle, you will find that most of the words will have a T/D or S/Z sound in the middle.

	List A	*List B*
403	Alberta, Canada	LaTe SHow
404	Atlanta, Georgia	PoTteR
713	Houston, Texas	ReSuMe
213	Los Angeles, California	aNaToMy
516	Long Island, New York	Go TeaM
305	Miami, Florida	LeTteR
514	Montreal, Canada	RaZoR
201	Newark, New Jersey	iNSaNe
202	Washington, DC	NeST
914	Yonkers, New York	MiSsLe

Now that you have mastered these associations you can apply them to a host of business and professional uses: model numbers, price quotes, ID numbers, and the like.

2. *Recalling stock market quotes.* Remembering stock prices is a good application of the system. The financial sections of newspapers quote stock prices as whole numbers plus fractions; $14 \frac{1}{8}$ means $14 and $\frac{1}{8}$th of a dollar (.12 $\frac{1}{2}$¢) or $14.125.

The fractions are always one of these seven values of 1/8th. We list them here along with a short word association:

$\frac{1}{8}$	haT
$\frac{2}{8}$ or $\frac{1}{4}$	heN
$\frac{3}{8}$	haM
$\frac{4}{8}$ or $\frac{1}{2}$	haiR
$\frac{5}{8}$	hiLl
$\frac{6}{8}$ or $\frac{3}{4}$	SHoe
$\frac{7}{8}$	HooK

A quote of $84 \frac{1}{8}$ would be remember as:

FR haT or FuR haT

The following four stock quotes were taken from the top 15 issues with the most shareholders on a given day. Cover the last column and see how many associations you can make. Compare them with those listed for accuracy of number association. Any association you make is fine as long as you use the correct consonants.

Bell Atlantic	$65\,^7/_8$	JaiL	HooK
Exxon	$77\,^1/_8$	CaKe	HaT
IBM	$95\,^3/_8$	PaLe	HaM
Sears	$39\,^5/_8$	MaP	HiLl

Look at the remaining stock quotes and come up with number-consonant associations:

AT&T	$64\,^3/_4$
Bell South	$37\,^1/_2$
General Electric	$66\,^3/_8$
General Motors	$47\,^1/_8$
PG&E	$29\,^3/_8$
US West	$31\,^1/_4$

3. *Applying this system to the Dow Jones Industrial Average.* You can now remember the Dow Jones easily and accurately using number-consonant associations. For example, during the writing of this book the DJIA has moved up from 2186 to 7081. You can remember that as from NeT FiSH to GooSe Fat.

For practice, encode these Dow Averages into two-word associations:

3250	_____	4543	_____
3763	_____	5129	_____
4115	_____	5213	_____

MEMENTOS

1. The key to remembering numbers is to convert the abstract digit into a more concrete form. This can be single letters, words, or phrases.

2. Study each system described in this chapter and decide which one or two are suited to your particular learning style.

3. Daily practice is essential if the system or systems you have chosen are to become natural to you and easily applied.

4. There are many numbers in your environment, such as auto license plates, model numbers, and financial figures. Make use of them by practicing converting them into concrete forms.

5. Make use of rhyme to help you remember numerical data.

6. Look for number patterns and apply them to your memorization of numerical data.

7. The number-consonant system takes the most time to learn. If you are serious about finding a foolproof way to convert numbers into an easy-to-learn alphabet system, this approach will be worth the time it takes you to master it. Break it up into two parts as we have done in this chapter.

8. There are many opportunities in your daily life to apply the number-consonant system: telephone area codes, stock market quotes, and the like. Make use of all of them.

Chapter Eight

Using Five Surefire Techniques for Remembering Names

There is nothing more important to a person that his or her name. We are usually flattered when a restaurant owner, storekeeper, or casual acquaintance greets us by name. Such recognition makes us feel important.

We have all found ourselves in situations when we draw a blank and just can't remember the name of a neighbor or colleague whom we have known for years. This makes us feel embarrassed, especially when we have used the name many times.

Most of us easily remember faces of people we've met but have much more trouble attaching the correct name to the face. This is because we are better at remembering what we see than remembering what we hear.

People claim they "forgot" a name when in actuality they never heard the name in the first place. For most of us, the problem is not a lack of *re*tention—it's a lack of *at*tention. We're so concerned about making a good impression, touching our hair or adjusting our necktie or belt, we don't hear the name in the first place. We do not attend to the name and so we say, a few minutes later: "I'm sorry but I forgot your name." We didn't forget it, we never learned it. We did not attend to it when it was given.

We all face situations when a name is on the "tip of the tongue," but we just can't retrieve it. When this occurs, the best thing to do is take a deep breath and try to relax. This chapter will give you a host of strategies for learning names and retrieving them when needed.

At any age, memory can be improved. Older people actually have some advantages over their younger colleagues. The techniques and strategies in this chapter have been tested and proven on thousands of people ranging in age from 18 to 85.

Once you acquire the essential skill of remembering names, a remarkable thing will happen. People will remember *you* better.

When you address a new acquaintance by name long after a cursory introduction, after getting over his amazement, he will make a point of learning and using *your* name. This is a valuable building block in business and social relationships.

You will also find that you make friends more easily and motivate people more effectively. We are all drawn toward people who radiate warm feelings toward us. A proven way to melt resistance in others is to learn their names and use them appropriately. People who are generally reserved or even standoffish tend to take a closer look at someone who has taken the trouble to learn their names. Sales figures can climb and minor conflicts can be resolved when individuals use the names of those they are trying to win over.

Very few people can just "naturally" remember names. Most of them are the first to admit that they *work* at remembering names. After interviewing hundreds of super salespeople and politicians I attempted to consolidate the tricks and strategies that they used to remember names. They came up with a variety of systems but all had these five bits of advice in common:

1. Pay *attention* to people when you are introduced.
2. Make *associations* or links between the person you just met and someone or something else that is familiar.
3. Become *observant* of details in the people you meet.
4. *Organize* the people you meet by putting them into categories and giving them labels.
5. *Visualize* the new person's name as you hear it.

PAYING ATTENTION TO INTRODUCTIONS

For most people, the problem is not lack of retention. Their problem is a lack of attention in the first place. So often when being introduced to a new person the individual is caught up in the impression she is making that she does not focus on the name of the person being presented. A few minutes later she apologizes by saying, "I'm sorry but I forgot your name." She did not forget the name. She did not get the name in the first place. You can make sure you are paying attention by making eye contact with the person being introduced. Do not look around the room or at anything other than the new person. Listen carefully to the name and silently repeat it to yourself.

Using the SUAVE System to Focus Attention

This system will help you pay attention when being introduced.

A frequent complaint is, "Soon after I hear the name it seems to vanish." To help you "get" the name right at the introduction and then "hold on" to it I have devised a five-step program called SUAVE. SUAVE is an acronym; each of the five letters stands for the initial letter of a step in the program, as follows:

S   =   Say the name.

U   =   Use it three times.

A   =   Ask a question.

V   =   Visualize the name.

E   =   End the conversation with the name.

Now, let's put this memory aid to work for you.

1. *Say the name when introduced.* Repeat it as soon as you have heard it. If you haven't heard it clearly, smile, and ask that it be repeated. People do not mind repeating their name. You may not be sure if it was "Jim" or "Tim." It's best to get this cleared up right away. Reinforce the name by saying something like, "Oh, Tim. Glad to meet you."

If it is an unfamiliar first or last name, ask for it to be spelled. The person will be flattered that you care enough to want it spelled. Visualize the letters as they are spelled out. Don't depend solely on your ears; use your eyes to "see" the name as it is spelled or repeated. For most of us, we learn better what we see than what we hear. "Write" the name on his forehead with your invisible felt marker.

2. *Use the name at least three times during your conversation.* You have already used it once when you repeated it, or said, "Hi, Tim." You will use it again at the end of the conversation.

Find one other occasion to add the name onto a sentence as you talk. For example, "That's very interesting, Susan." or "I agree with you, Mrs. Lee." If you use the name more than three times you may make the listener feel that you are going to try to sell her something. Using the name once or twice is not enough. It will not etch it into your mind. You need to use it three times.

3. *Ask a question and listen to your new acquaintance's answer.* As he responds to your question be sure you listen to the answer. This will give you additional cues to help you associate the name with the face. Ask questions that need more than a one-word answer. The more sustained response will provide you with more cues and more time to look at the name you "wrote" on his forehead.

Instead of, "Do you live nearby, Mr. Jensen?" ask, "Where do you live, Mr. Jensen?"

Instead of "When was the last time you visited the United States, Mr. Yamashita?" as, "What are your impressions of the United States, Mr. Yamashita?"

4. *Visualize the name by coming up with a vivid link between the name and the face.* There may be obvious ones such as: Mr. Taylor is in the clothing business, Marilyn has blonde hair and some of the glamour of Marilyn Monroe, Mr. La Rosa has rosy cheeks. (How to visualize less obvious names is discussed later on in this chapter.)

5. *End the conversation with the name.* Never end the conversation with a remark such as: "Glad to have met you," or "It was good chatting with you." These are generic, no-name comments that don't help your retention.

Instead, end the conversation with: "Glad to have met you, Mr. Heller." Or, "It was good chatting with you, Jean." In this way, as you turn to leave the last word you hear yourself say is the person's name. We always tend to remember the first and last items on any list. We also tend to commit the last thing we say to our long-term memory.

At the end of the meeting, on the way home from work, or whenever you are alone, review the names of the new people you met. Go over the names in order of their appearance. If there were several people and you want to remember them, by sure to write their names down. Jot a few comments alongside each name to help you associate the person and the name.

It is helpful to sketch a distinguishing mark or facial characteristic alongside the name; for example, a long nose, wild hair, large mouth, mustache, glasses. These need not be sophisticated sketches. Any crude drawing that will evoke a response in you is good enough.

Exercise for Using SUAVE

At a cocktail party you met four new club members. Take a few moments to study the names and the comments you jotted down. Then close your eyes and see if you can recall the four names. Once you have mastered the names, try to recall each characteristic. We have listed two characteristics for each person. You may not always want to list two; one might be sufficient to recall the face.

Vincent Gennaro	—	thick gray hair, dark mustache
Elaine Stern	—	tall with red eyeglass frames
Mike Donnelly	—	bald; powerful handshake
Jeanne Chin	—	slim; great smile

Now, close the book and see if you can answer these questions:

1. Who is the slim lady with the great smile? _____
2. One man had a powerful handshake; what was his name? ____
3. Who was the tall woman with the red eyeglass frames? _____
4. Which man had the dark mustache? _____
5. What did Mike Donnelly look like? _____
6. Describe Jeanne Chin. _____
7. Which one was Elaine Stern? _____
8. How would you describe Vincent Gennaro?_____

HOW TO USE ASSOCIATION

By this stage of your life, you have acquired a vast storehouse of information and names. A great hint for learning new names is to link them to names of people or things you already know. For example, you meet someone named Ruth. You immediately think of another Ruth you know and link the two Ruths. How are they alike?

How are they different? As you converse, your mind will be busy forming associations, comparisons, and contrasts to other people you know with similar names, appearances, hobbies, or occupations. Perhaps you don't know any other Ruth. In that case, make a link to a candy bar, Baby Ruth, or the baseball legend, Babe Ruth.

Twelve Association Techniques to Improve Name Recognition

If asked for the three techniques most often used by excellent name-retainers the answer would e: association, association, association.

When surveyed, people who seem to never forget a name passed along these tips:

1. Make an association that is personalized. It should be humorous, meaningful, or eventful to *you*. Don't rely on someone else's memory aid or mnemonic.

2. Substitute the name with *your* association. It may be something like Dolly = Dolly Parton; Jack = Jack Frost.

3. Repeat the name and association (substitution) until you are confident you know it. Practice in spare moments.

By using "association" as a technique of memory improvement, you will have many clues at your fingertips to assist you in learning and recalling names.

Here are a dozen suggestions for associating names and their owners. Go through the list twice to see which of these apply to you—which seem to meet your needs and your style. In helping business executives, retirees, and students boost their memory power, I have become aware that certain techniques appeal to some individuals and other methods appeal to others. In presenting 12 different approaches, I hope to offer some that are consistent with your particular learning style. No one uses all of them. Select those that appeal to you.

1. *The snapshot.* Pretend you have an instant camera and are going to photograph your new acquaintance. Where would you pose this person you just met? Recall what he spoke about and have him stand in front of a clue such as his new car, vacation home, or new granddaughter.

2. *The name tag.* Imagine your new colleague or friend holding up a name sign or wearing a prominent name tag. Be aware of this imaginary tag as you speak to her. Associate the printed name and the face.

3. *The introduction.* Visualize and hear yourself introducing this new person to another person. Hear yourself pronouncing his name as you look into his face.

4. *The interview.* Enhance the memory connection by interviewing this person on your imaginary talk show. What information do you want to highlight? What are some questions you'd like to ask? Associate the questions and answers with the face.

5. *The acrostic.* Form a phrase or list of attributes in which the first letter in each word makes up the name you're trying to learn, for example, BILL is a "big, intelligent, lovable lug" or, less favorable, a "bragging, immodest, leering liar."

6. *The paintbox.* Paint a colorful image. Use color to intensify your memory clues. If someone has a distinctly Irish-sounding name, visualize it in bright green letters. Use color clues in visualizing the name in "black is beautiful" for African Americans or any of these: true blue, golden girl, silver fox, carrot top, white knight, gray lady, brown bomber, and so on.

7. *The smell.* Associate the smells that surrounded you when you first met. Think back, was it in a Chinese restaurant, pizzeria, fish house, hamburger grill, or flower shop? Become aware of distinctive smells when you meet a new person, either on them, for example, perfume, tobacco, garlic, or the place. Does the name itself trigger a smell, such as Rose, Pepper, Ginger, Pine, or sound-alikes such as, Appel, Lyme, or Piazza?

8. *The taste.* Link the sound of the name, or a similar sound, with a familiar taste. Don't get caught up in the spelling, it's just the sound of the name that counts. For example, Mr. Sugarman, Mrs. Sweet, Dr. Coffey, Mr. Pepperdine, Saltz, Alfredo, Lamb, or Lemmon. Apply this as well to first names, such as, Frank, Sherri, Pop, or Candi.

9. *The same letter.* Link the name to an adjective that best describes the person for you and begins with the same letter as the name. Examples: Dapper Dan, Gorgeous George, Caring Carol, Jaunty Jack, Friendly Fran.

10. *The rhyme.* Aid your memory by rhyming the name with a hint that helps characterize the person, such as Slim Jim, Ruth Tooth, Plain Jane, or Fat Matt.

11. *The celebrity.* Match the person you just met with a well-known personality having the same or a similar name. Your neighbor Barbara with Barbra Streisand; Jacqueline with the late Mrs. Onassis; Larry with Larry King; and so on. There may be either a great similarity or a great contrast between the two. The important thing is that the technique helps you link the name and the face.

12. *The feature.* Locate one dominant feature—hair, eyes, nose, mouth, skin—and focus on associating this feature with the name. This should be a subjective feature that means something special to you, not one others would necessarily agree with. Associate those beautiful blue eyes with Allison, contagious grin with Greg, the dimple with Jethro, or round face with Charles.

These techniques force you to listen, attend, and concentrate. The more you practice, the better you'll get at remembering names. Practice makes permanent. It helps transfer the image from your transient memory to your permanent memory bank. No one has a perfect memory. But the more you practice, the more data you will transfer into your permanent memory.

Exercise for Making an Association with a Name

For each of the following names, come up with an association or substitution. Use the first association that pops into your head. Base the association on your own life experience, reading, or imagination.

To make the association vivid, use the same tactics as do TV commercials: exaggeration, humor, rhyme, color, action, sound. Read one name at a time. Close your eyes and develop an association for each name:

Bob   _____

Jill   _____

Dick _____

Rita _____

Sal _____

Tanisha _____

Miss Rivera _____

Mrs. Monroe _____

Mr. Larsen _____

Mr. Piazza _____

Mrs. Campbell _____

Ms. Reynolds _____

Write your association cue alongside the name. After six minutes, cover the name column. Using your association cues see how many names you can come up with. If you can recall only half the names, try again.

SHARPENING YOUR POWERS OF OBSERVATION

Detectives and FBI agents are trained to observe people carefully. People with good memories do this quite naturally. You can train yourself to be more observant of the people you meet and the surroundings and time of the meeting. In addition to facial characteristics, observe the body size and shape of the individual. Listen carefully to the voice—its quality and speech patterns. Tie these observations to the name, for example, Mr. Arena (met at sports complex), Daisy (so fresh early in the morning), Mr. Loring (such a boring voice), Mrs. Littleton (so petite, hardly a ton). Employ rhyme when possible. It is a short form to remember and is likely to stay with you. Advertising copywriters make use of this all the time.

Learn to Observe Faces to Better Learn Names

You have never heard someone say to you, "I remember your name, but I forgot your face." We are all better at pictures than we are at words. In order to strengthen your memory, you must enhance your picture-taking ability even further. A picture may be worth a thousand words, but only if it is a good picture.

By developing your powers of observation, you will provide your brain with better-quality pictures and these will give you more easily accessible words and names.

We begin by breaking down the faces of people into features for ease of recall. Think of one or two friends or relatives whom you see often. Try to recall the items described below. You may want to try this out with two people, one of each gender.

> Eyes: What is the shape and color of the eyes? Does he wear glasses? Does she wear eye makeup?
>
> Mouth: What is the shape and size of the mouth? Does she wear lipstick? What shade? Does his mouth have a mustache or a beard around it?
>
> Ears: What is the size, shape, and placement of the ears? Does this person wear one or more earrings?
>
> Nose: What is the size and shape of the nose? How does this person look in profile?
>
> Hair: What is the color and length of the hair? What is the texture? Is he bald or balding? Is there an obvious toupee?

Help yourself learn this technique by concentrating on a different facial feature each work day for a week. As you encounter people, study one feature per day, for example, Monday can be eyes, Tuesday is mouths, Wednesday is ears. If, at day's end, you haven't met any new person, apply this skill to the anchor on your favorite 11:00 P.M. news show. The important thing is to apply the skill for an entire week. The practice will help you match names and faces as a matter of habit. Once you establish the habit, your memory will take a quantum leap forward!

Exercise for Observing Faces and Matching Names

Assume you have met these ten people recently. Their names are listed in column one. You observed them carefully.

Let's also assume that you linked one facial characteristic with each new person. Column two contains a significant facial feature for the corresponding name in column one. For example, Bob wears half glasses, Judy has dark, wavy hair.

Study the names and visualize the matching facial characteristic that you observed and listed in column two.

Column One	*Column Two*
Bob	half glasses
Judy	dark, wavy hair
Jack	thick gray hair
Marlene	round face
Mario	bright smile
Roz	small button nose
Hal	single gold earring
Doreen	thin lips
Joel	neat, trimmed beard
Roberta	light blonde hair

Cover the lists before you answer these ten questions.

Questions

1. Who has the neat, trimmed beard?_____
2. What did you notice about Mario? _____
3. Who has the thick gray hair? _____
4. What did you notice about Roberta? _____
5. Who has the dark, wavy hair?_____
6. What did you notice about Hal? _____
7. Who has the thin lips? _____
8. What did you notice about Marlene? _____
9. Who has the small button nose?_____
10. What did you notice about Bob? _____

FOCUSING ON ORGANIZATION

If you are well organized when it comes to your desk, files, checkbook, closets, and so on, then you will be well organized when it comes to the data bank you carry around in your head. As you access new information, you "file it away in a suitable mental file cabinet, drawer, and folder." For example, you just met Dr. Ellison and you place his name and face with other physicians you know. Further, you place his name with other cardiologists. You even place his name with other doctors at City Hospital. You remember that you met him at the Spring Health Fair. This is what is meant by the correct mental file drawer and folder. The more specifics you "file," the more likely the recall.

Making the Most of Lists to Boost Name Recall

With a little organization, you can tap the gold mine of business cards, seating lists, and other printed material that you have accumulated.

Keep seating lists, rosters, directories, and other printed material that lists the names of people you've met and want to recall in the future. Set up a permanent place for storing these memory aids in the office or at home. Keep them in chronological order so you don't have to go through lists from three years ago when you want to familiarize yourself with the name of someone you met three months ago.

Make comments and notations directly on the printed list. For example, you return from a business dinner where a seating list was given out recording every attendee in alphabetical order and his or her table number. You were seated at table 8. Go through the seating list and put a check alongside every name assigned to table 8. Now, jot down a comment or association for each person at your table.

You may find it helpful to draw a circle, oval, or rectangle on the back of the printed program and place each person by initial around your table. This will help you visually recall who was on your left, your right, directly across from you, and so on.

Do the same with photos of groups of people. Promptly list the names of everyone on the back of the picture along with the date and location or occasion. You may have the information at your fingertips *now,* but you may draw a blank a month from now when you anticipate meeting these people again.

Using the Pen-and-Pencil Approach for Name Recognition

We have two kinds of memory: intrinsic and extrinsic. Infants cry for food because it brings results. They remember the people and objects that satisfy their needs. The memory that we carry around in our head is our intrinsic memory. Some of it we acquired by incentives, such as remembering how to obtain food. Other examples of intrinsic memory that we carry around in our head, although not related to natural needs, include rote memory items such as state capitals, multiplication tables, favorite beverages of guests in your home, or the names of friends' children.

Extrinsic memory consists of the pencil-and-paper memory aids that we don't carry around in our heads, such as notes, memos, calendars, lists. These are generally more reliable because intrinsic memory fades when not used or reviewed.

Confucius, the Chinese philosopher and teacher, said: "The weakest ink is stronger than the best memory." This is just as true today as it was in the fifth century. Very often we are certain that we won't forget a name because of the strong impression the person made. Life and pressures intrude, however, and unless we review the name it has a way of slipping out of our intrinsic memory. Extrinsic memory aids are habit forming, and it is a good habit for you to get into: Jot down the name, record the phone number in your personal directory; keep a pocket, desk, or wall calendar, and so forth. A good memory consists of both intrinsic and extrinsic memory.

Some examples of the kinds of personal notes of family and friends you may write down in name recognition include the following:

Their daughter, Melissa, expecting a baby next month.

Their son, Jonathan, will be attending Cornell.

Jack just bought a minivan.

Family recently sold their boat.

Susan got her real-estate license.

Go through your address book and greeting-card lists periodically. Make notations of recently acquired information. In this way, when you next phone the person or mail a greeting card you can add a personal note that is relevant and will please the recipient. These notations will serve to further link the name and face.

The notations suggested here provide personalized messages and inquiries that will delight and amaze your friends and colleagues. You will soon notice that by writing things down you will be building your data bank of intrinsic memory as well. If you refer to extrinsically stored items enough times they will transfer to your intrinsic memory.

How to Organize Names with First-Letter Cues

You can organize names and other data with simple memory aids or mnemonics. They serve as mental filing systems. Two proven approaches use the first letter of each name or word you want to remember.

For example, a nursing student wants to remember the five excretory organs of the body. She learns them by their first letter cues or SKILL (Skin, Kidneys, Intestines, Liver, Lungs). Such a mnemonic is called an *acronym*.

Another mnemonic that helps organize information is called an *acrostic*. It is a series of words in which the first letter forms a phrase. By remembering the simple phrase, you have at your fingertips the first letter of each item you want to recall. For example, music students use the phrase "*Every Good Boy Does Fine*" to remember the notes on the lines of the treble clef (EGBDF). Both acronyms and acrostics help you organize what you want to remember.

Exercise for Practicing Mental Organization of Names

1. Your errands for tomorrow are as follows: Auto inspection, Bank, Library, Deli. Form an acronym of four letters that will help you remember these four errands. _____

2. Suppose you have a shopping list that includes bananas, milk, eggs, bread, and lettuce. Form an acrostic for these items.

   _____

3. An investor wants to follow these five stocks in the financial section of the newspaper. How can he organize the names of these stocks so that he can recall all five names?

   Sandoz

   Enron Corp.

   Biosafe

   Roosevelt Financial

   Amgen, Inc.

   Form either an acronym or an acrostic. _____

USING VISUALIZATION

Most of us are better able to remember what we see than what we hear. When you meet someone for the first time and hear his name you should *immediately* visualize the name in large letters. Pretend you are writing his name on his forehead with a felt-tip pen. In this way, as you speak to him you will have the reinforcement of seeing his name above his eyes as you engage in conversation. As an additional cue, listen to his conversation and place him in front of a billboard that illustrates what he is saying. For example, you meet Bob Fitzsimmons and he is telling you about a new boat he just bought. Visualize him standing in front of a large outdoor billboard. On the billboard is a huge picture of Bob standing in front of his new boat. In your mental picture he may still have his name written on his forehead, in your handwriting. That's great—still another cue. This visualization will reinforce your recall of the name with the face.

Creating Colorful Pictures

Another word for visualizing is "picturing" or "imagining." Visualization is the ability to see a picture or image in your mind's eye. In order to help your memory, you must imagine with 20/20 vision. Make your visualizations vivid, in color, and in depth.

A concrete image is easier to visualize than one that is abstract. For example, the word *chair* stands for a concrete object: a piece of furniture for sitting with a back and four legs. The word *charity* represents an abstract concept: generosity for the poor, or a benevolent feeling.

With your imagination you can visualize both concrete and abstract pictures. A chair can be "seen" as a folding chair, an armchair, or a kitchen chair. Charity can be "seen" as a poor box, Mother Teresa, the Red Cross, and so on. The more elaborate the picture, the better will be the recall.

People who report vivid visual imagery perform better in recall than people who report poor visual imagery. Good visualizers learn and remember much more effectively than good verbalizers.

An example of the dominance of visual imagery over verbal cues is the fact that you more often remember a face than a name. The face represents a concrete image—a certain shape, skin color, eyes, hair, mouth. It is unique. The name is just an abstract collection of letters, such as Guzman or Brennan. We have less trouble with names that evoke a concrete picture, such as Baker, Woods, or Carpenter.

HOW TO VISUALIZE UNUSUAL NAMES

Some of the names of people you meet suggest obvious associations. It doesn't take much imagination to visualize names such as Taylor, Fox, Rivers, Brooke, or Black. They conjure up everyday images. By matching the picture with the name you are forging a link.

What can we do about unusual names that have unfamiliar spelling and even less familiar pronunciation? They key is to work on sound. Do you remember the parlor game Charades? In it you provided your teammates with a clue by tugging at your ear to suggest, "sounds like." Do the same when learning unfamiliar names.

Don't worry about spelling at this point. Instead, work on hearing the name correctly. Ask to have it repeated if you are not absolutely sure of how to say it. Repeat it and ask for correction, if necessary. When you do this you are forcing yourself to hear the name accurately in the first place. This, of course, is half the battle. We can't remember a name we never heard correctly. We can't pronounce a difficult name months after we hear it if we can't pronounce it seconds after we hear it.

Use capital letters and the color red to help you visualize as well as hear the accented syllable. Whenever possible, change the spelling of the syllable into a familiar word.

Example: MACHUCA becomes Ma CHEW ca (with CHEW in red letters)

SHALIKASHVILI gets broken up into five syllables: sha lee cash VEE lee

When listening, we catch the accent on the fourth syllable. We visualize the accented syllable in caps and in RED: sha lee cash VEE lee

Here are three more examples:

BOCCHICCO becomes bo CHEEK oh

PETRIDES becomes pet REED ease

SKLOVERWICZ becomes sk LOVER wits

Of course, there will be individual preferences when it comes to pronunciation. You must respect each individual's preference. That's why you say the name early in the conversation to validate the pronunciation.

With a little practice you will find unfamiliar ethnic names a stimulating challenge. And once learned, such names become hard to forget.

Exercises for Practicing Visualization

1. How many windows do you have in your house or apartment? Visualize each room to arrive at your total.

2. Pretend you are a helicopter pilot. Visualize your route to work each day as seen overhead by the pilot.

3. Being a good visualizer involves being a good observer. Think about these everyday objects. Visualize them in your mind and answer these questions:

   a. Describe the scams and markings on your sneakers or shoes._____

   b. What do the hands on your watch or clock look like? ____

   _____

   c. How many sections does your wallet have? _____Can you draw a picture of its compartments? _____

4. Visualize these abstract terms by coming up with a specific and vivid image.

   a. affection_____

   b. compassion _____

   c. generosity _____

   d. the number "76" _____

   e. the color "blue" _____

5. Use capital letters and color to help you visualize as well as hear the accented syllable in these names:

   a. Hochmeister _____

   b. Luciano _____

   c. Navarra _____

   d. Placido _____

FIVE THINGS NEVER TO DO
WHEN BEING INTRODUCED

When being introduced you want to make a good impression. This goes beyond flashing a smile and/or extending your hand. There are five definite no-no's:

1. *Don't look away.* Focus on the new person. Make riveting facial contact. If, in a few minutes after leaving her, you can't recall some distinguishing facial feature, you haven't maximized the opportunity.

2. *Don't guess at the name if you haven't heard it clearly.* If there's any doubt ask the person to repeat it. This is a compliment because you appear interested enough to have the name repeated.

3. *Don't think about yourself or your next appointment while your new acquaintance is speaking.* When you ask a question, *listen* to the answer.

4. *Don't wait until later to make an association with the name.* Do it while you are conversing. Listen to the voice and watch the mannerisms. They will give you hints as to the link or association you arrive at. This is personal and has to have meaning only for you, especially if it is negative. For example, Bess is a mess; Mr. Lemmon has a sour face; Ed has a face like Mr. Ed the horse.

5. *Don't hesitate to ask the person how his name is spelled.* This will reinforce your association between name and face. For example, you could ask "Is there an "e" at the end of your name, Miss Green?" or "Is it Kevski or Kevsky?" This will show an interest on your part and will help you etch the name into your memory.

WHAT TO DO WHEN THE NAME IS
ON THE TIP OF YOUR TONGUE

This is one of life's greatest frustrations. You know the name or word or number. You have used it correctly dozens of times. For some strange reason you just can't retrieve it at the present time. Sound familiar?

The best thing to do is to relax and try to put the frustration out of your mind for a little while. When you are relaxed and thinking about something else, the name will pop into your head.

But what can you do in the meantime? Try the alphabet search. This is the technique of going through the sounds of the letters of the alphabet from A to Z until you find one that serves as a cue to jog your memory.

For example, you want to describe the young lady you met last night to a friend but can't remember the name "Francine." You can go through the alphabet hoping that the beginning sound of the first letter will cue or jog your memory. Hearing the sound of "F" or visualizing the "F" may trigger the name.

Anxiety or depression can increase the incidence of "tip of the tongue" syndrome and memory meltdown in general. The opposite side of the coin is relaxation and self-confidence. Don't beat yourself up every time you're at a loss for a name of a person or thing. It happens to all of us—at every age level. Like many things, it is more prevalent as we get older.

It is also more likely to happen if you are asked to recall something you have not thought about for a long time. When you know you will be called upon to come up with certain information or are likely to meet certain people, reviewing ahead of time will often eliminate the problem. Here are some suggestions to follow.

- If you are planning to attend an annual meeting and are afraid you will not remember the names of key people, prepare ahead of time by going over a list of all who might attend. As you see the name, visualize the person and some association about her.

- If you are going to take a prospective client to lunch, review the names of the people you know in common and something about each of them that may come up in conversation.

- Don't become anxious when you forget a name. Think of all the names you already know and can access. Repeat instead, "I forgot that name, but by using memory-improvement strategies I will do better."

The strategies and techniques you learned in this chapter will help you develop the greatest asset of any career or item of personal satisfaction—people. We all need people, as the song goes, but first we have to remember their names.

There is an Eastern proverb that teaches:

Remember my name and I'll never forget you.

But forget my name and I'll never forgive you.

This is a little extreme; however, it illustrates the fundamental principle that remembering names helps lubricate all of life's transactions. Master it and you will feel good about yourself as you spread good feelings among all those who come in contact with you.

MEMENTOS

1. The five components of name recall are *Attention, Association, Observation, Organization,* and *Visualization.*

2. Use the SUAVE SYSTEM to focus *attention.*

3. Improve name recognition using some of the twelve *association* techniques.

4. Learn to *observe* faces better to learn names.

5. *Organize* names with first letter cues.

6. Practice *visualization* to master names.

7. To remember ethnic or unusual names, forget the spelling and break the name up into recognizable soundalike syllables.

8. Associate names and their owners by using a variety of cues. These include rhyme, color, action, and senses.

9. Place the face with the name by being more observant of the people you meet. Look for distinguishing features that you can link with the name.

10. Relaxation is memory's friend. Anxiety is its saboteur.

Chapter Nine

Age-Proofing Your Memory

The human brain is truly amazing. It can generate enough electricity to light a 25-watt lightbulb and has the ability to store as much information as a computer. Our bodies can heal wounds, repair broken bones, and spontaneously recover from disease. Yet many of us know people in their sixties and seventies who are a mere shadow of what they were a decade ago. Their spirit is depressed, their memory is all but gone, and they go through life joylessly and in confusion. Yet others, their age or older, remain active, alert, interested, and stimulating.

To some extent, memory does diminish with age but not in the dramatic way that most people imagine. Many who complain at age 75 that they are "not good with names" should ask themselves whether they were ever good with names? Many older adults use their advanced age as an excuse for not working at remembering.

In this chapter, we explore some proven methods that modern research has found can help age-proof our minds. There is no doubt that heredity plays a major role in how well our bodies and our minds adapt to the passage of time. Research has pointed out that in spite of this, there is much that each individual can do to keep alert in midlife and beyond.

HOW AGING AFFECTS MEMORY

Obviously, as people age they see some inevitable changes in their physical abilities as well in their cognitive skills. Although 5 percent of seniors succumb to some form of senile dementia, another 5 percent reach age 100 with their faculties intact. For those 90 percent in the middle, here are some facts of life worth considering:

1. *Metabolism changes with age.* Our body chemistry and processes do slow down in later life. Not only do we require fewer calories to survive, but our response time to stimuli also slows down. For people accustomed to thinking fast and acting immediately it seems as if their memory is impaired. It is not. It just takes a second or two longer to retrieve what you want to remember.

2. *Reaction time slows down.* Physical changes bring about a change in reaction time. A reduction in visual acuity or hearing make the questions harder to understand and so the answers tend to be slower and fuzzier. Doing two things at once, such as reading the paper and listening to the radio become more difficult or impossible.

3. *Isolation affects memory.* In later life, the loss of a mate deprives you of companionship and limits communication. Older people living alone remember *less* than their age mates living with someone. With fewer occasions to use it, their memory atrophies and rusts. Younger people who divorce or lose a mate find they must assume all the responsibilities and may actually have to remember *more*.

4. *Retirement brings still more changes.* Memory complaints often coincide with retirement. A reduction of motivation from the job and accompanying reduction of activities brings about a drop in mental stimulation. The consequences of forgetting are now minor. Instead of doing something today you can easily postpone it for tomorrow. Instead of reading for work-related information, we now read "for pleasure," which is less focused and usually less demanding. Once new, stimulating activities have replaced work, memory rebounds.

5. *Experience that comes with age is a plus.* An older person, like everyone else, can relate new information to material already mastered. The advantage to the older person is that you have so many more experiences to relate to. The number of memories is vast. Life experience also contributes to judgment, which enhances a good memory.

Using Memory Selection as a Technique for Age-Proofing

We are all faced with many routine chores each day. Some are more important than others. It's quite satisfying when we accomplish these tasks and get them out of the way. Unfortunately, we don't always remember to do the important things. Older people in particular tend to give equal attention to all the things they have to do.

Each day as you think ahead to what you want to accomplish, you should make *two* lists. List 1 consists of the various jobs you want to get done. List 2 contains the same items but in priority order. The items that are most important go to the top of the list. Those items that can wait a day or two go to the bottom of the list.

List 2 should be written down on a piece of paper. List 1 can be written out or kept in your mind as you write out List 2.

As you complete each item on List 2, you reward yourself by crossing it out. Those more difficult tasks, when completed, will give you great satisfaction when you cross them out. Keeping such a list will help prevent your "forgetting" something distasteful but really important, such as mailing your tax payment.

MEMORY SELECTION EXERCISE

The following items appear on someone's List 1 in random order. Rewrite the items into a List 2 in what you would consider to be priority order. The most important task will appear first and the least important item will appear last.

Call a friend to chat.

Order prescription-drug refill.

Select seeds from catalog.

Take new heart medication.

Pay newsboy for delivery.

Make appointment with eye doctor.

Get car inspected.

Buy milk.

Assemble income-tax papers for accountant.

Clean out litter box.

In later life, it is important to be selective when you focus your attention. It is not the quantity of activities you perform but rather their quality and their importance. Define what you want to remember, why, and for how long. Above all, pause, take the time to become aware of what you are doing. Consider its importance a week or a year from now. Search your memory, and your List 2, to see if there is something else, much more important, that you should be doing now. Don't rush it once you undertake an important task. Just take your time.

STEPS YOU CAN TAKE NOW TO ENSURE A STRONG MEMORY IN LATER LIFE

There are lifelong habits you can acquire now that will help you keep your mind and your memory alert. First, you have to recognize that a certain amount of memory loss is normal—at any age. Just as you notice certain changes in your body and physical abilities as you mature, there are certain changes in your memory as well. These are not the same for everyone.

There are many things you can do to ensure a strong memory throughout life. We will explore the effect of mental and physical exercises on memory. The benefits of sleep and mental attitude will also be presented.

What Is Normal Memory Loss?

Physicians now recognize that many healthy individuals are less able to remember certain kinds of information as they get older. They use the term "age-associated memory impairment" or AAMI to describe minor memory difficulties that come with age.

AAMI is neither disabling nor is it progressive. In no way should it be linked with senile dementia, which is both. When an otherwise healthy person is under pressure, the AAMI is most noticeable. Once relaxed, the individual is able to remember the forgotten material without difficulty.

Some common examples of AAMI are as follows:

Not recognizing a person you see fairly often.

Forgetting a word or phrase you use frequently.

Blocking out a familiar phone number completely.

Not remembering a travel route you use regularly.

REDUCING INSTANCES OF AAMI

While no "treatment" for age-associated memory loss is indicated, there are some preventive steps you can use to help age-proof your memory.

1. Write reminders and keep lists. This puts the pressure on the paper and not on you.

2. Repeat names and messages out loud. The auditory clue is another weapon you can add to your arsenal of memory aids.

3. Pay attention and make associations. This helps you focus on what's important and helps screen out distractions.

4. Visualize what it is you want to remember. By "seeing" what it is you want to remember you will encode it better.

5. Take your time. Don't rush from one thought to another. As we grow older, we need more time to process information.

MENTAL CALISTHENICS TO HELP YOUR BRAIN GROW

Scientists at the University of California, Berkeley, discovered that the brains of laboratory rats grew by 4 percent when they were forced to perform mental tasks every day, such as figuring out mazes, negotiating ladders, and relating to other rats. The control group did not have any problems to solve and lived alone. They tended to grow plumper with smaller brains. Those in the mentally stimulating environment received better scores on behavioral tests. Their better scores continued throughout their lives.

What about humans?

The Berkeley researchers concluded that the human brain is designed to respond to stimulation and will expand its powers to meet new challenges as well. The absence of mental challenges leads to atrophy.

Mental exercises can help boost the mind's ability and keep it fit for a lifetime.

Twelve Mental Calisthenics

1. *Train yourself to be more observant*. Look at your environment and record, mentally, what you see. Begin with the most

mundane items and move on to more complex observations. For example, describe the garage doors or mailboxes of your neighbors. What kind of vehicles do they drive? When you enter a restaurant or other public place, do you look for the location of emergency exits? How many serving people can you recognize in your favorite restaurant?

2. *Refine your senses.* No doubt you can distinguish the taste of foods you like from those you dislike. But, how aware are you of the scents and aromas around you? Can you select, from among the various street sounds, one that appeals to you more than the others? Do you work at being able to recognize voices on the telephone? Can you detect which fabrics contain polyester, and which are pure cotton?

3. *Think of friends' names and match the names with their telephone numbers.* See how many you can recall. Work on learning more of them.

4. *Learn something new.* This can be an introduction to computer software, fine wines, a foreign language, a modern artist, a composer or playwright.

5. *Train your hands to follow directions from your brain.* Learn to play the piano, another musical instrument, touch typing, needlecrafts, woodworking, and the like.

6. *Pursue a hobby.* Perhaps you like collecting memorabilia, oil paintings, or electric trains. Read all you can on the subject and discuss it with a fellow enthusiast.

7. *Memorize something you like,* such as a poem, a song, a passage from a book, a recipe or directions for building a birdhouse. Share your newly acquired information with another person.

8. *Review significant dates concerning family members, friends, or colleagues.* See how many birthdays and wedding anniversaries you can learn and recall.

9. *Use a reference book to learn the 50 state capitals as well as capital cities of foreign countries.* How many African or Asian countries can you name?

10. *Work on the chronological list of American presidents.* Break them into logical clusters for ease of recall: Colonial America, Westward Expansion, Civil War to twentieth century, the period up to World War II, and the present time.

11. *Recall your own personal history.* What were you doing last week at this precise time? How did you spend your last birthday? With whom did you spend Thanksgiving last year? What was the last film you saw? With whom did you see it? Where?

12. *Review everyday expenditures.* How much money is in your wallet now? What did you buy yesterday? When did you last add cash to your wallet? What expenses do you have in the next three days?

By doing these mental exercises, you will keep your brain cells active and increase the connective tissue between brain cells. Mental exercises more than compensate for any brain cell losses that occur with age.

We actually "grow" our brains by using them, say cognitive scientists. Challenging mental activities increase the number of active circuits or synapses in the brain. The more circuits, the more associations, the more associations, the greater the ability to remember.

How the Memory Benefits from Physical Exercise

There is a biochemistry to exercise. Many body chemicals are involved: lactose, glucose, androgens, testosterone, and chemical transmitters, among others. Those exercises that make demands on the cardiovascular system will provide better results for our memory than do sports such as bowling and golf. Most research has concentrated on running, but walking, swimming, cross-country skiing, aerobic dancing, jumping rope, and bike riding are all excellent aerobic activities.

THE BLOOD-BRAIN CONNECTION

Just like any other organ, the brain relies on the blood to provide oxygen and nutrients. The blood also carries away carbon dioxide and other waste products.

If the heart and veins become sluggish and don't work efficiently, our memory is quick to suffer. A number of studies point to cardiovascular problems as a key cause of progressive memory loss in later life. Researchers have used regular exercise to restore an unrestricted flow of cerebral blood. They have established that blood flow to the brain declines an average of 23 percent between the ages of 33 and 62. Less blood means less oxygen and glucose are made available to the brain, and so it has less energy to burn.

THE HEART-MEMORY CONNECTION

By establishing a pattern of regular exercise early in life, these cardiovascular problems can be reduced, postponed, or eliminated. While factors such as heredity play a role in cardiovascular disease, we do see the benefits of exercise in increasing blood flow to the brain.

In a remarkably short study of only 26 days, participants over 60 years old in a walking program scored better on memory tests than did the control group who did not exercise regularly. Not only did their hearts become more efficient, pumping a greater amount of blood with each beat, but also the exercise raised the levels of high-density lipoproteins in the blood. Exercise also reduces blood levels of certain fats that narrow arteries and cause them to harden.

THE OXYGEN-BRAIN CONNECTION

In addition to blood, exercise delivers more oxygen to the brain. Young people who keep fit have normal brain functioning patterns for their age, whereas sedentary young people's brains have taken on the patterns of older people.

The variable is oxygen. The brain needs oxygen to oxidize glucose in the production of electrical energy that sparks our memory. Our brain makes up only 2 percent of the body's weight, but its need for oxygen is tremendous—20 percent of the body's share. Shallow breathing and clogged arteries may leave the brain gasping for air, in a sense. Symptoms range from simple memory loss to full-blown senility. Exercising routines established early and continuing throughout life stimulate the memory and keep it from slipping as you age.

HOW SLEEP HELPS KEEP YOUR MIND SHARP

Adequate sleep is vital in keeping the brain alert and fully function-ing. Sleep-deprived individuals tend to be forgetful, with impaired functioning and depressed mood. Each person's need for sleep varies widely—from five to ten hours. The average duration of adult sleep is seven and one half hours. However, this is a meaningless figure. Thomas Edison slept only four or five hours a night. Albert Einstein needed ten hours of sleep each night to keep his mind sharp. Although our individual needs vary, it is important for each of us to find our optimum quantity of sleep to make it truly restora-tive. Many people report that too much sleep leaves them lethargic and their memory fuzzy.

Understanding the Memory-Sleep Connection

While you are asleep, your memory is being revised and stored in the brain. This is why you sometimes awaken in the middle of the night with an answer to a question or problem that has been troubling you during the day. Your brain doesn't sleep at night the way the rest of you does.

As people get older, their need for sleep diminishes. But in order to function with peak memory skills, it is essential to get enough sleep so that your brain can rest. Although the brain doesn't shut down completely as you sleep, it does operate on a different level.

Each night you pass through four or five sleep cycles. Each cycle lasts about an hour and a half. Each cycle is made up of several lev-els. During certain levels of deep sleep the brain disconnects from the senses and processes, reviews, consolidates, and stores memory. If you interrupt or interfere with this crucial sleep time, it will affect your performance the next day. So your brain needs sleep even if the amount of sleep is different from the amount you slept in the past.

Inability to sleep, because of bad sleep habits, not only deprives you of the valuable memory-consolidation periods during sleep but also interferes with learning during your waking hours. This is a special problem for older people because their levels of deep sleep diminish with age. It is during deep, or delta, waves of sleep that the brain recharges itself. Older people who don't get good sleep begin to live in a chronic state of fatigue. They find it difficult to pay attention or register information the way they did when they were younger.

Obviously, anything you can do to develop sound sleep habits will help you hold onto a strong memory throughout life. The following tips for restorative sleep have been tested and proven.

Six Life-Long Sleep Tips

1. *Be aware of what you eat.* Your stomach should be neither full nor empty at bedtime. Digestion involves increased metabolism and interferes with sound sleep. Eating a heavy meal shortly before retiring will keep you from getting a restful night's sleep. An empty or hungry feeling may keep you from falling asleep as well.

2. *Avoid late-day stimulants.* Coffee and tea will keep you from falling asleep as will cola drinks, chocolate, Anacin, and Excedrin. They all contain caffeine. Nicotine, diet pills, and certain prescription drugs work as a stimulant and will interfere with a good night's sleep. Performing strenuous exercise shortly before bedtime will also act as a stimulant.

3. *Watch your intake of alcohol.* Beverages containing alcohol make it difficult to stay asleep. They may help initiate sleep by making you drowsy; however, they keep you from getting to the deep sleep that your brain needs to rest. They may also keep you from sleeping through the night.

4. *Keep regular hours.* Stick to a regular schedule of awakening and retiring. Shift workers have five times the sleep problems as does the general population. Get up at the same time each day regardless of how much or how little you slept. This will help your body clock set its schedule.

5. *Develop bedtime routines.* Develop bedtime rituals or routines such as reading a book, soaking in a tub, listening to soft music. Avoid anything too stimulating. These regular rituals will tell your body that it is time to wind down and get ready for sleep.

6. *Expose your eyes to sunlight when you can.* Blind people have twice as many sleep problems as sighted people. This is because they are unable to use light cues to reset their brain's inner clock. Among sighted people, sleep problems are more common when

they spend most of their time indoors. During the short days of winter when sunlight is brief, there are more sleep and affective disorders. Get outside during your lunch hour or work break. Daytime sunlight is the yang that fosters the yin of nighttime sleep.

Sleep consolidates memory. We are able to solve problems and arrive at decisions when we "sleep on it." Sound sleep is both restorative and regenerative. To ensure a secure memory in later life, establish healthy sleep patterns now.

USING TECHNIQUES OF MEMORY SELF-MANAGEMENT

The world of tennis introduced us to a mind-control method originally called "yoga tennis" by Timothy Gallwey, a Harvard University-trained tennis teacher. He found that players hit their peak when they "let it happen" and directed the ball over the net first in their mind and then in actuality. This is done effortlessly. The mind is on the job, but quietly, without anxious thoughts of pressure or failure.

Today, athletes appreciate these findings, and many competitors now travel with a sports psychologist as well as a coach. But you don't have to be a professional tennis player to benefit from sports psychology when it comes to memory. Here are four basic tips adapted to strengthening your memory for the rest of your life.

Four Ways to Strengthen Memory Thoughts

1. *Visualize yourself in control of your memory.* See yourself remembering the dates, numbers, names, and facts necessary for your social and business success.

2. *Monitor your negative thoughts.* Remind yourself of the times your memory proved valuable. Don't belabor the occasional lapse of memory.

3. *Shut down inner dialogues in which colleagues or authority figures tell you "you'll probably forget" or "no one can possibly remember."* Dwell, instead, on those occasions when you surprised yourself and others with your memory skills.

4. *Center your mind on the here and now.* Stay within the concept of one thing at a time. Concentrate on each memory task as you face it, not on yesterday's or last week's memory task. Eliminate distractions; stay centered and on-task.

Avoid Leaving Memory to Chance

Too many of us leave memory to chance. We learn something and then hope that we will remember it when we need it. This is hardly good enough. It may work when your memory is at its peak in your twenties, but don't count on it later on. What you can do to prevent "losing it" in middle age and beyond is to take the advice of behavior psychologist and author B. F. Skinner and practice "good intellectual self-management."

His techniques are logical and very easy to implement. They emphasize doing something to enhance memory and not leaving memory to chance. We have paraphrased and abridged Skinner's suggestions for you.

1. *Do something.* If rain is expected, don't just think about it. Hook an umbrella over the knob of your front door as soon as the thought comes to mind.

2. *Capture your ideas.* Creative solutions and ideas frequently come to us in the middle of the night. Don't let them escape. You may not remember them in the morning. Keep a small recorder or pad and paper at your bedside.

3. *Carry a memo pad.* A spiral-bound, 3 × 5 memo pad in your pocket is invaluable for writing down names, numbers, and facts as they come up throughout the day. Review them each evening and record them in a more permanent location, such as a desk calendar or a phone directory.

4. *Keep it short.* Speak and write in sentences that are short and to the point. Beware of going of on tangents or making digressions that make you and your listener forget your point.

5. *Use an outline and stick to it.* When writing a business letter, personal correspondence or a report, draw up an outline first to guard against inconsistencies and memory lapses. Say it once and move on. You and your reader will remember it better this way.

If started early, these self-management skills will be worth their weight in gold later on in boosting memory.

Learning to Forget Constructively

Forgetting can have some major benefits in our lives. It's important to know when to forget. This is best learned early so that old age is not filled with frivolous, negative memories. We are constructive when we carefully choose which memories should be discarded.

Nature provides us with some basic forgetting skills. Without them, we would hold ourselves back. For example, a one year old is learning to walk. He falls and hurts his head. Fortunately, he forgets this injury the next time he has the urge to walk. If toddlers didn't forget such bumps they'd never master the skill of walking in an upright position.

Women forget the pain of childbirth and eagerly plan another pregnancy. A 60 year old forgets the pain of losing a mate and decides to marry again.

Yet certain pains must be remembered, and we use our judgment in deciding what should be remembered. Touching a hot pot on the stove is a memory worth recalling so that burned fingers don't become a habit.

For many, work is a haven for forgetting the pressure of a chaotic home life or a lonely, barren social life. We block out disturbing memories by immersing ourselves in a demanding schedule or task. Such escape gives us a short-term solution to our problems.

Amnesia, a disease frequently manifested on soap operas, is the blocking out of all memory by people facing unbearable tragedy. Most of us learn to handle traumatic experiences in a less dramatic way.

A technique worth learning early in life is to mix sad and vexing images with happy and satisfying memories to gain perspective. After a time, the unpleasant memories can be forgotten instead of your constantly going over them. This is an important survival tool.

CONSTRUCTIVE-FORGETTING QUIZ

Read each statement and then decide if it describes your behavior as occurring "frequently" or "seldom." Place a check in the appropriate column.

	F	*S*
1. Rude people make me angry for days.	____	____
2. When depressed about something, I can't think of anything else.	____	____
3. I count my change after each purchase.	____	____
4. Because many politicians have disappointed me, I no longer vote at election time.	____	____
5. I remember childhood humiliations.	____	____
6. The inefficiencies of my co-workers is a preoccupation of mine.	____	____
7. I have a regular routine for paying bills.	____	____
8. In crowded situations, I am careful to secure my handbag or wallet.	____	____
9. I hear myself say, "Forgive, but don't forget."	____	____
10. When recalling my childhood, I am usually happy.	____	____

SCORING: Each "Frequently" counts as 5 points.
                          Each "Seldom" counts as 1 point.

For statements 3, 7, and 8, a total of 11 or more points reveals a realistic view of the world. You are appropriately aware.

For statements 1, 2, 4, 5, 6, 9, and 10, a total of 7 to 12 points is good; 13 to 17 reveals you let too many things bother you; 18 to 21 shows you need to forget more; 22 or more means you need to purge yourself of bad memories and dwell more on good memories.

Selective forgetting is helpful. It's the trait that separates you from a computer. Learn how to pick through your memories the way you pick through a display of apples. The firm, ripe ones can nourish you emotionally, as well as physically. And you know what one bad apple can do to a barrelful.

PRESERVING MENTAL VITALITY

The enemy of mental vitality isn't growing older. The real enemy is the passivity that tends to creep up on us as we age. The fight is not with age—it is with boredom, with routine, with the humdrum.

Loneliness and isolation as well as the attitude of the people around us affect our memory. This is reinforced by our own expectation that we will become forgetful as we age.

If forgetfulness is thought of as age-appropriate, then once we reach our middle years we must begin not to act our age. Thomas Edison, Victor Hugo, and Pablo Picasso did not act their ages when they were in their seventies, eighties, and nineties. Although remaining active in a creative field doesn't necessarily prove your memory is intact, it certainly shows that you can remember what is necessary to stay at the top.

Memory Loss Is Not Inevitable

Prevention begins with fighting such stereotypes in midlife. Find things that you like to do and can do that are fun. Remember that memory loss in later years is not always inevitable. Controllable factors such as malnutrition, depression, and the side effects of certain prescription drugs all contribute to memory loss. Keep active physically, eat a variety of healthful foods, think positively, and review the possible side effects of the medicine you are taking.

The picture is getting brighter for older people every day. Most of them *won't* experience senility. Prepare yourself at age 50 for what your life will be like at 80. Most likely you'll live long enough to find out.

How You Can Maintain a Positive Attitude

As people grow older the single most helpful step they can take to ensure a strong, lasting memory is to work on maintaining a positive attitude.

Some specific steps you can take in this direction are as follows:

1. *Stay flexible.* Don't lock yourself into inflexible routines. Don't say, "Oh, but I always do it this way."

2. *Get involved in life.* Try new things and explore new areas. Say things such as, "I never tasted anything like that before, but I'll try anything once."

3. *Choose TV programs that are stimulating,* such as quiz shows, interview programs, and panel discussions. Avoid mindless,

repetitive dramas that dull your brain with dreary life stories or talk shows featuring dysfunctional people.

4. *Seek out positive, affirmative people* to spend your free time with. Their enthusiasm will become contagious.

5. *Share your expertise with others.* Teach a course, mentor a young person, or tutor a child. Such a contribution will make you feel positive and upbeat.

6. *Learn something new.* Attempt something different, such as a computer course. Use the hardware at your public library at first. Become computer literate. You'll find yourself surrounded by younger people. You'll exercise your brain.

Watching Your Language

Check yourself to see that you don't use the following expressions or their equivalent:

1. I'm too old for that kind of thing.
2. Clothes don't interest me anymore.
3. No, thank you. I've never tried that before, I'm sure I won't like it.
4. I just can't seem to remember names.
5. I eat very little. I don't get excited about food anymore.
6. I'd rather stay home, thank you. I'd rather watch TV.
7. I'm too old for exercise.
8. No thanks. I won't know anyone there.
9. I haven't heard from them in years. Let's leave it that way.
10. At my age, the best place is home.

Why Attitude Becomes More Important than Aptitude

How you feel is a decision you make every day.

Of course, painful chronic or acute illness will determine how you feel physically. In the absence of physical symptoms if you don't automatically feel upbeat, look around and find something to feel good about.

In the area of memory, you have to have the right attitude about your ability to remember what you need to know. Don't beat yourself up every time you make some slip. Instead, recall the many more occasions when you were able to retrieve some obscure piece of information from the past. A positive memory attitude will go far in reinforcing your memory skills.

WATCH THE MESSAGES YOU SEND

A new branch of medicine—psychoneuroimmunology—studies the relationship between mental attitude and health. Physicians have found that a positive attitude can result in faster recovery from such physical conditions as burns, surgery, and arthritis.

The brain produces neuropeptides, which transmit chemical messages that control the immune system. When you think positively, these messages are more emphatic. When you're depressed, the signal is actually weaker.

FOUR ROADBLOCKS TO AVOID

As we approach middle age, we set up roadblocks to developing a positive memory attitude. Here are some common obstacles of our own making and a suggestion for turning each one around.

1. *Personalizing:* Everyone remembers my memory lapse.
   Instead think: Everyone has slips. I don't dwell on theirs and they won't remember mine.

2. *Generalizing:* I'm losing my memory. I probably have Alzheimer's disease.
   Instead think: I occasionally forget something. It's probably overload. There are things that I remember more clearly than my younger colleagues.

3. *Negativity:* I'm having difficulty learning this year's price schedule.
   Replace this with: It's always hard getting it straight in January. By February, I'll have it down pat—as usual.

4. *Perfectionism:* I really messed up my sales presentation.
   Instead think: With a little more preparation I can get it straight next time.

As you go about your day's activities, expect positive outcomes. Start your day with enough time to prepare for its activities. Don't begin by rushing. Eat a good breakfast. Don't drug yourself with coffee and cigarettes. People who cultivate positive attitudes expect good things to happen, and they usually do.

UNDERSTANDING THE MEDICAL FACTOR IN MEMORY

The medications you take may have an effect on your memory. If you are experiencing a sudden change in your ability to remember you should consult your physician. Be sure to take along a list of all the prescription drugs and over-the-counter medications you take on a regular basis.

Certain medical conditions may have an effect on your memory. Your physician will apprise you of them.

How Your Blood Pressure Affects Memory

Researchers at the National Institute on Aging found that subjects with high blood pressure in midlife are much more likely to have trouble remembering things when they are old.

These findings underscore the value of having your blood pressure checked regularly in your forties and fifties. One study tracked 3,735 men for 30 years. On average, the subjects were 48 years old at the start and 78 years old when the study concluded. They learned that men who had high systolic blood pressure (the higher of the two numbers in a reading) during midlife were almost two and half times as likely to have poor memory functioning and other cognitive impairment in old age as men with low blood pressure. Other studies show that the same is true for women.

For this reason, it is essential that you have your blood pressure checked by your physician and that you are guided by her recommendations concerning control of hypertension.

IDENTIFYING SECRETS OF LIFELONG MEMORY AGILITY

The greatest fear about advancing age for most adults is loss of memory. By their mid-eighties, about 20 percent of that age group can expect to face cerebral atrophy sufficient to cause a loss of memory. But what about the majority of older people who manage *not* to lose their memory?

Actually, there are several well-documented characteristics of those older people with agile memories. A survey of 40 men and women between 70 and 95 from Seattle, Washington, had some fascinating results. More than three fourths of this group kept their memories intact and functioning. Researchers found that the people with good memories had three broad characteristics in common: they were mentally stimulated, maintained a healthy lifestyle, and built a support system of friends and family.

Three Characteristics of Seniors with Good Memories

You can learn from their experiences by studying their characteristics:

1. *They were mentally stimulated.* The group studied demonstrate that mental activity and stimulation are the key to mental sharpness in later life. Those with good memories enjoy doing crossword puzzles, playing bridge, or reading widely. These people are decidedly the majority in the disease-free population. Brain cells, like muscle tissue, atrophy with nonuse. The seniors studied far exceeded the national norm for their age group in engaging in provocative discussion and enlivening activities. They sought out people with a similar outlook.

2. *They maintained a healthy lifestyle.* This group of seniors were blessed with good genes and also wholesome patterns of living. For example,

- They were generally free from cardiovascular disease. Heart disease and stroke constrict or block blood vessels, which can lower oxygen levels in the brain and lead to cell damage. Such damage affects memory and its functioning.
- They enjoyed a high level of satisfaction with their accomplishments and their present life. They were less likely to express regrets over missed opportunities and wrong choices in life.
- They were generally better educated than average. Those who did not have years of formal education were nonetheless avid

readers, curious about the world around them, self-taught in many areas, and pursued hobbies.

- They married someone they perceived to be smarter than themselves. As a rule they credit their mates for their stimulating life.

- They were flexible and less likely to adhere to rigid rules and routines. They appeared to be able to accept change more easily than did their senile contemporaries.

- They were generally "up" about life. They did not acquire the general malaise about living that infects so many of their less able age mates.

- They were more likely to engage in some regular physical activity. Such exercise benefits the memory by lowering blood pressure and the risk of hypertension. It also reduces weight and the risk of diabetes. Aerobic exercise increases the flow of oxygen to the brain.

3. *They built a support system of friends and family.* The seniors with good memories were different from their age mates in one other important area. They worked at building and maintaining friends throughout life. They also stayed in touch with family members. They were frequently the initiators of phone calls, greeting cards, and notes to other people. They looked for opportunities to be with other people for meals, conversation, walks, or shopping.

People who stay close to family members and friends throughout life are less likely to shut themselves off in later life. Of course, in this age group, many of their friends die or move into institutions, thus limiting contact.

Many physicians report that large numbers of older Americans who are isolated and alienated are more likely to present dementia-like symptoms, such as memory loss and confusion. Such isolation, frequently self-imposed, produces a kind of depression that mirrors senility or may actually be a precursor.

On the contrary, those who work at their social contacts throughout life keep their memory well into advanced age. The lesson there is that early in life people need to seek out stimulating activities, a healthful lifestyle, and a network of family and friends that they can maintain through the years.

SPECIAL TECHNIQUES FOR THE
OLDER LEARNER TO USE

Some aspects of memory change little as people age. The short-term memory capacity is much the same in older and in younger people. An 85 year old can look up an address and address an envelope as well as her granddaughter since this task requires only short-term memory.

The slowing down of memory ability in the elderly is most apparent in encoding or transferring data into long-term memory and in recall or retrieving information on demand. Adding new names and faces to those already mastered becomes more difficult. Coming up with information once known but not recently used is another area of difficulty in later life.

Four Major Reasons for Change

Although there is a wide range of individual differences among this population, the reasons are usually as follows:

1. *Distractions.* Older adults find it harder to pay attention to more than one thing at a time. Someone talking, the TV sound, or the doorbell ringing may disrupt your concentration easily. The doctor's questions in the examining room may interfere with your concentration. You forget the questions you were going to ask. Writing out questions before you leave home is a good hint.

2. *Time.* It takes a little more time for you to learn something new. "You can teach an old dog new tricks" if the teacher is patient with you and provides you with a little more time and a little more reinforcement to learn the "trick." Once you make up your mind that you can learn, the addition of a little more time will ensure mastery.

3. *Access.* It becomes increasingly more difficult to retrieve familiar names and vocabulary words on demand. The sensation that the word or name is on the tip of the tongue occurs more frequently in old age. The best advice is to relax, take a deep breath, and try to access the information by thinking of related items. If that fails, accept the fact that it will come to you while you are thinking of something else.

4. *Effort.* Information that could be learned with little effort in the past may now require greater effort to remember. There is a need to focus attention and stay on task. With a little more work on intensifying concentration, you can encode what you want to remember.

Ten Ways to Remember Better in Later Life

People in their eighties and nineties are attending college courses and doing well. The media feature stories on them all the time. After interviewing dozens of these elderly high achievers we consolidated their success stories and hints into ten practical suggestions. In general, they agreed that it takes a little more time, a little more effort, and a high degree of motivation. These are their suggestions:

1. *Provide yourself with a good place to read and study.* Be sure the lighting is adequate, the ventilation and temperature are comfortable, and your glasses are appropriate.

2. *Give yourself enough time to do and learn what is necessary.* Don't squeeze cognitive tasks into a few minutes between other activities. Program enough time for you to succeed at remembering.

3. *Write things down.* Keep a calendar of dates and refer to it often. Write "To Do" lists every evening for things you want to do the next day. Write shopping lists and remember to take them with you.

4. *Space your learning.* Study for several short periods of time, with rest in between. Things you want to memorize are best reviewed just before you go to sleep. Sleep helps to consolidate memory.

5. *Analyze the memory strategies you use.* Is it rote, association, pairing? Which ones work best for you? Use the techniques that suit your particular learning style.

6. *Learn through repetition.* We all learned the multiplication tables through rote. As infants we learned to respond to our names the same way. Review and repeat the material you want to master.

7. *Ask questions.* If you don't comprehend what is being presented, the fault may be in the presentation. Ask questions to help clarify the situation.

8. *Develop tricks to give yourself the extra time you may need.* Clear your throat, take off your glasses, take a deep breath to get a few extra seconds. That's all it may take to bring up the slow-moving word or thought.

9. *Break the new material down into small bites.* By dividing up the material into logical, manageable pieces, you will ensure mastery. This is in addition to scheduling short periods of time for study.

10. *Relax and think positively.* Anxiety and depression are the greatest barriers to a good memory. Reward yourself with an incentive. After mastering several bites of information, stop for a cup of coffee.

A VISUAL-AUDITORY MEMORY INVENTORY

As people age, they become more dependent on one major sense of learning. Some people remember best what they see. Others do a better job with what they hear. This inventory will indicate which skill is more developed for you at this time.

After you read each item, look away or close your eyes to picture the image in your mind. Take about 30 seconds for each item, then rate how clearly you were able to imagine the item. Complete all items.

Rating Scale: Very clear = 4

Clear = 6

Fairly clear = 2

Fuzzy image = 1

Can't imagine = 0

1. Visualize the face of a close friend or relative.   _____
2. Imagine this person's laugh or voice.   _____
3. Picture a can of food—any food or drink.   _____
4. Imagine a car door slamming.   _____
5. Picture your childhood bedroom.   _____
6. Hear a car engine starting up.   _____
7. See a wide green lawn.   _____
8. Listen to the voice of a popular singer.   _____
9. Look into the window of a favorite store.   _____

10. Hear a favorite song or musical selection. _____

11. Visualize a scene from a favorite movie or TV show. _____

12. Imagine the sound of a bus or a train. _____

13. Picture yourself reading a book or newspaper. _____

14. Imagine the sound of a baby crying. _____

15. See yourself at your favorite restaurant. _____

16. Hear the sound of a nail scratching a chalkboard. _____

17. See a large bouquet of flowers. _____

18. Imagine a car alarm going off. _____

19. Visualize a beautiful sunset. _____

20. Hear the sound of door chimes. _____

     Scoring: Grand Total = rating for all 20 items _____

       Total your ratings for the odd-numbered items _____

       Total your ratings for the even-numbered items _____

       Your total for the even items + odd items should =
the Grand Total.

Look at your total score for the odd-numbered items. They represent the _visual skills._ Look at your score for the even-numbered items. They represent the _auditory skills._

If your score for the odd-numbered items is much higher than for the even-numbered items, you are primarily a _visual learner._ If your even-numbered score is higher, then you are an _auditory learner._ A small percentage of people will have both scores approximately the same. They learn equally well visually and auditorily.

How You Can Use This Information

Let's assume that someone is going to make a short speech, deliver a eulogy, or introduce a guest speaker, for example. A visual learner would be better off writing out his remarks and then reading them over several times until he feels comfortable that he knows what he is going to say. He learns by seeing.

An auditory learner will not get very far this way. She should make a cassette tape of what she wants to say and then play it over several times. She learns best what she hears. If no tape recorder is available, she can learn the material by reciting it aloud several times.

This inventory can help you determine your stronger orientation to learning—visual or auditory. Now that you know your strong side, pursue it in all the memory tasks you take on.

TEN BASIC PRINCIPLES OF MEMORY RETENTION FOR SENIORS

1. *Interest.* Keep up your interest in the world around you. Be interested in what you're reading or listening to.

2. *Selection.* Be selective in what you try to remember. Many things can be written down and later consulted. Use calendars. memo books, lists, and so forth, for those.

3. *Attention.* Focus on what it is you want to remember. The problem is not so much retention for seniors as it is attention.

4. *Understanding.* Increase your understanding by asking questions. You're never too old to show your curiosity or seek clarification.

5. *Intention.* Make a conscious effort to intentionally remember. "See" yourself remembering.

6. *Confidence.* Recall all the things you *do* remember. Tell yourself you can and will remember.

7. *Externals.* Look outside yourself at what you want to remember. Avoid getting caught up in ego-related items.

8. *Association.* Link new data to things you already know. The more connections you make, the stronger the recall.

9. *Organization.* Take the time to classify similar things together. Put them into logical categories.

10. *Practice.* Spend a few minutes each day applying these basic principles.

As you go over these ten principles, personalize them to meet your particular needs. Review them from time to time. The only thing separating you from a great memory is your willingness to give it a try. Pay attention to "how" you remember. Which techniques work best for you?

Pay attention to how you "forget." Which situations and what kinds of items do you have trouble remembering? Work on those items and see how much you can improve. Memory is a skill and like any skill it can be learned. Like any skill, it can improve with practice—at any age.

MEMENTOS

1. There are steps you can take now to ensure that your memory will be active throughout your life. These include keeping your mind active as well as your body, getting adequate sleep, practicing good memory habits, and forgetting some things without guilt.

2. The middle years have an effect on your memories. Handling the changes in your life, keeping a positive attitude, and eating properly all help keep your memory agile.

3. People in their later years have special memory considerations. Some normal memory loss is to be expected.

4. Consult your physician to check your blood pressure regularly because hypertension may contribute to memory loss. Also, review different medications you are taking to see if their interaction can be the cause of confusion or interference with memory.

5. Older people with agile memories display some common characteristics: They stay mentally stimulated, they maintain a healthful lifestyle, and they develop a support system of friends and family.

6. Memory selection grows in importance as people age. It's important to prioritize activities and not treat each one with equal importance.

7. Elderly high achievers employ many hints and practical suggestions in remembering and learning. These include taking a little more time on mental tasks, putting forth a little more effort in learning, and staying motivated and eager to learn throughout life.

8. Our senses play an important role in how we learn. Analyze how you absorb new material. Some people depend primarily upon their vision while others depend more on their hearing. Be sure to employ your stronger sense when trying to remember.

Chapter Ten

Mental Math Shortcuts

There is no substitute for memory power plus thinking skills. Mental math goes hand in hand with memory power. By learning the shortcuts in this chapter, practicing them, and using them every day, you will solidify your memory power. Here are some of the benefits that you will gain:

- Handle shopping chores with ease and accuracy. You will be able to anticipate your correct change rapidly.

- Approximate the return you can earn on your investments. You will learn how to figure out when your memory will double—in your head.

- Estimate the percent of your money that is spent in different areas. You will be able to calculate percent with ease and accuracy.

- Calculate in advance your take-home pay, with overtime or a bonus. You will become more adept at all calculations.

- Project profit-and-loss figures for your company. You will be able to "see" numbers and handle large numbers more easily.

These shortcuts are mental exercises that, while not specifically memorization techniques, are helpful in keeping the mind flexible and in gear. In short, they make it possible to remember more efficiently.

Start by taking the diagnostic test at the beginning of the chapter. For this, you will need pencil and paper. Then, read the shortcuts, study the example for each, and do the mental exercises. After you complete the shortcuts, you will take another test, this time without pencil and paper—coming up with the answers in your head.

You will gain personal satisfaction as you see your speed and accuracy grow as you apply these mental math shortcuts.

A DIAGNOSTIC TEST OF YOUR BASIC MATH SKILLS

See how many of these calculations you can complete in three minutes using pencil and paper.

1. $900 \div 25 =$ _____
2. $45 \times 22 =$ _____
3. $40 \times 7.9 =$ _____
4. $19 \times 25 =$ _____
5. $630 - 485 =$ _____
6. $17.6 \div 0.4 =$ _____
7. $726 \times 11 =$ _____
8. $62 \div 99 =$ _____
9. $170 \times \$10.75 =$ _____
10. $5824 \div 64 =$ _____
11. If an investor pays 8% interest per year, in how many years will the principal double? _____

The last problem seems insoluble to most readers. But before you complete this chapter you will be able to solve it in your head and with speed and accuracy. Read on!

SEVEN SHORTCUTS FOR MENTAL MULTIPLICATION

SHORTCUT 1: SPEEDING UP THE WAY YOU MULTIPLY

A large number can be broken down into two smaller numbers without changing its value. When numbers are too big to multiply easily, divide one number into two smaller numbers.

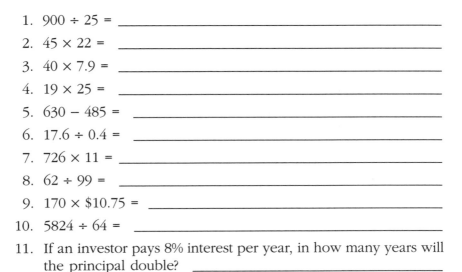

Example One: $6 \times 14 =$ _____

Step 1: Split 14 into two parts 7 and 2

Step 2: The problem now reads $6 \times 7 \times 2 =$ _____

Step 3: $6 \times 7 = 42$ $42 \times 2 = 84$

Answer: $6 \times 14 = 84$

Example Two: $90 \times 1.4 =$ _____

Step 1: Split 90 into two parts 9 and 10

Step 2: The problem now reads: $9 \times 10 \times 1.4 =$ _____

Step 3: $10 \times 1.4 = 14 \quad 14 \times 9 = 126$

Answer: $90 \times 1.4 = 126$

EXERCISE FOR SHORTCUT 1:

1. $60 \times 1.6 =$ _____

2. $7 \times 120 =$ _____

3. $17 \times 22 =$ _____

4. $15 \times 320 =$ _____

5. $78 \times 12 =$ _____

6. $7 \times 1.8 =$ _____

7. $0.9 \times 15 =$ _____

8. $8 \times 160 =$ _____

SHORTCUT 2: MULTIPLYING A TWO-DIGIT NUMBER

By cross-multiplying and working from right to left you can easily multiply by a two-digit number without paper and pencil.

First multiply the ones digit. Then cross-multiply; and finally multiply the tens digits.

Example $21 \times 23 =$ _____

Step 1: Multiply the ones digits $1 \times 3 = 3$

Step 2: Cross-multiply. Do this by multiplying the tens digit of the first number by the ones digit of the second. Then multiply the ones digit of the first number by the tens digit of the second. Add both.

$(2 \times 3) + (1 \times 2) = 6 + 2 = 8$ (tens digit answer)

Step 3: Multiply the tens digits: $2 \times 2 = 4$ (hundreds digit answer)

Step 4: Combine answers: 483

Note: If the product is larger than 9, be sure to carry, as in this example:

Example Two: 34 × 23 = _____

Step 1: Multiply the ones digits: 4 × 3 = 12

The 2 of the 12 becomes the ones-digit answer, and you carry the 1.

Step 2: Cross-multiply and add (also add the 1 you carried).

(3 × 3) + (4 × 2) = 9 + 8 + 1 + 18

The 8 of the 18 becomes the tens digit, and you carry the 1.

Step 3: Multiply the tens digits and carry the 1.

(3 × 2) + 1 = 7

The 7 becomes the hundreds digit.

Step 4: Combine partial answers to get: 782

Answer: 34 × 23 = 782

EXERCISES FOR SHORTCUT 2:

1. 31 × 24 = _____

2. 72 × 54 = _____

3. 67 × 89 = _____

4. 81 × 38 = _____

5. 43 × 16 = _____

SHORTCUT 3: MULTIPLYING BY 11

To multiply a two-digit number by 11 (or 0.11, 1.1, 110, and so on) add the two digits and insert the sum between the two digits.

First write the number, leaving some space between the two digits. Then add the two digits and write the sum between the two digits themselves.

Example One: 35 × 11 = _____

Step 1: Write the number, leaving a space between the two digits

3 ____ 5

Step 2: Add the two digits 3 + 5 = 8

Step 3: Insert the 8 in the space, producing 385

Example Two: 5.4 × 1.1 = _____

Step 1: Ignore the decimal point and zero.

Think 54 × 11 = _____

Step 2: Write 5 _____ 4 (Add 5 + 4 – 9)

Step 3: Insert 9 between 5 and 4, producing 594

Quick Estimate: Since 5 × 1 = 5, then 5.4 × 1.1 will equal a little more than 5. So, 594 is really 5.94

Answer: 5.4 × 1.1 = 5.94

Example Three: 9.7 × 1.1 =

Note: Here, 9 + 7 = 16 results in a two-digit number. Insert the 6 between the 9 and 7 and carry the 1.

9 (16) 7 becomes 9 6 7, and by carrying the 1 becomes as the final answer, 10 6 7 or 1067.

Quick Estimate: 9.7 is almost 10. 1.1 is a little more than 1. 10 × 1 = 10. So, 9.7 × 1.1 will yield a number a little more than 10. Therefore, the partial answer, 1067 becomes 10.67.

Answer: 9.7 × 1.1 = 10.67

EXERCISES FOR SHORTCUT 3:

1. 45 × 11 = _____

2. 56 × 1.1 = _____

3. .65 × 110 = _____

4. 9.3 × 11 = _____

5. 4.7 × 110 = _____

SHORTCUT 4: HOW TO MULTIPLY USING GROUPING

This is similar to Shortcut 1 in that you reduce difficult calculations to two steps.

Group one of the numbers into two easy-to-handle parts.

Example One: 13 × 12 = _____

Regroup: (12 × 12) + (12 × 1) = 144 + 12 = 156

Example Two: 507 × 6 = _____

Regroup: (500 × 6) + (7 × 6) = 3000 + 42 = 3042

EXERCISES FOR SHORTCUT 4:

1. 58 × 7 = _____

2. 74 × 9 = _____

3. 6 × 93 = _____

4. 45 × 21 = _____

5. 102 × 30 = _____

SHORTCUT 5: SPEEDING UP MULTIPLICATION BY ROUNDING OUT

It's easier to multiply by tens. In this technique you raise one number to reach the nearest ten. You then adjust the second number down by the same amount.

Example One: 9 × 28 = _____

Step 1: Raise 28 by 2 to reach 30. (9 × 30 = 270)

Step 2: Reduce 270 by 2 × 9, or 18

Step 3: 270 − 18 = 252

Answer: 9 × 28 = 252

Example Two: 39 × 99 = _____

Step 1: Raise 99 by 1 to reach 100 (39 × 100 = 3900)

Step 2: Reduce 3900 by 1 × 39 or 39

Step 3: 3900 − 39 = 3861

EXERCISES FOR SHORTCUT 5:

1. 79 × 5 = _____

2. 29 × 12 = _____

3. 14 × 48 = _____

4. 17 × 25 = _____

5. 89 × 30 = _____

SHORTCUT 6: A FAST WAY TO MULTIPLY BY A FRACTION

When multiplying two numbers, you can double one of the numbers and halve the other before multiplying. To multiply a fraction by a whole number, double the fraction and halve the whole number.

Example 2 $\frac{1}{2}$ × 42 = _____

Step 1: Double the 2 $\frac{1}{2}$ to make it 5

Step 2: Halve the 42 to make it 21

Step 3: 2 $\frac{1}{2}$ × 42 now becomes 5 × 21 = 105

Answer: 2 $\frac{1}{2}$ × 42 = 105

EXERCISES FOR SHORTCUT 6:

1. 3 $\frac{1}{2}$ × 50 = _____

2. 4 $\frac{1}{2}$ × $12 = _____

3. 5 $\frac{1}{2}$ × 11 = _____

4. 2 $\frac{1}{2}$ × 44 = _____

5. When insurance is paid in advance for 3 years, the premium is
2 $\frac{1}{2}$ times the one-year premium. If the premium for one year
is $320, what would it be for 3 years? _____

SHORTCUT 7: THE QUICK WAY TO MULTIPLY BY $\frac{3}{4}$

When multiplying by $\frac{3}{4}$, .75, or 75 percent, this easier method
ignores multiplying by 3 and then dividing by 4.

To multiply by $\frac{3}{4}$ or its equivalent, halve the number and add
it to half the half.

Example One: 3/4 × 84 = _____

Step 1: Half of 84 = 42

Step 2: Half of 42 = 21

Step 3: 42 + 21 = 63

Answer: 3/4 × 84 = 63

Example Two: 75% of $5600 = _____

Step 1: Half of $5600 = $2800

Step 2: Half of $2800 = $1400

Step 3: $2800 + $1400 = $4200

Answer: 75% of $5600 = $4200

EXERCISES FOR SHORTCUT 7:

1. $\frac{3}{4}$ × $9.60 = _____

2. $.75 \times \$4.80 = $ _____

3. 75% of $\$16.00 = $_____

4. $^3/_4 \times \$37.00 = $ _____

5. $.75 \times 1760 = $ _____

EIGHT SHORTCUTS FOR MENTAL DIVISION

SHORTCUT 1: HOW TO DETERMINE A NUMBER'S DIVISIBILITY

To figure out when a number can be divided without a remainder, the following rules should be memorized:

A number is exactly divisible—

by 2, if its last digit is an even number, for example, 1996

by 3, if the sum of its digits is divisible by 3, for example, 396 (3 + 9 + 6 = 18)

by 4, if the last two digits are divisible by 4, for example, 384

by 5, if the last digit is 0 or 5, for example, 225

by 6, if the number is divisible by both 2 and 3, for example, 114

by 8, if the last three digits are divisible by 8, for example, 992

by 9, if the sum of the digits is divisible by 9, for example, 423

by 10, if the last digit is 0, for example, 240

by 12, if the number is divisible by both 3 and 4, for example, 144

Note: The rules for 7 and 11 are too complicated to learn.

EXERCISES FOR SHORTCUT 1:

1. Which of these numbers is not divisible by 3?

   111   183   166   141

2. Which of these numbers is not divisible by 4?

   348   488   834   384

3. Which of these numbers is not divisible by 6?

   282   474   390   256

4. Which of these numbers is not divisible by 9?

   239   234   918   630

5. Which of these numbers is not divisible by 12?

   156   384   468   150

Shortcut 2: Using Simple Factors to Divide

When dividing by a large number, you can get the same result by dividing by the two factors of that number.

Instead of trying to divide a number by 24, break the 24 up into its factors, 2 and 12, or 3 and 8, or 4 and 6. Divide the number by each of the factors to get the answer.

Example $4488 \div 24 =$ _____

Step 1: Break up 24 into 4 and 6

Step 2: Divide 4488 by 4 and get 1122

Step 3: Divide 1122 by 6 and get 187

Answer: $4488 \div 24 = 187$

Variation: $4488 \div 24 =$ _____

Step 1: Break up 24 into 8 and 3

Step 2: Divide 4488 by 8 and get 561

Step 3: Divide 561 by 3 and get 187

Answer: $4488 \div 24 = 187$

Exercises for Shortcut 2

1. Divide 1300 by 25 _____

2. Divide 390 by 15 _____

3. Divide 168 by 14 _____

4. Divide 252 by 36 _____

5. Divide 5824 by 64 _____

Shortcut 3: How to Divide Any Even Number

To divide any even number, we halve both the dividend and the divisor.

Example: $136 \div 8 =$ _____

Use a mental monologue where you say silently: "136 divided by 8 is the same as 68 divided by 4, which is the same as 34 divided by 2, which is 17; so 136 ÷ 8 = 17."

EXERCISES FOR SHORTCUT 3:

1. 192 ÷ 24 = _____

2. 496 ÷ 8 = _____

3. 198 ÷ 18 = _____

4. 322 ÷ 14 = _____

5. 228 ÷ 12 = _____

SHORTCUT 4: DIVIDING BY USING THE DOUBLE-DOUBLE METHOD

In division, if you double the divisor and double the dividend you will get the same answer as if you divided without doubling.

When the divisor contains one half or .5, it is easier to double the number and get a whole number, for example, $3 \frac{1}{2}$ doubled is 7 and 4.5 doubled is 9.

Example One: $36 \div 4 \frac{1}{2} =$ _____

Step 1: Double $4 \frac{1}{2}$ to produce 9

Step 2: Double 36 to produce 72

Step 3: 72 ÷ 9 = 8

    Answer: $36 \div 4 \frac{1}{2} = 8$

Example Two: $145 \div 2 \frac{1}{2} =$ _____

Step 1: Double $2 \frac{1}{2}$ to produce 5

Step 2: Double 145 to produce 290

Step 3: 290 ÷ 5 = 58

EXERCISES FOR SHORTCUT 4:

1. $28 \div 3 \frac{1}{2} =$ _____

2. $300 \div 7 \frac{1}{2} =$ _____

3. $369 \div 1 \frac{1}{2} =$ _____

4. $315 \div 4 \frac{1}{2} =$ _____

5. 42.5 ÷ 2.5 = _____

Shortcut 5: How to Divide Variations of 5 Quickly

Multiplication is easier to do in your head than is division. Certain variations of 5, such as 15, 7.5, 37.5, lend themselves to rapid division by multiplication. These numbers don't always resemble 5.

1. To divide by 5, multiply by 2 and divide by 10.

   Example: Divide 725 by 5
   $$725 \times 2 = 1450, \text{ which when divided by 10 equals } 145.$$

2. To divide by 15, multiply by 2 and divide by 30.

   Example: Divide 135 by 15
   $$135 \times 2 = 270, \text{ which when divided by 30 equals } 9.$$

3. To divide by $7\,\frac{1}{2}$ or 7.5, multiply by 4 and divide by 30.

   Example: Divide 390 by $7\,\frac{1}{2}$
   $$390 \times 4 = 1560, \text{ which when divided by 30 equals } 52.$$

4. To divide by $12\,\frac{1}{2}$ or 12.5, multiply by 8 and divide by 100.

   Example: Divide 175 by 12.5
   $$175 \times 8 = 1400, \text{ which when divided by 100 equals } 14.$$

5. To divide by $37\,\frac{1}{2}$, multiply by 8 and divide by 300.

   Example: Divide 675 by $37\,\frac{1}{2}$
   $$675 \times 8 = 5400, \text{ which when divided by 300 equals } 18.$$

Exercises for Shortcut 5:

1. $795 \div 5 =$ _____
2. $195 \div 15 =$ _____
3. $105 \div 7\,\frac{1}{2} =$ _____
4. $162.5 \div 12.5 =$ _____
5. $300 \div 37.5 =$ _____

Shortcut 6: Dividing by 9

When dividing a number by 9, 99, 999, and so on, a repeating pattern will appear. These repeating patterns will help you check your calculations for accuracy. If there is no repetition, then you have made an error.

If the first number is smaller than the second, the first number will repeat itself.

Examples: 1. 5 ÷ 9 = 0.5555

2. 73 ÷ 99 = 0.737373

3. 18 ÷ 999 = 0.018018

Note: When the first number is larger than the second number (9, 99, 999, and so on), a repeating pattern will still appear, but in a different way.

Examples: 1. 40 ÷ 9 = 4.4444

2. 900 ÷ 99 = 9.090909

3. 2500 ÷ 999 = 2.502502

EXERCISES FOR SHORTCUT 6:

1. 53 ÷ 99 =   _____

2. 763 ÷ 99 =   _____

3. 514 ÷ 9 =   _____

4. 2000 ÷ 999 = _____

5. 760 ÷ 99 =   _____

SHORTCUT 7: DIVIDING BY 15

To divide a number by 15, multiply it by $^2/_3$.

The easiest way to divide a number by 15 is to take $^1/_3$ of the number and double your answer.

Example: 180 ÷ 15 = _____

Step 1: Ignore the zero.

Think of the calculation as 18 ÷ 15

Step 2: Multiply 18 × $^1/_3$ = 6

Step 3: Double the 6 to get 12

Quick Estimate: If we were to divide 180 by 10 (instead of 15) we would get 18 as our answer. Since 15 is larger than 10, the answer will be less than 18; 12 satisfies that requirement and is the answer.

Answer: 180 ÷ 15 = 12

EXERCISES FOR SHORTCUT 7:

1. $240 \div 15 =$ _____
2. $39 \div .15 =$ _____
3. $48 \div 1.5 =$ _____
4. $57 \div 15 =$ _____
5. $36 \div 1.5 =$ _____

SHORTCUT 8: SPEEDING UP DIVISION BY LARGE NUMBERS

It is easier to divide by a single digit than by a two-digit number. By doubling a two-digit number, you can often get a one-digit number to work with.

Example $420 \div 35 =$ _____

Step 1: If we double 35 we get 70, which is essentially a one-digit number, 7. (Remember to later divide by 10.)

Step 2: Double 420 as well, to produce 840.

Step 3: Problem is now $840 \div 7 = 120$

Step 4: Since we divided by 7 and not 70 we must now divide by 10. $120 \div 10 = 12$

Answer: $420 \div 35 = 12$

EXERCISE FOR SHORTCUT 8:

1. $510 \div 15 =$ _____
2. $3600 \div 150 =$ _____
3. $1525 \div 25 =$ _____
4. $1800 \div 45 =$ _____
5. $5100 \div 25 =$ _____

FOUR SHORTCUTS TO USE IN BOTH MULTIPLICATION AND DIVISION

SHORTCUT 1: HANDLING ZEROS IN MULTIPLICATION AND DIVISION

When multiplying with zeros, eliminate the zeros that follow the last figure. Compute. Count up the zeros and tack them on to your partial answer.

Example: Multiply 3200 by 30

Step 1: Remove all three zeros and compute: $32 \times 3 = 96$

Step 2: Return all three zeros to partial answer: 96,000

Answer: $3200 \times 30 = 96,000$

Dividing with zeros: Cancel an *equal* number of righthand zeros when dividing. Do not cancel a zero that is followed by a number.

Example: $8400 \div 120 =$ _____

Step 1: Change to $840 \div 12 =$ _____ (Cancel one zero from each number)

Step 2: Divide $840 \div 12 = 70$

Answer: $8400 \div 120 = 70$

EXERCISE FOR SHORTCUT 1:

Multiply

1. 2300 by 30 _____
2. 1600 by 40 _____
3. 330 by 60 _____
4. 1500 by 120 _____
5. 600 by 90 _____

Divide

6. 2400 by 30 _____
7. 80,000 by 160_____
8. 6000 by 750 _____
9. 10,800 by 90 _____
10. 40,200 by 20 _____

SHORTCUT 2: USING THE RULE OF 25

There are four quarters in a dollar, or $\frac{1}{4}$ of 100 is 25.

Multiplying a Number by 25: To multiply any number by 25, divide the number by 4 instead. Then insert any zeros or move any decimal points as needed. A *quick estimate* will tell you if any zeros or a decimal point are needed.

Example One: 32 × 25 = _____

Step 1: Divide 32 by 4,   32 ÷ 4 = 8

Quick Estimate: Since 32 × 10 = 320, then 32 × 20 would be 640. So, 32 × 25 has to be more than 640.

Step 2: Adding one zero to 8 would give an answer of 80, which is too small. Adding two zeros would produce an answer of 800, which is in line with the quick estimate.

Answer: 800

Alternate Solution: 10 × 25 is 250. So 30 × 25 = 750. Since 32 is a little more than 30, the answer will be a little more than 750, and 800 makes sense.

Example Two: 2.5 × 86 = _____

Step 1: Divide 86 by 4,   86 ÷ 4 = 21.5

Quick Estimate: If 1 × 86 = 86 then 2.5 × 86 has to be more than twice 86.

Step 2: Move the decimal point one place to the right.

Answer: 215

Dividing a Number by 25: To divide a number by 25, multiply the number by 4 and add any zeros (or insert or move any decimal point).

Example One: 900 ÷ 25 = _____

Step 1: Ignore the zeros for now and multiply 9 × 4 = 36

Quick Estimate: Since 100 ÷ 25 = 4, then 900 ÷ 25 would be 9 times 4 or 36. There is no need to add zeros or a decimal point in this example.

Answer: 36

Example Two: 450 ÷ 2.5 = _____

Step 1: Ignore the zero and decimal point for now and multiply 45 × 4 = 180

Quick Estimate: Mentally you can estimate the answer to be more than 100 but less than 200 because,

    100 × 2.5 = 250 (too little, less than 450)

    200 × 2.5 = 500 (too big, more than 450)

    180 × 2.5 = 450 (just right, and the answer)

There is no need to add zeros or a decimal point.

Answer: 180

EXERCISE FOR SHORTCUT 2:

1. Multiply 25 by 88. _____

2. If you have a toy bank with 92 quarters, how much money is that? _____

3. A charity admission ticket is $2.50. If 320 tickets are sold how much money is raised? _____

4. Divide 2,200 by 25. _____

5. A cashier has $95 in quarters. How many quarters does she have? _____

SHORTCUT 3: A FAST WAY TO MULTIPLY OR DIVIDE BY 4

To multiply or divide by the number 4 (or 0.4, 40, 400, and so on) all you need to do is double the number twice (if multiplying) or halve the number twice (if dividing). Note: Ignore any decimal points or zeros when calculating. Insert decimal point or tack on zeros after completing the calculation, if they are needed.

Example One: $1700 \times 0.4 =$ _____

Step 1: Ignore the zeros and decimal point.
    Think of the calculation as 17×4

Step 2: Double the 17 and get 34
    Double the 34 to get 68 (partial answer)

Quick Estimate: Since 0.4 is a little less than $^1/_2$, the answer must be a little less than half of 1700. Look at the partial answer of 68. If we add a zero and make it 680 that would be a little less than half of 1700 (850) and would make sense.

    Answer: $1700 \times 0.4 = 680$

Example Two: $620 \div 40 =$ _____

Step 1: Ignore the zeros.
    Think of the calculation as $62 \div 4 =$ _____

Step 2: Halve the 62, $62 \div 2 = 31$
    Halve the 31, $31 \div 2 = 15.5$ (partial answer)

Quick Estimate: 40 goes into 100 more than twice. 620 is more than six times 100. Therefore, the final answer will be more than 2×6 or 12. The partial answer of 15.5 makes sense.

    Answer: $620 \div 40 = 15.5$

EXERCISES FOR SHORTCUT 3:

1. 85 × 4 =   _____
2. 4 × 83 =   _____
3. 40 × 7.9 =   _____
4. .44 × 400 =   _____
5. 360 × 0.4 =   _____
6. 220 ÷ 4 =   _____
7. 440 ÷ 40 =   _____
8. 17.6 ÷ 0.4 =   _____
9. 24.4 ÷ 4 =   _____
10. .84 ÷ .4 =   _____

Postscript: To multiply or divide a number by 8, you simply multiply or divide the number one more time.

SHORTCUT 4: A QUICK WAY TO MULTIPLY OR DIVIDE BY 5

The numbers 5 and 2 are examples of reciprocals because they equal 10 when multiplied together. To multiply a number by 5, divide the number by 2. To divide a number by 5, multiply the number by 2. Note: Ignore any decimal points or zeros when calculating. These can be taken care of after the calculation.

Example One: 480 × 5 = _____

Step 1: Ignore the zero

Step 2: Divide 480 by 2, 480 ÷ 2 = 240

Quick Estimate: 5 × 500 = 2500, so the answer must be a little less than 2500. Therefore 240 is too small. Tacking on one zero, we come up with 2400, which makes sense.

Answer: 480 × 5 = 2400

Example Two: 22.2 ÷ 5 = _____

Step 1: Ignore the decimal point

Think of the calculation as 222 ÷ 5 = _____

Step 2: Multiply 222 × 2 = 444 (partial answer)

Quick Estimate: 20 ÷ 5 = 4, therefore 22.2 ÷ 5 must be a little more than 4. So, 444 becomes 4.44

EXERCISES FOR SHORTCUT 4:

1. 53 ÷ 5 = _____

2. 85 × 5 = _____

3. 2.1 × 50 = _____

4. 6.8 × 500 = _____

5. 17.5 ÷ 5 = _____

THREE MORE SHORTCUTS TO GAIN MASTERY IN MENTAL MATH

SHORTCUT 1: ADDING QUICKLY IN YOUR HEAD

It is easier to add by 10s than it is to add numbers ending in 6, 7, 8, or 9. When adding numbers ending in 6, 7, 8, or 9, round out the digits to 10; add, then subtract the value you added from the answer:

Example: Add 578 and 216.

Step 1: Change 578 to 580 by adding 2.

Step 2: 580 and 216 are 796.

Step 3: Since you added 2 in Step 1, you must now subtract 2 from 796, 796 − 2 = 794

Answer: 794

EXERCISES FOR SHORTCUT 1:

1. 245 + 57 = _____

2. 354 + 38 = _____

3. $21.49 and $12.33 total $_____

4. $12.66 and $5.48 total $_____

5. $27.88 and $13.25 total $_____

SHORTCUT 2: A SIMPLE METHOD FOR SUBTRACTING IN YOUR HEAD

It is easier to subtract by 10s than by any other number. Take the number to be subtracted and increase it to the nearest multiple of 10. Then increase the other quantity by the same amount.

Example: 624 − 348 = _____

Step 1: Increase 348 to 400 (by adding 52)

Step 2: Increase 624 by the same amount (624 + 52 = 676)

Step 3: 676 − 400 = 276

Answer: 624 − 348 = 276

EXERCISES FOR SHORTCUT 2:

1. 234 − 159 = _____

2. 478 − 259 = _____

3. $40.64 − $1.36 = _____

4. A home purchased for $129,750 was sold for $233,500. How much profit was made on the sale? _____

5. 55 − 16 1/2 = _____

6. 75 + _____ = 123

7. 200 − 37.5 = _____

8. 23.64 − 22.91 = _____

9. 102 − 91 = _____

10. 245 − 189 = _____

SHORTCUT 3: FIGURING OUT WHEN YOUR MONEY WILL DOUBLE

You can compute when your money will double if you divide the number 72 by the rate of interest.

Example: An investment pays 90% interest per year. In how many years will the principal double?

72 ÷ 9 = 8

Answer: 8 years

You can also compute the rate of interest by the "Rule of 72." Divide 72 by the number of years needed to double the principal and you will have the rate of interest.

Example: If $1,000 grows to $2,000 in 12 years, how much simple interest is the investment paying?

72 ÷ 12 = 6

Answer: 6% interest.

EXERCISE FOR SHORTCUT 3:

1. A bond pays 7.2% interest. In how many years will the principal double? _____

2. An investment pays 4.5% tax-free interest per annum. If all the interest is left to accumulate, in how many years will the interest equal the principal? _____

3. If an investment doubles in 6 years, how much interest is it paying? _____

4. Which of these two bonds is paying the higher rate of interest?

    Acme Productions at 9% per annum or
    Zebra Enterprises, which doubles in 10 years _____

5. A tax-free bond doubles in 16 years. What is its rate of interest?

    _____

REPEATING THE DIAGNOSTIC TEST

See how many of these calculations you can complete in three minutes _without_ using pencil and paper.

1. $900 \div 25 =$ _____
2. $45 \times 22 =$ _____
3. $40 \times 7.9 =$ _____
4. $19 \times 25 =$ _____
5. $630 - 485 =$ _____
6. $17.6 \div 0.4 =$ _____
7. $726 \times 11 =$ _____
8. $62 \div 99 =$ _____
9. $170 \times \$10.75 =$ _____
10. $5824 \div 64 =$ _____
11. If an investor pays 8% interest per year in how many years will the principal double? _____

Check your answers with those at the end of this chapter. No doubt you did much better than when you began this chapter. Not only can you do more of the calculations rapidly, but you now know how to do each of them in your head.

MEMENTOS

The shortcuts you have learned will serve two purposes: You will be able to compute quickly and sharpen your memory skills while exercising your mental powers.

This chapter gives you a deftness with numbers that is a valuable plus to memory improvement. Such "paperless" skill in handling numbers will help you in many everyday personal, business, and professional situations such as the following:

- Anticipate the correct change when making a purchase.
- Compute the waiter's tip quickly at the end of the meal.
- Estimate your grocery bill before you reach the check-out.
- Calculate the best deal when borrowing money.
- Invest your money at the highest return easily.
- Foresee next year's tax bill using your current tax bracket.
- Save your employer money by calculating expenses rapidly in advance.
- Develop confidence in your ability to handle numbers.

ANSWER KEY

Diagnostic Test

1.	36	2.	990	3.	316	4.	475	5.	145
6.	44	7.	7986	8.	.6262	9.	$1827.50	10.	91
11.	9 years								

Seven Shortcuts for Mental Multiplication

Shortcut 1

1.	96	2.	840	3.	374	4.	4800	5.	936
6.	12.6	7.	13.5	8.	1280				

Shortcut 2

1.	744	2.	3888	3.	5963	4.	3078	5.	688

Shortcut 3
1.   495   2.   61.6   3.   71.5   4.   102.3   5.   517

Shortcut 4
1.   406   2.   666   3.   558   4.   945   5.   3060

Shortcut 5
1.   395   2.   348   3.   672   4.   425   5.   2670

Shortcut 6
1.   175   2. $54   3.   60 1/2   4.   110   5. $800

Shortcut 7
1. $7.20   2. $3.60   3. $12   4. $27.75   5.   1320

Eight Shortcuts for Mental Division

Shortcut 1
1.   166   2.   834   3.   256   4.   239   5.   150

Shortcut 2
1.   52   2.   26   3.   12   4.   7   5.   91

Shortcut 3
1.   8   2.   62   3.   11   4.   23   5.   19

Shortcut 4
1.   8   2.   40   3.   246   4.   70   5.   17

Shortcut 5
1.   159   2.   13   3.   14   4.   13   5.   8

Shortcut 6
1.   .5353   2.   7.7070   3.   57.1111 4.   2.0020   5.   7.6767

Shortcut 7
1.   16   2.   260   3.   32   4.   3.8   5.   24

Shortcut 8
1.   34   2.   24   3.   61   4.   40   5.   204

Four Shortcuts to Use in Both Multiplication and Division

Shortcut 1

1. 69,000	2. 64,000	3. 19,800	4. 180,000	5. 54,000
6. 80	7. 500	8. 8	9. 120	10. 2010

Shortcut 2

1. 2200	2. $23.00	3. $800	4. 88	5. 380

Shortcut 3

1. 340	2. 332	3. 316	4. 176	5. 144
6. 55	7. 11	8. 44	9. 6.1	10. 2.1

Shortcut 4

1. 10.6	2. 425	3. 105	4. 3400	5. 3.5

Three More Shortcuts to Gain Mastery in Mental Math

Shortcut 1

1. 302	2. 392	3. $33.82	4. $18.41	5. $41.13

Shortcut 2

1. 75	2. 219	3. $39.28	4. $103,750	5. $38 \frac{1}{2}$
6. 48	7. 162.5	8. .73	9. 11	10. 56

Shortcut 3

1. 10 years	2. 16 years	3. 12%	4. Acme	5. 4.5%

Diagnostic Test

1. 36	2. 990	3. 316	4. 475	5. 145
6. 44	7. 7986	8. .6262	9. $1827.50	10. 91
11. 9 years				

Chapter Eleven

Mental Creativity Boosters

Your brain is truly amazing. Besides being able to store endless bits of information, it can search your memory to rearrange these pieces of data or experience to create new unique items and solutions.

In this chapter, we provide you with a "plus" to basic memory improvement. Until now you have tried a variety of memory aids or mnemonics to help you remember names, dates, facts, or numbers. You are now going to explore two other avenues to memory enhancement: intelligence and creativity. These advanced techniques plus the basic mnemonic approach you have already employed will enhance your memory to the maximum. By using all three approaches, you will forge vivid memory links that will make recall faster and more accurate.

Neuroscientists refer to the brain's plasticity—its ability to acquire more information the more you challenge it. The worst thing you can do is let your memory "rest."

Your brain's processing circuits are put to work when you use your intelligence to remember. Learning how to use your brain's neural connections to approach memory and creative tasks will help you function better and on a higher level.

Before you can tap the creative force of your memory you have to understand how various kinds of intelligence affect our creativity and our memory.

IDENTIFYING THE SIX KINDS OF INTELLIGENCE

Most people think of intelligence as some global, all-inclusive kind of superior mental ability. They even think of people with good memories as being smarter than the general population. Respected psychologists prefer to think in terms of *many* kinds of "intelligence." Here are six kinds to consider.

239

1. *Verbal intelligence.* No matter what our work or social position we all require verbal or written communication skills. Improved language ability would certainly help. Language has many functions that include the sounds of words, their meaning, usage, and memory of words (vocabulary). Whether you are a professional writer or a shy talker, you have to flex your linguistic muscles daily. If not, you will suffer from writer's block or self-consciously search for everyday words. As you practice and improve your language ability, you will become more facile with words—more creative in your writing and speaking.

In addition, as your language fluency improves so will your ability to remember word definitions, key terms, and names of things. By improving your proficiency with words, you will also improve your memory and your ability to recall verbal images.

Exercises for Using Verbal Intelligence

EXERCISE 1   Choose a favorite beverage you enjoy. Prepare a 30-second radio commercial for this product. Plan what you will say. Write out a brief outline. Stand in front of a mirror and "deliver" your commercial. See how much of this you can commit to memory.

EXERCISE 2   Look through your daily newspaper. Find some news event or comment that interests you. Write a letter to the editor giving your views on this topic. You may or may not choose to mail this letter. Revise it with an eye toward improving its language and impact. Try to remember the main points.

EXERCISE 3   Tell a friend or family member about a TV program you saw or a book you read. See how accurately you can retell the story. Work on a clear presentation without any need for backtracking.

2. *Logical thinking.* Logic is the ability to think matters through to their natural conclusion. This type of smarts is shown by scientists and others whose work is dependent upon reasoning. It is especially useful in the computer age. Logic entails a prediction of the future based on present or past experiences. When we develop logic intelligence, we also become better able to see the truth of conclusions others make. In addition, we avoid jumping to conclusions of our own. This valuable skill helps us apply reason to solv-

ing our everyday problems. By practicing logic, you are adding order to your memory bank. Logic enhances retrieval of stored memories.

Exercise for Using Logical Thinking

Study this series of letters. Try to find a logical way in which the missing letters have been taken out. The answer is at the end of the chapter.

A B D E F I J K L P Q R S T Y Z A B C J K L M N O P

3. *Spatial Reasoning.* Every time you walk across the room, park your car, rearrange your living room furniture, or put together an unassembled item, you are using spatial abilities. Although artists and sculptors personify the highest functioning of this skill, all of us can improve our level of performance in the spatial world.

This kind of intelligence is the knack for grasping how things orient themselves in space. The ability to imagine what something looks like from different angles is frequently tested on aptitude tests. For example, a cluster of rectangles are joined and the person taking the test has to imagine how these shapes will look from another view. This is a unique form of intelligence. Young people who do poorly in academic subjects often demonstrate a strong spatial intelligence.

One way in which we exercise our brain's spatial ability is by doodling. While talking on the telephone or listening to others at a business meeting, we often doodle—make an aimless or casual scribble, design, or sketch. Instead of just processing the verbal information that is coming our way, we relax by providing our brain with some needed spatial stimulation. The types of doodling vary with the individual: geometric shapes, irregular contour lines, or sketches of people or things. Anyone who has parked a car in a large parking lot without "registering" spatial reasoning knows how frustrating it is to locate the car later.

Exercise for Using Spatial Reasoning

EXERCISE 1   Use your visual memory to picture a room in your house or in your workplace. Mentally remove the furniture, one piece at a time. Visualize the bare room. In your mind's eye picture a totally different room. Use the same furniture to come up with a new look. After a few minutes, return the furniture to the original placement. As you practice this skill, you will not leave out any items and will find it easier to reproduce the actual room in your imagination. This is an excellent memory exercise as well. You have to remember where each piece is placed.

EXERCISE 2   This exercise can be done while you commute to work by car or during a familiar weekend drive. The object is to reduce your mental route to a mental map. As you travel from your home to your destination, visualize the route as it might be seen from a helicopter above.

Mentally draw the route from start to finish on this imaginary map. Pay attention to the route as it changes direction or passes familiar landmarks. When you get home, draw this imaginary route on a piece of paper. Include the compass points on your paper map. Sketch in the landmarks. Compare your map to an actual street or town map. As your brain's spatial reasoning improves, your mental maps will more closely resemble the actual maps. Your memory skills will also develop as you recall the route you took.

EXERCISE 3   Computer games will help you enhance your spatial skills. They are easy to set up, and just a few minutes of use each day will reward you with greater spatial reasoning ability. They activate neurons that process spatial information as they force you to follow and manipulate images on the screen. The games are restorative because they shift your brain out of analytical thought modes and into purely spatial modes. Computer games often have different skill levels. Some even keep a record of your previous scores allowing you to plot your progress.

4. *Knowledge-of-People Skills*. Intelligence is more than just knowledge of the world of ideas and facts. One facet deals with knowledge of the world of persons. The ability to motivate, work with, lead, or care for people is a valuable skill. The traditional I.Q. test ignores this skill for a variety of reasons; mainly because it's difficult to measure.

Interpersonal skill includes understanding people—what motivates them, how to size up their feelings, and how to get along with them. People with such skills are drawn to fields such as sales, teaching, therapy, and politics. This special kind of creative gift has also sparked vast social movements. Charismatic leaders have changed the course of world history.

Many of these interpersonal skills can be learned if there is sufficient motivation. They require a good memory, especially for names and faces. The many how-to-succeed books, tapes, and seminars attest to this. Shy, withdrawn individuals, if motivated, can become more open and extroverted, as the many learning aids claim.

Practicing these interpersonal skills will help you better visualize what you want to remember, especially recognizing people and what they tell you. For example, by increasing your knowledge of people skills, you will be more likely to remember people's names, occupations, family members, preferences, background information, and business associations.

Exercises for Using People Skills

EXERCISE 1   Make an effort to really look at the people you encounter in your daily activities. Too often, people are so concerned about their own appearance or thoughts they ignore details about the people they meet socially or in business. At the end of each day, for one week, jot down the names or positions of all the people you interfaced with on that day. Alongside each name, write a few words describing these individuals. Your descriptions may include, but not be limited to, the person's eye color, hair style, and approximate height, age, and weight. Also list topics discussed, as well as the other person's voice, diction, and general manner. By week's end, you should be able to write a significantly more detailed description and remember it better. Observation skills are basic to memory and creativity.

EXERCISE 2   Each day, attempt to involve a stranger or mere acquaintance in conversation. During your conversation, ask questions that will elicit a response concerning the person's family, home community, career, interests, and aspirations. Force yourself to reveal something about yourself in these areas. These may be people you're unlikely to see again or people you've seen for years but never took an interest in. By increasing your involvement, you will hone your people smarts.

EXERCISE 3   Find someone who needs a little empathy or emotional support. This can be done on the telephone from home or in the workplace. It's not difficult to find a relative, neighbor, colleague, or church member who has lost a loved one, suffered an accident or illness, been terminated from a job, or is planning to move. Give this person a phone call or visit and consciously provide some emotional encouragement and support. Give them an opportunity to vent their feelings as you validate what they're saying and spend most of your time listening. Their gratitude for your interest and concern will encourage you to do more of this.

5. *Intrapersonal Intelligence.* People with a high degree of intrapersonal intelligence know their strengths and weaknesses, their aspirations and fears; in short, they know themselves.

This skill helps people persevere when faced with obstacles or frustrations. They know what they can and what they cannot do to change situations.

This ability is different from others in that it is likely to grow and deepen as we gain life experience. Being introspective, analyzing our desires, and facing our limitations, as well as recognizing our talents all contribute to our self-knowledge.

This special kind of skill is often invisible.

Self-knowledge is a big help in memory improvement. You must know what your own weaknesses and strengths are before you can capitalize on them. Ask yourself a series of questions in order to assess your memory weaknesses and strengths.

For example: Am I comfortable with numbers? Am I more likely to remember what I hear or what I see? Can I visualize technical diagrams in my head? Can I recall them later? Do I have a strong sense of direction? Can I find a place I have visited just once before?

Exercises for Using Intrapersonal Intelligence

EXERCISE 1   Think about your ability to relax. We all have some favored activity that helps us unwind and restore our sense of recreation. It may vary from a hot bath to a game of golf. Make a list of three activities that are your personal favorites for relaxation.

EXERCISE 2   Consider how you are different. Each individual possesses personality traits, desires, and interests that make him or her unique. Think about those personal qualities that make you special—and different from your friends and relatives. List three of them.

EXERCISE 3   We all have goals and aspirations—personal and professional. List three accomplishments you would like to achieve in the next year. By reducing them to writing, you have taken a vital step toward achievement.

6. *Motor Skills*. Kinesthetic or motor skill is no less a form of intelligence than any of the others we have explored. A child who learns to swim or ride a bike at a young age will retain her "memory" of this motor skill throughout life. In a similar way, a good typist is amazed that his fingers "remember" the appropriate keys after years of not typing.

In our culture, people have made a distinction between mind and body. This is fading as we see that in many ways they are one. Your capacity to use your whole body, or parts of your body (such as your hand) to solve problems or to produce a piece of art is as intellectually challenging an activity as figuring out a math problem.

From surgeons to sculptors, we see examples of people who rely on movement skills to solve a problem or fashion a product. Star athletes use their bodies to solve problems—orchestrating winning plays or breaking existing records.

In a similar way, we can use body movement to enhance our memory. For example, try writing a new name with your index finger in the palm of your other hand. The act of using your finger like a pen helps store the name in your brain.

An actor will "walk through" her part in a stage play to reinforce the lines of dialogue she has committed to memory. Walking through the role helps build a series of cues to the various lines.

Golfers and tennis players frequently practice a stroke or movement in their home or office before going out to the links or court. Building up your kinesthetic intelligence will boost your memory power as well.

Exercise for Using Motor Skills

Take a few minutes to walk across a room or down a street. Pay careful attention to every movement you make with your feet, knees, thigh muscles, hands, arms, shoulders, and so on. Pretend you are teaching a recently recovered accident victim to walk again. What suggestions would you make as to balance, motion, and coordination? What part does your brain play in this? After you have thought about this, go on to create some new dance step. Use your memory of other steps to create it.

HOW YOUR MEMORY BENEFITS FROM CREATIVITY

Now that you better understand intelligence, you can use that knowledge to focus on the main idea of this chapter—how to use creativity to strengthen memory.

Creativity involves seeing the usual things in unusual ways. Creativity involves making unexpected combinations of conventional elements and bringing unity to disorder. We are all capable of it. It is not the private domain of artists or inventors. Even more important, we can all exercise and enhance our innate capacity for creative thought.

For example, you may be struggling with a problem for days looking for a solution. Suddenly, a lightbulb turns on in your head and the solution appears. Most problems do not lend themselves to such simplistic solutions. More often, we feel close to the final answer or the feel of the idea but it eludes us. Our brain has to sift through its memory bank of raw information before it can come up with an answer or solution.

Problem solving depends on memory. Stored in your memory bank are potential cues and clues to solve problems.

Ten Creative Methods to Help with Problem Solving

When the solution to a problem eludes you, try one of these methods. Some may appear familiar, and others seem new. Some may even seem contradictory because we never know just what will work. Try them all.

1. *Generalize.* Go beyond the set of problems you are facing to a more general area or domain, for example, instead of focusing on the one specific problem that presents itself at the office—the staff's resentment about needing to punch in and out at the time clock—look to the generalized area of staff morale. By pushing your thinking from the narrow problem to the more global area you are more likely to arrive at a mutually acceptable solution.

2. *Specialize.* Look for details in the problem that may point to a solution. Is there a certain characteristic that all the elements have in common? This common element may hold the secret to solving the larger problem. Look carefully at details that may fine-point the issue and reveal the solution.

3. *Analogize.* Compare or contrast this situation to another similar one. In the courtroom, judges and lawyers frequently look for precedents established in similar cases. A previous case may involve problems similar to the current case. By establishing an analogy between the two, a solution can be worked out.

4. *Miniaturize.* Try to find a smaller problem within the larger one. Then build on that solution to solve the larger problem. "Bite off" a small piece of the larger one and work at it. Arriving at a successful solution to this smaller problem will often transfer to the larger one.

5. *Change direction.* Come up with several possible solutions and go off in different directions from this central point. Don't get stuck on one possible solution. You may assume the only way to improve earnings is to lower the unit price. One creative solution would be to raise the price but offer additional service, more choices, or a longer guarantee at the new price.

6. *Accessorize.* Add features to the basic product if it is moderately successful at what it does. Don't stop when a satisfactory product or service is developed. Add a new application or design to make it more successful. Search the competition for ideas.

7. *Be flexible.* Allow your brain to flex its muscles just as your limbs do when you're at the gym. Develop the ability to be flexible in the exercise of several of your brain's functions. Creativity is not the use of just one ability. It is the exploration of a variety of approaches. Use one approach and then another. Don't get locked into a pattern that is fixed. Instead, stay loose and flexible.

8. *Suspend judgment.* Learn to silence that inner voice that tells you "it can't be done" or "it was never done that way before." Although not every idea is necessarily a good one, your voice of judgment can make it hard for you to believe that you have had any good ideas at all.

9. *Incubate.* You need time to digest all you have gathered. This incubation stage comes after you have weighed and examined all the relevant pieces and pushed your brain to its limit. It is a pas-

sive stage, when the mind's unconscious works on it. The answer may come to you in a dream, while in the shower, or when driving your car. Your unconscious mind allows your ideas to freely combine with other thoughts in your head.

10. *Realize.* The final stage is action. In this stage you realize what you have and go with it. Translating your idea into reality makes it more than just another thought. It becomes an idea—useful to you and to others. This is the point that you have waited for. The light is on but you must give it the heat of action.

This list of creative methods simplifies a process that is fluid and can take many forms. Some methods seem contradictory. All are complex.

Your brain has a capacity to learn in direct proportion to the challenges you put before it. The exercises in this chapter provide prods and nudges to creativity expansion on your part. You will recognize many of the elements of creative capability as the same ones we use to develop a strong memory.

- *Association*—relating unknown objects or ideas to those already known.

- *Classification*—grouping of objects and ideas according to criteria.

- *Organizing*—arranging thoughts and materials according to purpose.

- *Facility*—quick, easy generation of ideas and images. All you need do is apply these creativity exercises and let those circuits strengthen to become better at their normal functioning.

EXERCISES FOR CREATIVITY TRAINING

Now that you have a basic understanding of how creative ability works, we are going to give you some basic training in exercising your creativity. Many of the following exercises tap your memory skills in such areas as association, visualization, observation, an categorizing. As you have seen, creativity and memory go hand in hand.

Visual Images

Our ability to recall and use words is basic to our communication skills. The ability to recall and visualize images in space is essential to creative thinking.

Many people don't think they have the ability to visualize spatial relations. All of us can improve this important skill with a little practice and concentration. Repeat this exercise several times until you can do it easily and accurately. At first you may want to check your response by using a pencil and paper.

Exercises for Visual Images

Visualize a row of three coins. The coin in the center is a penny and those on the ends are dimes.

Mentally move the penny to the right end of the row.

What is the order of the coins now?

Now, move the coin in the center to the left end and the coin that was on the left end to the right end. What does the row of coins look like now?

This time visualize two rows of coins. The first row has three dimes and the second row has three pennies.

Take the dime on the left end and trade it with the penny in the middle.

Then take the penny on the right end of the second row and trade it for the dime in the middle of the first row.

Now take the coin on the left end of the first row and trade it for the coin in the middle of the second row.

What is the order of coins in the two rows now?

Note: If you had trouble visualizing the various moves, try reading one at a time and then close your eyes, fixing it in your memory. Concentrate until you "see" it clearly in your mind's eye. Do this for each move until you see the final pattern of coins. Do this slowly to ensure accuracy.

Answers are at the end of the chapter.

Creative Language

Memory assists us in building and retaining a large vocabulary. How we use the language we know depends on our creative ability. In these exercises, you will use your creative ability with language to complete the tasks.

Exercises for Creative Language

1. Imaginative store owners have used creativity in coming up with amusing and memorable names for their businesses. Here are some examples:

Maternity clothes—Coming Attractions

Beauty salon—The Mane Event

Resale shop—Repeat Performance

Assume that you are going to operate one of these business establishments. Think of a clever store name that is both creative and memorable:

Pizza parlor— _____

Dry cleaner—_____

Bakery—_____

Deli— _____

Greeting card store— _____

Shoe store— _____

Diner— _____

Fitness center—_____

2. In order to overcome language barriers, certain nonverbal symbols have become commonplace. For example, "No Smoking" is expressed as a cigarette with a red circle and diagonal slash superimposed. The symbol for a hotel is shown as a horizontal figure on a bed.

Assume that you have been retained to design information signs for an international exposition. Your symbols cannot use words and must be clear, distinctive, and easy to remember.

Come up with a simple drawing that will represent the international symbol for each of these items:

Parking lot

Shopping center

Bus stop

Ticket office

Interpreter

Barber shop

Beauty salon

Post office

Visualization

If you want to remember certain objects, it is best to visualize the item as well as the word. Visualization can be improved with practice. Try these exercises that depend on your ability to visualize or "picture" what is sought.

Exercises for Visualization

1. Study these letters as they appear in each column. Then, make up four words, as follows:

Two *four*-letter words, one made up from letters in column one and the second made up from letters in column two.

One *five*-letter word from the letters in column three.

One *thirteen*-letter word made up of *all* the letters.

Column One	*Column Two*	*Column Three*
V D O E	E I N M	T A S T R
_____	_____	_____

2. Each of these pairs of letters are the first two letters of words representing food items on a shopping list. List the ten food items alongside the pairs of letters:

BA _____   BE _____   CE _____

ON _____   OR _____   PL _____

SQ _____   TO _____   ST _____

TU _____

Answers are at the end of the chapter.

Auditory Concentration

Many people remember what they hear better than what they see. Much creative work is based on capitalizing on the everyday sounds we all encounter but don't really take in. We are usually too busy attending to our other senses to hear everything going on around us.

Exercise for Auditory Concentration

For this exercise, first imagine the following sounds:

A fire engine

Screeching auto brakes

A car alarm

Footsteps on a bare floor

Voices in another room

Dogs barking

A commuter bus motor

Then, take a walk on a busy street or ride on a busy street with your car window down. Pay attention to the sounds that are out there.

Aim to identify seven different sounds. They may be from this list or they may be other sounds. List them here:

1. _____
2. _____
3. _____
4. _____
5. _____
6. _____
7. _____

Analytical Thinking

In problem solving, logical and analytical thinking are needed to process information used to arrive at solutions. We are sometimes overwhelmed by the large amount of information that often accompanies problem situations. We don't know how to make sense of the information surrounding the problem.

Exercise for Analytical Thinking

Some kind of systematic procedure is needed to make sense of the data we have. For this exercise, set up four columns—one for each brother. From the family data provided, you want to find out which brother is the teacher and where he lives. Answers are at the end of the chapter.

The Four Brothers

1. The four brothers were born in Illinois.
2. Dave married Doris.
3. Danny moved to California.
4. The doctor brother moved to New Jersey.
5. Dan married Debra.
6. Deidre married the doctor brother.
7. The dentist brother married Dora.
8. The computer analyst brother moved to Connecticut.
9. Dean married Deidra.
10. Doris lives in Texas.

Teacher brother—_____   Teacher lives in—_____

Creative Adaptation

One way to exercise your creative abilities is to come up with a different ending to a familiar story that is well known in our culture. For each of these familiar stories change either the ending or a basic element of the story.

Example: *Hansel and Gretel*. Make them both computer whiz kids who venture out into the woods with a laptop computer, which keeps them from getting lost. The evil witch tries to electrocute them with her microwave oven but the children hot-wire it in such a way as to temporarily stun the witch. They then use the Internet to get assistance.

Exercise for Creative Adaptation

Use your creative talents to adapt these familiar stories:

Sleeping Beauty   _____

_____

Tom Sawyer   _____

_____

Beauty and the Beast   _____

_____

Aladdin   _____

_____

King Arthur   _____

_____

Numerical Relationships

You can bring the world of numbers into your creative orbit with this exercise. Fit numbers into the blank spaces so that all the equations equal 20. The equations have more than one solution so that you can individualize your response.

Example: $\underline{12} + \underline{3} - \underline{5} + \underline{10} = 20$

1. $\underline{} \times \underline{} + \underline{} = 20$
2. $\underline{} - \underline{} + \underline{} - \underline{} = 20$
3. $\underline{} \times \underline{} + \underline{} - \underline{} = 20$
4. $\underline{}\,\underline{} \times \underline{} - \underline{} = 20$
5. $\underline{}\,\underline{} + \underline{} - \underline{} = 20$

Exercises for Numerical Relationships

1. Now use the same grid but have the five equations add up to 35.

2. Look at these numbers for 30 seconds. Then close the book and try to remember all the *different* numbers. Several numbers appear more than once. You need only to remember the seven different numbers.

4	8	3
6	10	6
8	5	10
3	12	4

Creative Writing

Throughout literature, certain mythical animals have been created combining body parts from existing animals.

Examples:

Centaur—half man and half horse

Griffin—part lion and part eagle

Sphinx—a woman's head and a lion's body

Exercise for Creative Writing

Create three of your own mythological animals. Give names to your made-up menagerie members. Also, ascribe some characteristics or traits to your animal. In Greek mythology the sphinx was a female monster noted for killing anyone unable to answer its riddle.

	Animal	*Physical Appearance*	*Characteristics*
1.	_____	_____	_____
2.	_____	_____	_____
3.	_____	_____	_____

Verbal Perception

How we "see" or perceive words provides another creative cue to memory. Sometimes pairs of words share a common element that triggers recall. At other times, we search to build a word or name from a mere fragment.

For example, the words "piano" and "lock" share a word that can be associated with each of them: "key."

Exercises for Verbal Perception

EXERCISE 1   List the common word each of these pairs share:

ship—playing cards _____

training exercise—carpentry tool _____

stage—airplane _____

flashlight—artillery _____

tuft of hair—canal device_____

snooze—fabric surface _____

EXERCISE 2   Here is an opportunity to look at some ordinary objects and find ways in which they are the same. Many problems can be solved if you search your memory to find a commonality between or among situations or things. For example: book—window

  a. both can be opened and closed

  b. both are usually rectangular in shape

See if you can come up with a least two common elements for each of these word pairs or trios:

  1. tree—dime   _____

  2. bucket—egg _____

  3. hat—blanket _____

  4. paper clip—thumb tack _____

EXERCISE 3   Sometimes we have to build a structure around a fragment. Following are six two-letter word fragments. See if you can build six words around each of these word fragments. The two letters may appear at the beginning, middle, or end of the word. The first one is done for you.

OR	*MA*	*EN*
1. b**OR**der	1. _____	1. _____
2. _____	2. _____	2. _____

3. _____   3. _____   3. _____
4. _____   4. _____   4. _____
5. _____   5. _____   5. _____
6. _____   6. _____   6. _____

RI	*NT*	*CT*
1. _____	1. _____	1. _____
2. _____	2. _____	2. _____
3. _____	3. _____	3. _____
4. _____	4. _____	4. _____
5. _____	5. _____	5. _____
6. _____	6. _____	6. _____

Answers are at the end of the chapter.

Logical Reasoning

The following two logic exercises require you to read carefully and use the information you're given. In the first exercise, remember that *one* person can be a mother, daughter, and grandmother to three different people. In the second, you may want to use scrap paper and make a five-column chart to check off the clues.

Exercises for Logical Reasoning

EXERCISE 1   Sitting around the Thanksgiving dinner table were one great-grandfather, two grandfathers, one grandmother, three fathers, two mothers, four children, three grandchildren, one great-grandchild, one brother, three sisters, two husbands, two wives, one father-in-law, one mother-in-law, two brothers-in-law, three sisters-in-law, two uncles, three aunts, two cousins, one nephew, and two nieces. What is the smallest number of people who could have been present?
Answer: _____

EXERCISE 2   An apartment house is occupied by five people. They all live on different floors, have different jobs, and were born in different states. From the following clues, work out the job and birthplace of each person and the floor on which he or she lives. Write your answers on the lines below.

> Sal lives on the floor above the dancer.
>
> The architect lives one floor above the man from Pennsylvania.
>
> The person on the fourth floor was born in Florida.
>
> Peter lives on the first floor.
>
> Carl lives on the floor between the engineer and the man from South Dakota.
>
> The person who was born in Washington lives on the fifth floor.
>
> The person born in California is not an architect.
>
> The baker lives on the second floor.
>
> The man living on the floor between Butch and the chemist was born in Pennsylvania.
>
> Fred does not live on the third floor.
>
> The dancer lives on the fourth floor.

	Name	*Job*	*Birthplace*
1.	_____	_____	_____
2.	_____	_____	_____
3.	_____	_____	_____
4.	_____	_____	_____
5.	_____	_____	_____
6.	_____	_____	_____

Answers are at the end of the chapter.

This last exercise is similar to the one you did under "Analytical Thinking." We end with this exercise because it offers your creative memory the greatest challenge.

MEMENTOS

1. Many of the same skills needed to be creative are required for good memory. They are the ability to make associations, classify, organize, and generate images quickly.

2. There are ten creative methods described in this chapter that can be learned and put to use. They are as follows:

> Generalizing—look beyond the specific to a more global view.
>
> Specializing—look for details in the problem that may point to the solution.
>
> Seeing analogies—compare and contrast the situation to one more familiar to you.
>
> Biting off small pieces—work on just one aspect of the larger problem as a first step.
>
> Changing focus—go off in a different direction to find a solution.
>
> Adding accessories—add new applications or services to your product to make it better.
>
> Being flexible—try a variety of approaches and don't let yourself get boxed in by a rigid approach.
>
> Suspending judgment—listen to your inner voice before abandoning a project.
>
> Incubating an idea—take time to let all the information you gathered digest and develop.
>
> Taking action—realize what you have and go with it.

3. There are different kinds of intelligence. Six different types were discussed in this chapter. They are as follows:

> Language skills—using verbal or written communication.
>
> Logical thinking—applying reasoning to solving everyday problems.
>
> Spatial reasoning—grasping how things orient themselves.
>
> Understanding people—developing the ability to work with people.
>
> Understanding yourself—knowing your own strengths and weaknesses.
>
> Movement skills—using motor skills to enhance your life.

4. Creative training exercises can sharpen memory skills.

ANSWER KEY

The Six Kinds of Intelligence

EXERCISE FOR USING LOGICAL THINKING

First, one letter: C. Then, two letters: GH.

Then, three letters: MNO. Then, four letters: UVWX, etc.

Creative Training Exercises

EXERCISES FOR VISUAL IMAGES

1. Dime, Penny, Dime.
2. Dime, Penny, Dime.

   Penny, Penny, Dime.

EXERCISES FOR VISUALIZATION

1. dove, mine   start or tarts   demonstrative
2. bananas, onions, squash, turnip, beets, oranges, tomatoes, celery, plums, strawberries

EXERCISE FOR ANALYTICAL THINKING

Dave, Texas.

Exercises for Numerical Relationships

2. 3, 4, 5, 6, 8, 10, 12

EXERCISES FOR VERBAL PERCEPTIONS

1. deck, drill, wing, battery, lock, nap
2. 1. Both round, rough outer edge, can be recycled, can grow in value if rare
   2. Found on farms, can carry something, sold in stores, round in girth
   3. Used as covering, can be made of wool, at least one in every household, used by all age groups, can cause emotional attachment

    4. Made of metal, found in offices, can cause injury, used with papers, cold to the touch

3. OR = border, cordon, porter, ordain, morass, sordid

   MA = remain, remand, amazed, remake, matter, matrix

   EN = tendon, renter, intend, mentor, sentry, woolen

   RI = ripper, priced, ripple, strict, shrine, scrimp

   NT = antler, recant, intend, resent, entire, untied

   CT = indict, strict, action, factor, direct, rector

EXERCISES FOR LOGICAL REASONING

1. Seven people.

2. Sal is an engineer, was born in Washington, and lives on the fifth floor.

    Peter is a chemist, was born in California, and lives on the first floor.

    Fred is a baker, was born in Pennsylvania, and lives on the second floor.

    Carl is a dancer, was born in Florida, and lives on the fourth floor.

    Butch is an architect, was born in South Dakota, and lives on the third floor.

Chapter Twelve

Mental Aerobics Workouts

"Use it or lose it."

This often-repeated adage of the physically fit is applicable, as well, to those yearning to remain *mentally* fit. A strong memory is kept strong by constantly exercising one's ability to remember.

Until now, the emphasis has been on strategies and skills for reinforcing your ability to remember names, faces, dates, facts, numbers, and so on. In this chapter, the emphasis is on keeping your mind limber, agile, and alert in a variety of mental activities.

In a gym or health club, people perform many exercises that have no specific outcome such as walking on a treadmill or riding a stationary bicycle. They get nowhere on the treadmill or on the bicycle, but they do exercise muscles that help them keep fit and better able to perform the physical challenges of their everyday life.

So, too, with this chapter. The exercises here are designed to strengthen those mental skills that you need in your daily life, such as paying attention, concentrating, categorizing, using mental pegs, and memorizing.

You are shown a complete mental workout. As with any soundly conceived physical exercise program, the strenuous but invigorating exercises will be preceded by a warm-up and followed by a cool-down exercise.

We begin with the warm-up—seven exercises or daily procedures that we suggest you work at every day. They provide your brain with enough stimulation to keep it from becoming lazy and lethargic.

Some of the warm-ups should be done as soon as you open your eyes in the morning. They will serve to get the cobwebs out of your head and prepare your mind for a stimulating and productive day. Other warm-up procedures can be done at any time.

The main thrust of this chapter is the basic workout, which contains more challenging mental exercises that will stretch your memory muscles.

The chapter concludes with a cool-down exercise that you can perform every night, just before going to sleep. This will help you maximize your mind's ability and give you increased confidence in your mental powers.

SEVEN DAILY WARM-UP EXERCISES FOR MENTAL AGILITY

These seven warm-up exercises will help you jump-start your day with a sharp memory. Some of them can be done during those small pockets of time that are ordinarily overlooked, such as standing in line, waiting for transportation, or waiting for a meeting to start. The first one can be done even before you start your day—at the breakfast table.

1. How to Sweep the Clutter from Your Mind

Many people begin the day with a cluttered brain. No wonder they can't focus their *attention*—the first characteristic of a good memory. People with cluttered minds are referred to frequently as "scatterbrained" or "absentminded."

This exercise will clear out the litter in your mental attic. It resembles meditation, a form of mental discipline that has been used by millions of people for hundreds of years.

You will be able to clear your mind of any anxiety or confusion so you can start the day clearheaded and with an open, alert outlook.

- Choose a time and place—soon after arising is best; any place where you won't be disturbed is fine.
- Pick a comfortable sitting position—on the floor, on a cushion, or in a chair. Your hands should be in your lap.
- Concentrate on your breathing. Count each exhaled breath up to ten and then start over. Pay attention to the rise and fall of your stomach as you breathe.

- Close your eyes and tune into what's going on in your head. Try to turn off this mental activity. Aim for an empty, clean feeling in your brain. Erase all anxious thoughts about the past and the future. Concentrate on the here and now—on your breathing and nothing else.

- Limit your session to five minutes. Use a timer or a watch with an alarm so that you can keep track of the time.

That's it. At first the five minutes will seem like an eternity. Stick with it. Making this warm-up an integral part of your morning routine will get your memory off to a flying start.

2. Five Ways to Exercise Your Attention Muscles

We have five senses: sight, sound, taste, smell, and touch. As mentioned in Chapter 1, these senses can help us forge memory links, for example, Rose uses a floral perfume; Dr. Coffey reminds me of my morning beverage.

The following exercise will help you sharpen your ability to focus your attention, one sense at a time.

Choose one type of attention sense you want to concentrate on for a day. Choose one day of the work week for each sense. For example:

Monday is sight.

Tuesday is sound.

Wednesday is taste.

Thursday is smell.

Friday is touch.

From the moment you wake up to the time you prepare for bed, try to tune into that sense.

Assume you choose "touch" for Friday; concentrate on how often you use your sense of touch that day. Think about your legs and feet as you walk feel your car steering wheel; touch the doorknob of your house with greater concentration.

After doing this for a while, link up a particular errand or appointment with the feel of your spoon, keys, change, and the like.

This skill is acquired by constant practice. Once mastered, you will have a built-in reminder for many of the things you have to remember. By waking up awareness of all your senses, you will lay the foundation for a more efficient memory.

3. Use Categories to Hone Your Mental Skills

You can do this exercise at any time of the day. The only equipment you need is a single sheet of paper and something to write with. Each time you do this, choose any five-letter word that comes to mind. It should have five different letters. Then, select a category such as Foods, Cities, Birds, Flowers, Islands.

Draw four lines down the paper and four lines across. This will give you five boxes down and five across. Write one letter of your word atop each column, for example, CHORD.

Now, refer to your category. Let's assume you chose Birds. Your paper, after much concentration would look something like this:

C	H	O	R	D
canary	hawk	owl	robin	dove
cardinal	heron	ostrich	raven	duck
cuckoo	hummingbird	oriole	roadrunner	dodo
chickadee				
chicken				

You may not be able to come up with 25 bird names nor will you always be able to fill even a single column. That's not important, however. What is vital is that you exercise your memory by trying to find as many items as you can.

This exercise will warm up your mind all day long as you mentally go back to your list of categories. Refer to it in spare moments and add to your list.

The next day, change the five-letter word and also the category. You can do this in your spare minutes—while waiting for an activity to start or while waiting in line. It's a lot better than anxiously reliving some past hurt or some future event you dread. More importantly, you will be honing your memory ability.

4. Use Anagrams to Strengthen Word Recognition and Word Memory

Words made by transposing the letters of one word into another are called anagrams. For example, MARCH is an anagram of CHARM. Some words can be transposed into three or four other words, as in

SHARE

SHEAR

HEARS

HARES

Anagrams are a great mental warm-up because they are based on word recognition and word memory. As you construct anagrams, you are exercising these two abilities.

For variety, put letter groups of five letters on index cards—one five-letter group per card. Take one of these cards and see how many anagrams you can construct from those letters. Keep the cards on hand to work on during your spare time.

Just making up these cards from five-letter words will provide you with mental stimulation. The cards can be used over and over, if you write the new words on a separate piece of paper. Here are a few letter groups to help you get started:

ERDAS   PEGAS   STELA   ADELS

5. Amaze Your Friends with Statistics

You can amaze your friends or fellow workers while performing a mental warm-up.

Select some numerical facts or statistics that are of interest to you and memorize them. These can be baseball batting averages, populations of major cities, or the length of major rivers. Try bringing them into a conversation and quote them.

This is good practice and you get an immediate positive feedback from your listeners about your memory. In most cases, you will quickly forget the data because you won't transfer them into your long-term memory—unless you choose to and use reinforcement techniques.

It doesn't matter if you choose to retain or forget the data after using them. The important thing is that you proved to yourself that you can memorize abstract information when you want to. Impressing your listeners is merely the motivation for learning the statistical information in the first place.

For variety, try learning non-numerical facts such as the names of recent vice presidents and their years in office or Hollywood Oscar winners from the previous year.

6. Use a Clock to Develop Your Sense of Concentration

When you wake up in the morning, include this exercise in your warm-up routine:

- Choose some thought that you want to recall at a fixed time later that day. It can be an errand or a thing; for example, call California at 11:00 A.M. Eastern Standard Time, or at 10:30 A.M. I will think about my cat.

- Concentrate on this image and fix it firmly in your mind. This is the hard part.

- Dismiss it from your mind after this and go about your regular business. Do not make a conscious effort to return to this thought until the appointed time.

At the end of the day check to see if you brought it to mind at the appointed time. With practice you will learn to do this. The obvious transference will be your new ability to keep track of appointments and dates.

It's helpful to visualize the hands of the clock or watch you are likely to be consulting at that time.

After a month of daily practice you should be quite good at this. It's helpful if you practice this exercise with a friend or family member. You should each have your own hour and item. Then compare notes.

This exercise further develops your sense of concentration and helps you master the art of keeping appointments and other time-related responsibilities.

7. *How to Use Interactive Imagery in Your Daily Life*

Mental pictures are enhanced if you combine them, when appropriate. Practice this before you take on some complicated memory task.

For example, a salesman is driving to his next call. He wants to remember some of the things the customer spoke about last time. He concentrates on some interactive images he created during his last call. He wants to have them at his fingertips for this follow-up visit.

The customer mentioned that he and his wife enjoy sailing. His wife is a judge and he, the customer, enjoys playing tennis. The salesman created the following interactive image:

There are two people on the deck of a sailboat. The customer is wearing tennis shorts and his wife is wearing a black robe. They are both enjoying their sailboat.

Alternate images could have been:

The customer is holding a tennis racket while his wife holds a gavel. They are both laughing on the deck of a sailboat.

This imaginary sailboat has a black robe for a sail and a tennis racket for a rudder.

These single, vivid, amusing interactive images are easier to remember than a list of separate items: customer-tennis; wife-judge; both like sailing. By making them interactive you are reducing the number of individual items you have to remember. This alone will make it easier to remember. Putting them together into a cartoon-like picture further enhances your chances of remembering them. This is both a memory technique and a perfect warm-up before you go on to remember more technical items such as prices quoted, model numbers, and inventory.

TEN WEEKLY BASIC WORKOUT EXERCISES

These ten exercises are the heart of your mental aerobics program. They are quite varied in format and in level of difficulty. Start by doing just one or two. Gradually build up to including all of them in your week's workout.

1. Build Concentration with Number Expansion

This is one of those exercises that can be done anywhere at any time. It comes in handy while commuting to and from work, waiting in line, or when trying to get your mind off a repetitive activity.

The value of this exercise is that you must concentrate and also use some visual imagery as you "see" the numbers.

- Count backward from 100 in 7's. After some success try starting at 200 and subtract by a two-digit number.

- Keep doubling a number for as long as you can. For example, 4, 8, 16, 32, 64, 128 . . .

- Count in 9's, as in 9, 18, 27, 36, 45, 54 . . . Then, try a two-digit number.

- Convert some fractions into decimals. Do this by dividing the denominator into the numerator. For example: $^3/_4$ = .75. What about $^1/_8$, or $^5/_8$, or $^3/_{16}$?

- Add consecutive numbers mentally, such as 1 + 2 + 3 + 4 + 5 + 6 + = ____

After practicing these, you will, no doubt, make up some number expansion of your own.

The idea is to do them in your head with accuracy and some degree of speed. You're remembering these numbers in place.

2. Improve Your Memory Using Ordinary Recipes

Here's an exercise you can perform while preparing a favorite dish.

- Lay out the ingredients you will be using. Make a mental note about each one. Where did you get it? Where did you place it on the counter?

- Announce the name of each item as you reach for it.

- Become aware of the feel, smell, and/or appearance of each ingredient.

- Visualize the quantities needed of each; for example, 3 eggs, $^1/_2$ cup sugar, and so on.

- Re-create the sequence in which you use the ingredients.
- Mentally list the processes you will use. Reduce them to one word. Make a chain of these words, such as stir, mix, blend, beat, pour, bake.
- Recall the recipe while the dish is baking, cooking, or chilling.
- Refer to the written recipe and make corrections, if any, from your mental recitation.
- Pretend you are giving the recipe to a friend; go over it with the corrections, if any.

By making this exercise a regular habit, you will be improving your memory while engaged in a totally different task.

Don't limit it to cooking. Whenever you are engaged in any recreational or craft activity, be aware of the various steps. Say them to yourself. Do it with woodworking measures, musical selections, and the like.

3. Sharpen Your Mind by Opening a Combination Lock

Combination locks don't use a key, but they do depend on your memory of three-number combinations to open. Not remembering or confusing the numbers or sequence can be frustrating and humiliating. Following these steps will exercise your mind while doing away with the need for keys, which are sometimes misplaced.

- Begin by recording the combination as insurance in case you forget it.
- Practice getting the feel of the lock and spinning the dial.
- Memorize the sequence of directions; for example, right, left, passing the number once, and then right.
- Visualize the numbers in their positions. Associate the numbers with ages of your life or years or some other vivid memory.
- Pay attention to the mathematical properties of the numbers (doubles, odd-even, high-lower-lower).
- Use your mind's eye to visualize the process without handling the lock.
- Practice opening the lock after not using it for an extended period of time.

In this activity, you are using visualization and association to hold on to your recall of the numbers and their sequence. These are two vital aspects of memory that benefit from exercise.

Using a combination lock will also help reinforce your memory of numbers.

4. How to Use a Calendar to Enhance Your Memory Potential

Remembering appointments is an easy task if there are just a few of them. Busier people face a more daunting task. Everyone needs to use a calendar.

The most meticulously kept calendar is useless, however, unless it is referred to on a regular basis so that you can transfer the appointments from your calendar into your memory. Follow these steps and exercise your mental datebook:

- Force yourself to look at your calendar twice a day. To get into the habit, put a small dot in each day's "box" each time you look at it. Once the habit of consulting the calendar twice daily is firmly established, you need not make the dots.

- Use the calendar to record appointments, birthdays, bills to be paid, calls to be made, and so forth. Also, use it to record the names of new people you meet. This is helpful when you want to recall the name a month from now and it has gone out of your head. You should also note phone numbers that you looked up so that you won't have to repeat that process in the future. Periodically transfer this information to your personal telephone directory.

- Every Sunday night look at your appointments and reminders for the week ahead. Walk away from the calendar and see how many appointments you can recall. Do the same thing each morning. Each evening you should look at what you have planned for the next day.

- On your way to work or to your first appointment, review the day's calls. Do this mentally and check your recall with your calendar.

- Reread your calendar at day's end to review phone numbers, new names, and other entries you want to commit to memory or record in some other place, or both.

Using the calendar in this way will reinforce your memory potential while keeping track of your appointments. By jotting down new data on your calendar, such as names and phone numbers, you will be capitalizing even further on calendar use.

5. Learn to Use Body-Parts Pegs to Fortify Your Mind

We are aware of our bodies and surely can't forget their major parts. This exercise depends upon your use of *pegs* that are linked to various parts of your body.

In doing this exercise, you must first identify these ten body parts in sequence. We are going to go from top to bottom. Study this list of body parts, the number, and the related item listed alongside it.

Number	*Body Part*	*Related Item*
1.	head	hat
2.	eyes	glasses
3.	mouth	teeth
4.	shoulders	pads
5.	chest	pocket
6.	waist	belt
7.	hips	pocket
8.	knees	pads
9.	ankles	socks
10.	feet	shoes

These ten parts of your body have become memory pegs. Learning them is easy because they're already in your knowledge bank. The only challenge is learning to link them with the appropriate number. The fact that "shoulders" and "knees" both have the same related item, "pads," is not a problem because shoulder pads and knee pads look different.

The reason for learning the related item is that sometimes it is easier to link what you want to remember with "belt" than it would be with "waist." Both "waist" and "belt" tell you it is number 6 in the list of ten items.

Exercise for Body-Parts Pegs

Practice by listing the numbers from one to ten—on paper or in your mind. Then match the correct body part and its related item with the number. Close the book and do it now. See each peg vividly in your mind.

Remembering a List of Daily Errands

Assume you want to do these errands in exactly this order:

1. Get gas for the car.
2. Go to the bank.
3. Pick up a newspaper.
4. Buy milk.
5. Pick up the repaired watch.
6. Drop off dry cleaning.
7. Attend the department-store sale.
8. Buy towels.
9. Make a duplicate car key.
10. Have lunch with a friend.

By using either the body-parts list or the related-item pegs, you can commit these ten items to sequential memory with ease and the accuracy. You can mix and match the body parts and the related item pegs. It makes no difference. Use the one that provides the stronger image. You can even use two, as in numbers 2, 5, and 7 on the following list.

Here are some suggested images. You may want to make up others of your own.

1. I'll fill my *hat* with gas.
2. My *eyes* see dollar bills through the lenses of my *glasses*.
3. I'll carry my newspaper in my *mouth* like a dog.
4. On my *shoulders* I am balancing containers of milk, one on each shoulder.
5. My repaired watch is in my *chest pocket*.
6. My *belt* is holding my dry cleaning.

7. My department-store credit card is in my *hip pocket.*

8. My *knees* are covered with thick towels.

9. In my *sock* is my car key.

10. My *feet* will rest when I sit down with my friend for lunch.

Keep these body parts in your permanent memory bank. They come in handy for remembering things that must be recalled in sequence.

6. Remember Better with This Location List

This is a second peg list that can serve as an alternative to the body-parts list. The advantage of this list is that you can include up to 20 items on it.

Instead of using your body parts as pegs, you will use items in four rooms of your house or four areas of your workplace. Mentally visit those rooms and select five items in each room. These are items of furniture or appliances that will serve as pegs and "hold" the object or errand you want to remember. For example: The book is on the *bed.* Or, the checkbook is in the *sink.*

It is important that you go through whatever rooms or work stations you choose in the same order each time. For example, the kitchen is first, the dining room is next, followed by the living room, and ending with the bedroom. The choice is yours; just keep them constant.

The pegs should be large and different from one another. Don't select two similar chairs or two matching tables. Remember them in some logical order within the room: from right to left, clockwise, or from floor to ceiling. Keep this sequence the same in all the rooms.

Here is a sample list of 20 pegs that will hold the object you want to remember.

Room 1: Kitchen

counter—theater tickets

stove—doctor's appointment

sink—library books

dishwasher—shoe-repair ticket

refrigerator—car-wash coupon

Room 2: Dining Room
   buffet—return recyclables
   table—supermarket discount coupons
   chair—shopping list
   breakfront—wallet
   plant stand—car keys

Room 3: Living Room
   arm chair—prescription
   lamp—photo finishing
   fireplace—bakery
   couch—wine
   bookcase—haircut

Room 4: Bedroom
   dresser—travel agent
   mirror—lunch
   bed—post office
   night table—dentist
   chest—video store

Practice walking through each room in sequence. "Pick up" each errand or object as you sweep through each room in order.

As in all memory tasks, exaggeration and humor will help make the items more vivid in your mind. For example, "see" huge theater tickets sitting on your kitchen counter. Imagine the doctor's shingle sitting on your stove top; the library books piled in the sink like dishes; the large shoes in the dishwasher, and so on.

You can use these same locations to list your appointments:

Mr. Jones is on the counter.

Martin is in the stove.

Jane is in the sink.

Ms. Watson is in the dishwasher.

The vice president is in the refrigerator.

Some verbal elaboration can fix the person and peg even more:

Mr. Jones, the accountant, is on the counter.

Martin is warming up in the stove.

Jane is "all wet" in the sink.

Ms. Watson is agitated by the dishwasher.

The V. P. is cooling down in the refrigerator.

After you fix these locations in your memory, you will be amazed at how many applications you will find to use these 20 pegs: appointments, lists of presidents of organizations, product lines, price codes, model numbers, and so forth.

7. Develop a Sharper Mind with Magic Pairs

This is a mental exercise that will stimulate your memory while you have a good time. What makes it unusual is that you can amaze your friends with it. They will see it as a magic trick while you will use it as an exercise. You can do this with one, or up to four people looking on.

- Select 20 playing cards from a deck as ten pairs. Picture cards or number cards may be used, but just two of each picture or number.
- While you are out of sight, each viewer picks up one or more pairs, studies the pair, and then places them face down onto a single pile.
- You pick up the pile of cards, keeping them in pairs. All the cards are face down.
- You turn each card over one at a time, and then place it, face up, on a table in what appears to be a random order.
- You make four horizontal rows of five cards each. But you don't place the cards in order. You may start with the first card in the first row and the next card in the third row and so on.
- After you have placed all 20 cards in random order on the table, you ask your viewers, one at a time, to point out the row or rows in which their pair appears, without saying which cards are theirs.

- You immediately announce which pair of cards is which person's. You repeat this with each person until you have announced each pair correctly.

The success of this exercise depends on your learning four magic words: LIMIT, MOOSE, PEARL, and STRAP. You may remember them in any order. It's best to learn them in one order and then always use that same sequence.

STRATEGY

- After you learn these four five-letter words, they become locations on a mental map that you place on the tabletop. The map looks like this:

L	I	M	I	T
M	O	O	S	E
P	E	A	R	L
S	T	R	A	P

- When you lay out the pairs of cards, you are careful to place them on letter-spots that are themselves pairs, L's, I's, M's, and so on. It appears as if you are spreading the pairs out in a random manner, but you are mentally visualizing this map.

- Ask your friend or viewer to tell you which row or rows contain his pair of cards.

- If he says "Row 1 and Row 3," you know his pair of cards are resting on the "L" spots on the table. The only pair of same letters on those two rows are the "L" spots.

- When you place the ten pairs face up, you seem to be doing so haphazardly. Actually, you are practicing your mental map. You are providing your brain with additional practice when you visualize each letter after it is covered.

   Examples: Rows 1 and 2 on this map would have to be the M spot. Rows 3 and 4 would be the R spot. Rows 2 and 4 would be the S spot.

For a more invigorating workout, after you have done this one several times, you can change the position of these four words. An even better workout is to make up new words.

8. How to Use Free Recall to Strengthen Your Mind

This is a short-term memory workout called Free Recall. You will look at a string of items to remember which can be recalled in any order. This is different from *serial recall*, in which you must remember them in sequence.

Here are four lists. Go down each list, covering up each word with a piece of paper as you go.

When you reach the bottom of list 1, write down as many words as you can recall, in any order. Then, proceed to the other one at a time. The lists vary in length.

List 1	*List 2*
folder	tablet
menu	cookie
window	doorbell
table	bench
arm	lipstick
trip	butter
daughter	soldier
star	tractor
apple	carpet
tire	paint
giraffe	school
boat	camera
	airplane
	stove

List 3	*List 4*
knife	garage
sofa	tiger
truck	van
diploma	refrigerator
stapler	capsule
shed	piano
stove	armchair

furnace	carpenter
liver	microwave
wine	coupon
graph	computer
rubber band	plant
spine	electrician
plumber	fender
baker	trumpet
bookkeeper	fireplace
dishwasher	parchment
windshield	flowerpot
	beverage
	pharmacy

- See how many words you can recall from list 1. Move on to list 2.
- Before going on to list 3, try list 1 again. This time move up the list, starting with the last word.
- Go on to lists 3 and 4. Move up and down. Use these lists to practice applying your short-term memory.

9. Flex Your Memory with an Eight-Digit Number Series

This memory exercise flexes your mental "muscles" while you amaze others with your recall prowess.

To do this workout, you will need 22 index cards. Number each card separately from 1 to 22. Write these numbers large on the face of each card.

On the back of each card you are going to write an eight-digit number, separated by commas. For example: 12,345,678. Each card will have a different eight-digit number. You will surprise your friends and viewers by calling out the large number when they tell you which one of the 22 cards they are looking at.

This is a great mental workout for you and a baffling "memory trick" for the viewer. You will be exercising your mind as you do each card. You can obtain the same benefit doing this exercise without any audience, but like many physical exercises, the time passes more quickly when you have company. Here goes:

1. Number each card from 1 to 22.

2. Announce that you have memorized the eight-digit number that appears on the back of each card and that each of the 22 cards has a different number.

3. Choose one card from the pack. For example, let's assume that you or your viewer chose card 14. To "get" the large number written on the reverse side of the card, go through these mental calculations as you "concentrate" on the card.

   * Add 9 to the card number that is called out. (14 + 9 = 23)

   * Reverse this total to begin your eight-digit number. (23 becomes 32) Your number is now: 32,——,——.

   * Obtain the remaining six digits by repeatedly adding the last two numbers. For example, 3 + 2 = 5, so the next digit, the third digit, becomes 5, 32,5—,——.

   * Get the fourth digit by adding the last two: 2 + 5 = 7. You now have: 32,57-,——.

   * Get the fifth digit by adding the last two, digits three and four, or 5 + 7 = 12. When your total is 10 or more, you keep the second digit and drop the first. In this case, 12, you keep the 2 and drop the 1. You now have 32,572,——.

   * Continue to add the last two digits to obtain the next one. We add 7 + 2 = 9. Resulting in: 32,572,9-.

   * Adding 2 + 9 = 11 we now have: 32,572,91-.

   * Finally, adding 9 + 1 = 10 we keep the 0 and drop the 1 to get 32,572,910, our eight-digit number.

This memory exercise takes much longer to explain than it does to actually do. Try this two or three times with different numbers and you will be astonished at how quickly you can do the calculations in your head.

Exercise for the Eight-Digit Number Series

Assume card 8 has been selected. Try to figure out the eight-digit number written on the reverse of this card. Do not look at the explanation that follows until you have tried it yourself.

As a check, compare your answer with this one:

Card 8

- Add 9 to the 8 to get 17. Reverse 17 to get 71,—,—.
- 7 + 1 = 8 or 71,8—,—.
- 1 + 8 = 9 or 71,89-,—.
- 8 + 9 = 17 or 71,897,—. (8 + 9 = 17, keep the 7 and drop 1)
- 9+7=16 or 71,897,6—. (9 + 7 = 16, keep the 6 and drop 1)
- 7 + 6 = 13 or 71,897,63-.
- 6 + 3 = 9 or 71,897,639, the eight-digit number.

Making up the cards is easy and worth the effort. It will provide you with mental dexterity in handling numbers. This workout can double as an amusing parlor trick.

10. How to Memorize Playing Cards with Pegs

In this, the last of the basic workout exercises, we are going to show you how you can memorize a pack of playing cards with an easy-to-use peg system.

Once you learn these card pegs, you will be able to apply them when you play Bridge or any other card game in which you need to remember the cards that have been discarded.

As with every exercise, it may seem difficult at first, but with repetition it gets easier. What makes it somewhat different is that you will be exercising your memory while engaged in a favorite recreational activity. Even if you do not play cards, you can still use this exercise; make up your own form of Solitaire or other card game.

This exercise requires practice, but it is not difficult to master with a little patience. It is based on the Peg System you learned in Chapter 2.

Review of the Peg System

1 = penny (one cent)	8 = skate (figure 8) (rhymes)
2 = shoe (a pair) (rhymes)	9 = cat (9 lives)
3 = tree (rhymes)	10 = dime (10 cents)
4 = door (4 sides) (rhymes)	11 = skis (parallel lines)

5 = nickel (5 cents)   12 = dozen (12 items)

6 = six-pack (6 items)   13 = witch's hat (unlucky 13)

7 = dice (lucky 7)

You'll recall that we used everyday coins: penny, nickel, dime. Also, we chose rhyming words when suitable: shoe, tree, door, skate. Finally, some symbols lent themselves to become obvious pegs: a six-pack, dice, cat, skis, dozen, witch's hat.

Once you have learned these number pegs, it's a simple matter to convert them into cards.

Playing-Card Pegs

Ace = penny   8 = skate

2 = shoe   9 = cat

3 = tree   10 = dime

4 = door   Jack = skis

5 = nickel   Queen = dozen

6 = six-pack   King = hat

7 = dice

The last step is the easiest. Superimpose the peg with the particular suit: Clubs, Hearts, Spades, or Diamonds. In your mind's eye, these become a golf club, a valentine, a garden spade, and a diamond ring.

The idea as to have interactive images. That is, the two items, number and suit, are merged into one. Example: A 9 of diamonds would be imagined as a cat with a diamond ring on its paw.

Notice that we are suggesting a single image, a cat with a ring. This is better than a cat and a ring. The latter forces you to remember two images. The first is just one silly picture. The more ludicrous or exaggerated the picture, the easier it is to remember. Just think of the outlandish TV commercials that have been so successful: dry-cell batteries walking across the screen, or dancing raisins.

Some suggested examples:

Ace of hearts = a heart-shaped box of candy with a penny on the cover

Ace of clubs = a golf club with a large copper penny on its head

Ace of spades = a garden spade with a large curved penny as its blade

Ace of diamonds = a penny surrounded by a diamond ring

These examples are suggestions. The best images are the ones you make up yourself. Just remember to unify the two images into one picture.

Three Exercises for Using Playing-Card Pegs

EXERCISE 1   Form peg associations for each of these playing cards:

4 of hearts	3 of hearts
6 of clubs	5 of diamonds
8 of spades	7 of clubs
King of diamonds	Jack of spades

EXERCISE 2   Look at these playing-card peg images and figure out which playing cards they represent:

1. A large door with a spade as its handle
2. A nickel with a diamond mounted on its face
3. A six-pack of hearts
4. A dice with clubs instead of dots
5. A cat with a club in its mouth
6. A pair of skis with spades instead of poles

You are free to personalize or even change any of these suggested pegs. For nines you can imagine your own cat. A door can be your front door. You can miniaturize any item. For example, a 6 of spades can be an empty soda-can six-pack filled with 6 miniature garden spades.

EXERCISE 3   In a game of gin rummy, your opponent has discarded these cards, which you remember by their peg images:

A cat with a heart in its mouth

A black, pointed hat with a diamond painted on it

A dozen golf clubs

A skate stuffed with valentines

A tree with garden spades instead of branches

What were these five discarded cards?

After some practice, you will quickly recall certain images: a ten of diamonds will quickly come up as a dime with a diamond ring surrounding it. Before long, you will have a storehouse of 52 silly pictures. As you begin to use these pegs when you play your favorite card game, however, they will not be silly at all. They will become interactive images that trigger a response in your head.

In addition, you can use this same system to remember price quotes, code numbers, Personal Identification Numbers, and so on. Just match the pegs with the number.

BUILD MENTAL DEXTERITY WITH THIS COOL-DOWN EXERCISE

How to Set Your Mental Alarm Clock

At day's end, you can cool down your memory by doing one more exercise. Tell yourself to awaken at a certain hour. This is a skill that anyone can acquire with a little practice. Until you have mastered it, continue to use your alarm clock or clock radio.

- Begin by doing it tonight. Decide what time you want to awaken tomorrow. Let's assume you choose 7:00 A.M. As you close your eyes, "see" 7:00 A.M. on the face of the clock or watch near your bed. Fix it in your mind's eye.

- Visualize a second picture. Visualize the clock at one minute before the time you selected, in this case, 6:59 A.M. See the minute hand move to the appointed time, from 6:59 A.M. to 7:00 A.M. Now "hear" your alarm or clock radio go off.

- Get out of bed at the appointed time tomorrow morning. This is important. Your brain must get reinforcement that you are serious about this "wake-up call."

Practice until you have confidence that you can awaken at any desired hour without an alarm clock. At that point you will! (Some of my clients continue to set the alarm as a form of "insurance.")

Don't be discouraged if occasionally your "inner clock" is off. Be aware that our body clocks are sometimes affected by plane travel, medication, alcohol, or illness. But this is the exception.

MEMENTOS

1. Memory needs to be exercised constantly. "Use it or lose it" applies to memory power just as it does to physical fitness.

2. Warm-up exercises can be done as soon as you awaken. They help you clear your mind and get ready for the mental challenges of the day.

3. The eight warm-up exercises in this chapter will help you to

    focus your attention

    forge memory links

    learn to categorize

    form anagrams

    learn statistics

    concentrate on appointments

    enhance your mental images

4. The basic workout will give you

    ability to "see" numbers

    recall a recipe

    open a combination lock

    recall dates and appointments

    use your body as a memory aid

    use your house as a memory aid

    memorize cards and numbers

    recall short-term memory items

    recite a series of eight-digit numbers

5. The cool-down will help you set your mental alarm clock.

A FINAL MEMENTO

You have in your hands a guidebook for keeping your memory sharp and your mind agile. By applying the suggestions presented here, you will increase your ability to store and use knowledge. As you build your greatest personal and business asset—a good memory—you will achieve greater personal satisfaction, build confidence, and enhance your career goals.

Good luck and pleasant memories!

Index